Michael Adams is an author, journalist, TV producer and screen-writer. His memoir *Showgirls, Teen Wolves and Astro Zombies* is about a year-long search for the worst movie ever made. His book *Shining Lights* is a profile of Australian Oscar winners, based on interviews with Cate Blanchett, Nicole Kidman, Russell Crowe and Geoffrey Rush.

Michael also contributed to *The 100 Greatest Films of Australian Cinema*, edited the AFI yearbook, and hosted Showtime's *Movie Club* and SBS's *The Movie Show*. For a decade Michael was reviews editor of the Australian edition of *Empire* and has written extensively on film and pop culture for *Men's Style, Yen, Rolling Stone*, Rottentomatoes.com and Movieline.com. He most recently worked as a writer and producer for a TV show about Australian inventors for the History Channel. Michael is also the creator of the podcast Forgotten Australia – www.forgottenaustralia.com

T0385141

AUSTRALIA'S
Sweetheart

MICHAEL ADAMS

hachette
AUSTRALIA

Internal photos: Bina, Mary, Mick and Carmel Maguire, 1936 (page 1); Mary on board the *Mariposa* as it arrives in Los Angeles, 1936 (page 129) (Los Angeles Public Library); Mary on board the *Queen Mary*, heading for London, 1938 (page 225); Lupe, Joan, Mary and Carmel Maguire, 1938 (page 347) (Los Angeles Public Library). Unless otherwise credited, all photos are from the author's collection.

Published in Australia and New Zealand in 2019
by Hachette Australia
(an imprint of Hachette Australia Pty Limited)
Level 17, 207 Kent Street, Sydney NSW 2000
www.hachette.com.au

10 9 8 7 6 5 4 3 2 1

A catalogue record for this book is available from the National Library of Australia

ISBN: 978 0 7336 4029 2

Cover design by Christabella Designs
Cover photographs courtesy of Alamy and Trove
Author photo by Ava Adams
Typeset in 12.2/17 pt Bembo Std by Bookhouse, Sydney
Printed and bound in Australia by McPherson's Printing Group

The paper this book is printed on is certified against the Forest Stewardship Council® Standards. McPherson's Printing Group holds FSC® chain of custody certification SA-COC-005379. FSC® promotes environmentally responsible, socially beneficial and economically viable management of the world's forests.

In memory of Chris Murray,
a great friend and a great friend to Australian film

CONTENTS

PROLOGUE

19 AUGUST 1936

Australia's Sweetheart is leaving for Hollywood and the Sydney pier is crowded with people who've come to watch her set sail on the *Mariposa*. Standing on the promenade deck of the mighty white liner, Mary Maguire waves to the multitude five storeys below. There are two thousand people down there on Darling Harbour's Wharf 1A. Most are seeing off family and friends. But many are fans of Australia's newest movie star. Trying not to sob like she did yesterday at her Brisbane farewell, the raven-haired seventeen-year-old smiles for everyone braving this winter morning to wave and shout best wishes.

The ship's whistle gives two blasts, then there's the cry of 'All visitors ashore!' The boys from *The Sun*, *Truth* and the *Sydney Morning Herald* take their final pictures of Mary. She tries to look composed in her black fur coat as she clutches a floral bouquet and poses beside a lifebuoy on the railing. Raising a gloved hand in a farewell wave, wind whipping her hair every which way, she laughs as the flashbulbs pop and the Fox Movietone newsreel camera whirs. After wishing her good luck, the reporters, photographers and cameramen go ashore.

Mary has a last round of hugs and handshakes with some of the friends and film colleagues who have just put on a huge cocktail party for her in the ship's ballroom. When they've left she stands with her father, Mick, at a railing lined with other passengers. Stewards hand out rolls of coloured streamers, and the Maguires and their fellow passengers rain these down on the well-wishers below. Within seconds a dazzling paper rainbow connects ship to shore.

It's 10.57 a.m.: just three minutes until they begin their voyage. A tiny part of Mary wishes she could get off the boat. Go back home. Go back to the way things were. Go back to a life where she's not always the centre of attention and always expected to smile even if she feels like crying. Just for a day.

But Mary chides herself for such an ungrateful thought. Upon boarding the *Mariposa* she signed many autographs for excited young Australian girls. She knows they can't expect much more from life than school and shop or secretarial work for a few years before they marry and become their mothers. Any of them would kill to be in her shoes: adored, beautiful, wealthy and setting sail for even greater fame and fortune. Mary knows she has a duty to be happy. She isn't just living her dream – she's living all of their dreams.

'The most famous girl in Australia' and 'The envy of many a girl in Australia': they're phrases the newspapers have used to describe her. Mary can't deny how lucky she is; just like she can't help the hurt in her heart. Mother, sisters, best friends: this morning they're more than six hundred miles away in Brisbane. Although making movies has meant such separation before, this is very different because soon the people Mary loves most will be more than seven thousand miles distant. There's no way of knowing when she'll see them again – any more than she knows what really awaits her on the other side of the Pacific Ocean.

At least Mary has her dad. Big, tough Mick: blue eyes twinkling as he smiles proudly; he's well padded these days but still dapper in his three-piece suit. He may no longer be a welter-weight champion, yet with him in her corner everything will be fine. Surely.

Moments before eleven o'clock, the *Mariposa*'s whistle sounds three times. The hawser lines are tossed off deck, the boat's engines rumble and its twin stacks belch smoke. This is it. She's really leaving. It seems like just yesterday she was Peggy Maguire, Brisbane convent girl, destined only to see Hollywood glamour from her seat in the local picture palace.

As the wharf band strikes up 'Aloha 'Oe', which translates to 'Farewell to Thee', passengers and well-wishers sing along and whisper its haunting refrain, 'Until we meet again'. Tugboats help the big liner away from shore. It's a marvellous and melancholy spectacle as thousands of colourful streamers strain and then snap, symbolising all the ties broken by this departure.

The *Mariposa* rounds Miller's Point and slides beneath the mighty arch of the Sydney Harbour Bridge. Gaining speed, saluted by honking ferries, the ship steams eastwards as Mary takes a last look at this city. While it was never really home like Melbourne or Brisbane, Sydney holds a place in her heart because it was where she was first considered for Hollywood.

Swell deepening, air saltier with sea spray, the ship surges past Sydney Heads and into the open ocean. Mary is leaving Australia behind for the first time. As the cliffs and beaches recede in the ocean haze, it's far from clear what her life will be like when she next sees these shores. Countless hopeful young women wash out in Hollywood every year. She might become one of them. She may have been better off staying a big fish in a small pond. But if she *does* make it in America, then the next time she sees Australia she might be a star as big as . . .

Janet Gaynor? Helen Hayes? Luise Rainer? Maureen O'Sullivan? Thinking of these goddesses conjures a reverie of shiny limousine doors held open at gala premieres as searchlights sweep the sky above Grauman's Chinese Theater and –

The cries of the dozens of seagulls following the boat shatter any reverie. Australia has slipped out of sight behind the liner. Unable to know that she will never again lay eyes on the country of her birth, Mary seeks out the luxury of the *Mariposa* and starts counting down the days until she takes on Hollywood.

PART ONE

Australia

1.

Hollywood as we know it didn't exist when Mary Maguire's mother was born on 20 November 1890. American moving pictures were then just starting to be made in Thomas Edison's New Jersey laboratory, and the world's future filmmaking capital was nothing more than a modest farming community perched on the edge of the California desert. In this respect it wasn't dissimilar to Mary Carroll's birthplace of Lillimur, home to a hundred hardy souls living off the land in arid north-western Victoria. This tiny town was where her father, Daniel Carroll, who ran a horse-breeding business with his brother, had brought her mother, also named Mary, after they married at St Patrick's Church in Adelaide in 1887. A good Irish Catholic couple, they set about having a big brood. Their first daughter was born in 1888. Baby Mary, who'd be known to all as 'Bina', came along two years later. A son followed in 1891.

Carroll Bros. had prospered in the 1880s but the business faltered as Australia slid into economic depression. Unable to pay the rent on the farm, they were forced to liquidate, with Melbourne's *Leader* noting that the sale of all their worldly possessions – from furniture and farm equipment to pigs and horses – raised a dismal few pounds at auction. Daniel and his

wife and children started over on a farm in Goyura, another
flyspeck on the map of north-western Victoria, and had two more
surviving children in the next few years. Life on the land didn't
get any easier, not with depression followed by drought, and the
family moved to Melbourne around 1897. They settled where
there was work, in the industrial and shipping hub of Newport,
and Daniel got a job as a railway signalman. It was a position he
would keep for fifteen years – which was just as well because,
with another two children added to the family, he wound up
with nine mouths to feed.

Bina grew up knowing she could only have a better life
through hard work, a willingness to seize opportunity and an
abiding faith in God. She saw proof of this as her people came
up in the world. By 1909 the family had moved to a cottage in
Middle Park, where the air was fresher, the streets were wider
and they were just a short walk from the bay. Three years later
the Carrolls were within a block of the beach, in a handsome
two-storey brick terrace house in Middle Park's Ashworth Street.
This upward mobility was made possible by Daniel's steady salary,
supplemented by the contributions his children made as they left
school at age fourteen and got jobs.

By 1912 Bina was working as a confectioner and had come of
age as a compact but voluptuous Black Irish beauty. In 1913, at
a time when many young women remained at home until they
married, she showed her independence by moving to Bendigo,
where she worked as a waitress.

How Bina came to meet Mick Maguire isn't recorded. She may
have known of him before they laid eyes on each other because
he was a minor Melbourne celebrity – and quite the catch, even
if a bit of a bad boy.

———

Mick was the eldest son of Michael Maguire, a bareknuckle boxer and Schweppes soft drink company salesman, who had married Ellen Shaw in 1892. Like the Carrolls, they were good Irish Catholics. After their first son died as an infant, they had Mick, born on 6 June 1894, then four more children. The family lived in working-class Abbotsford, which, like adjacent suburbs Richmond and Collingwood, was known for its hardscrabble conditions. Even so, Mick went to Christian Brothers College up the hill in East Melbourne, his father's salary either sufficient to cover fees or the school waiving expenses as they sometimes did for Catholic families in need. In any event, the young Maguire was an asset for CBC because, while no academic achiever, he was a great sportsman.

So great that, in addition to captaining his school's football team to a Grand Final win in 1910, fifteen-year-old Mick that year played professionally for Richmond's beloved Tigers in the Victorian Football League (VFL). Despite being the youngest player in the club's history, that season he triumphed as its leading goal kicker – and claimed the title again in 1911. Photos show a cockily handsome chap with hooded eyes, Roman nose, full lips and strong jaw beneath dark hair slicked in a centre part. Standing five feet eleven and already full of brash charm, this local hero was surely a hit with the ladies.

Mick was also tough. He had to be. The VFL was then a blood sport, with much handwringing done by columnists, club officials, politicians and policemen about how to curb outrageous on-field violence. But Mick could handle himself better than most. Trained in the 'fistic art' by his father, he wasn't just a brilliant young football player but also a promising young boxer who had his first public match when he was eleven years old. By early 1911, aged sixteen, he was fighting professionally, and in March that year won £20 by beating future Australian featherweight champion

Jack Green. For a kid living at home, Mick was doing well for money. In addition to his fight winnings, he and his fellow football players were from that year paid up to thirty shillings a week, which was close to the minimum male wage then calculated to take into account supporting a wife and three children.

Yet Mick wasn't content to coast along, defecting from the Richmond Tigers to the Melbourne Redlegs halfway through the 1912 season. In a sport dominated by suburban loyalties — not to mention Christian denominations, for Richmond was Catholic and Melbourne was Protestant — the decision had to have made him a few enemies. But it showed he was a young bloke willing to follow opportunity.

Not that Mick was *too* sensible. He took pleasure in punching on and partying, and he was an enthusiastic brawler and boozer on a Redlegs trip to play 'friendly' games in Tasmania. His fondness for on-field fisticuffs saw him make history at the start of the 1913 football season. The VFL had just set up the first independent tribunal to investigate complaints and issue punishments. On 7 May it held its first inquiry into a player — Mick. He had the previous Saturday not only kicked four goals against the University side but also punched out two of its players. After hearing evidence — including Mick's unconvincing claim to have acted in self-defence — the committee disqualified him for four games. 'Let this be a warning to other players,' the chairman said. 'As far as Mr Maguire is concerned, he must learn to control his boxing proclivities on the football field and keep them for the gymnasium.'

As he copped this suspension, Mick knew he was about to be judged on a far more serious matter. In his pocket was a summons to appear at Richmond Court for missing fifteen days of the compulsory military training then required of all men aged eighteen to sixty. Defending the charge, he offered a laughable excuse for a man earning a good living as a boxer and footballer: he hadn't been physically fit enough to do his sworn duty. That Mick even tried this excuse suggests a chancer always ready to see what he could get away with. Fined ten shillings, he was ordered into military police custody for fifteen days to do his drill.

Mick played for the Redlegs through 1913 and finished with the team early in the 1914 season. Though his goal-scoring had slowed, he had another reason for quitting. Boxing greatness beckoned – if only he could knuckle down to knuckling up. 'Our fighting footballer,' remarked a 1913 *Referee* article, 'generally trains in a lackadaisical manner.' Nevertheless, Reginald 'Snowy' Baker saw potential. Australia's Olympic hero and all-round sporting champion had become a boxing promoter and praised Mick's great punching power and ability to take hard knocks. Snowy booked him for major fights at the Melbourne Athletic Pavilion, promoting his 'clever, quick, splendid judgment and defence' in matches against local, interstate and international boxers. Mick won more often than he lost. 'If young Maguire would only train seriously there is no telling how high he would rise in the game,' wrote *Referee* in July 1914. Respected boxing journalist 'Solar Plexus' weighed in with the observation: 'A more promising or finer-looking youngster I don't ever remember seeing.'

After the Great War began in August, pressure built for young men to enlist, as Les Darcy, Snowy Baker's most famous boxer, would soon discover when he was taunted as a coward. But, just like Darcy, Mick was under-age. He couldn't legally sign up without parental consent before his twenty-first birthday in June 1915.

In any event, married men, especially those with children, weren't expected to enlist – and Mick was soon to be both.

On 17 March 1915, Mick and Bina married at the Carmelite Church in Middle Park. The bride and groom adored and complemented each other. He was a strong, popular man of independent means who would be a good provider and father. She was an independent and hard-working woman whose pragmatism would help rein in his unruly energies. That Bina was more than three years older than her new husband also gave her more authority in the relationship. They moved into a rented house in Port Melbourne and started planning a family.

Mick had by then taken work as a clerk for a rails bookmaker at race meetings. Managing hordes of excited punters was a stressful job, but it gave the popular sportsman the chance to expand his contact network in racing-mad Melbourne. In mid-1915 Mick finally listened to his critics and got serious about boxing, heading to Sydney to spend several months training and trying to rustle up big fights. He scored one in August at the Stadium against British welterweight champion Arthur Evernden. By the twelfth round Mick's eye bled freely and he was snorting crimson spray. But he slugged on to victory in the twentieth. Returning to Melbourne, Mick, with his dad in his corner, took on Britain's Nicol Simpson. Though 'loose-fleshed and loose-limbed' and half a stone lighter than his 'fine, muscled up' opponent, *Referee* reported Mick was 'wonderfully improved' since his last home-town fight. Mick won on the referee's decision, and the crowd 'cheered and cheered'. Three months later in Brisbane, he vanquished Henri Demlin, a victory that later saw him claim to have bested Australia's most famous boxer. 'I beat Les Darcy, too,' he would say, blue eyes twinkling. 'Of course, I did. I knocked out that Frenchman in sixteen rounds, and it took Darcy twenty rounds to beat him, so doesn't that prove that I beat Darcy?' A great bit of Irish blarney, just so long as his drinking buddies forgot Demlin was *Belgian*, Darcy *KO'ed* him in round five and that Mick won after *twenty rounds* when the referee gave him the decision – with half the audience this time loudly dissenting.

Briefly promoted as Victoria's welterweight champion, Mick could make reasonable money boxing. He pocketed up to £30 for big fights and, with side wagers reaching £100, he might walk away from a win with close to what an average office worker earned in a year.

But John Wren's shadow loomed over his career. Melbourne's powerbroker had become Snowy Baker's business partner in January 1914 and was infamous for fixing sports events. Mick's last big fight – against American Fritz Holland in Brisbane in December 1915 – certainly had a stink about it. Mick seemed scared from the start. He retreated continually until the fourth round when he dropped to the mat, apparently felled by a left hook. Mick stayed down for the count. But the crowd was incensed, and the referee ruled no contest. 'I was chased from the ring, chased by embittered fans, pasting me with chairs,' Mick would later say. 'They reckoned I was loafing on it. They chased me down the aisle and into the street.'

His career took a dive after the Holland fight. Anyway, by now his little brother Andy, also a bookmaker's clerk, was proving the better boxer. Mick took genuine pleasure in his sibling's success, sparring and travelling with him. But brotherly affection would sour for Andy as he realised that no matter how good he was, Mick would always be their father's favourite.

———

Mick's winnings had been welcome, but Bina was glad her handsome husband – who already had one cauliflowered ear – would no longer come home beaten black and blue. Now pregnant with their first child, she had even more reason to be concerned about his health. Their baby was born in early 1916 and they named her

Mary. But she died in infancy. Bina was soon pregnant again, and on 17 November 1916 welcomed baby Patricia at Coonara Private Hospital in St Kilda. Happily, this little girl thrived.

Planning a boxing comeback, Mick organised an exhibition match against Andy in February 1917. 'He entered the ring, mud fat,' wrote the *Weekly Times*. 'Mick made an inglorious showing, being dropped in the second round, while he had great difficulty despite a 2½-stone advantage in seeing three rounds out.'

His life as a professional boxer over, Mick's new career began that November when he and Bina took over the London Hotel in Collingwood. To economise – and get help with baby Patricia – the couple moved into the Ashworth Street home of Bina's parents. While Mick would work the bar, Bina officially held the licence. This arrangement reflected her take-charge attitude and, at a time of much concern over illegal betting in pubs, also averted the possibility that her husband would be turned down because of his ties to the gambling game – legal and perhaps otherwise. Six o'clock closing had been introduced a year earlier, making it a tricky time to get into the hotel business. To stay on the right side of the law, Mick had to ensure drinkers were out the door by that time. It wasn't an easy or pleasant task, particularly when ejecting drunk men recently maimed and/or made mad in places like Gallipoli, Fromelles and Bullecourt. No doubt Mick was often asked whether he – the famous fighter – had done his bit 'over there'. In January 1917, *Referee* had reported he 'once looked like moving to the front', suggesting Mick tried to sign up and was rebuffed.

In the autumn of 1918, Mick tried to restart his VFL career by signing with Collingwood. But the old magic eluded him – he played only nine games, scored a modest ten goals and was off the team when the Magpies faced South Melbourne in that year's Grand Final. Collingwood lost in a nailbiter, but Mick had consolation for his double disappointment because by then Bina was expecting another baby.

————

The weeks leading up to the birth of the girl who would be known as 'Australia's Sweetheart' were dramatic, tragic and terrifying. Early February 1919 saw a heatwave engulf Melbourne, and the air was hazy and harsh with smoke from bushfires on the city's outskirts. Yet the threat posed by Spanish flu was far worse. The pandemic had reached Melbourne on 21 January and was soon putting a hundred citizens a week into their graves. Authorities tried to dispel rumours that the pestilence was actually bubonic plague. But they couldn't deny the disease's horrific virulence: people in perfect health in the morning could by evening have drowned in their own mucus and blood. Frighteningly, the most vulnerable were people Mick and Bina's age, with pregnant women at greatest risk and their unborn babies in danger of dying in utero even if their mothers recovered. To prevent the spread of infection, race meetings and other sporting events were cancelled, and hotels, theatres, cinemas, music and concert halls were closed. The Maguires could still go to church, provided they wore masks at indoor services or endured the heat at alfresco masses offered in gardens and on tennis courts. Authorities urged people to engage in a 'quiet, cheerful life' at home – though life at Ashworth Street wouldn't have been that quiet, not with toddler Patricia, or that cheerful, not with heat and smoke let into the house by anti-influenza directives that doors and windows be left open for ventilation.

Conditions eased in the third week of February. Rains doused the fires, temperatures slipped back to bearable and influenza deaths decreased. However, with hospitals still overflowing, it was far safer for Bina to give birth at Ashworth Street.

Yet even the sanctity of the Australian family home wasn't guaranteed in Middle Park that weekend. The night before Bina's baby came, the quiet of a suburb under virtual quarantine was shattered by gunshots when a returned Digger ran amok with a revolver. Storming into the house he had shared with his estranged wife, he shot dead their two-year-old daughter, put four bullets into the man he believed to be his wife's lover, and then blew out his own miserable brains. Melbourne was reeling from this tragic news when Hélène Teresa Maguire – who would be called Peggy and later Mary – was born on Saturday, 22 February 1919.

2.

Little Hélène thrived. Melbourne was on the road to recovery. Temperatures eased, infections and deaths dropped, public buildings reopened. But in mid-autumn another influenza wave hit, killing nearly thirteen hundred people in six weeks. This time, though, the defiant city didn't come to a standstill, and soon the Maguires took over the Carters Arms Hotel in Northcote. As the year progressed, the epidemic burned itself out and life gradually went back to normal. Quarantined soldiers came home, cars were more common on the streets, and films like *The Man from Kangaroo*, starring Snowy Baker, and *The Sentimental Bloke*, directed by Raymond Longford, showed that Australians could make movies every bit as good as those coming from Hollywood.

The Roaring Twenties was more an American than an Australian concept, yet Melbourne would soon exhibit some of the trappings of the era with the birth of broadcast radio and the strains of jazz coming from clubs where smart young women adopted the flapper style. As the decade got under way, the Maguires enjoyed a new era of prosperity as hotel proprietors. Hélène was by then a plump, healthy toddler. A photo of her at eighteen months of age shows her in a grassy backyard, sunlight in her short curls, dressed like a prize fighter in shorts and booties with one hand in a little boxing glove.

Not long after this picture was taken Mick and Bina added another daughter to their brood – Joan, born in April 1921 – and sold the Carters Arms licence to take over the Yarraville Hotel in Footscray. Over the next fifteen months, the Maguires bought and sold numerous hotel licences, with their eldest daughter, Patricia, later recalling that as a child she and her sisters frequently travelled with their parents in taxis between these pubs. Though they were short-term investments, records indicate the family sometimes lived on the premises, as with the Yarraville Hotel, the Palmerston Hotel in South Melbourne and the Gilbert Club Hotel in Kerang in country Victoria. It was a peripatetic lifestyle that showed the couple would take risks and move to further their interests – just as Mick had done as a teenager by defecting from Richmond to Melbourne, and as Bina had demonstrated by striking out for Bendigo as a single woman. Husband and wife were similar in this respect, yet one of Mick's mates later confirmed that she was the brains behind their business strategy. 'Lunching with the clan Maguire, I decided that Mick had been lucky in his matrimonial choice,' the friend wrote in a newspaper column. 'Mrs Maguire was a sparkling and radiant personality in any class or company . . . Under the wife's direction the family fortunes prospered.'

In July 1922, Mick and Bina poured these fortunes into the Bull & Mouth Hotel in Melbourne's busy Bourke Street. This historic hotel, with its famous gold-painted plaster bull's head mounted over the public bar, formed the backdrop for Hélène's earliest childhood memories. The three-storey Bull & Mouth had been built around 1851, when Victoria's gold rush was just beginning. With its central Bourke Street location, near the corner of Swanston Street, it held a prime position opposite the staging post for Cobb & Co coaches bound for Ballarat, Bendigo and beyond.

With Melbourne's population quadrupling in three years, business boomed at the Bull & Mouth. Predating similar saloons in the American west by several years, it was a wild place where men pounded cheap drinks in a fug of tobacco smoke, sought out other pleasures in upstairs rooms and occasionally concluded arguments with their fists. On an infamous occasion around this time, a jealous husband pulled out a revolver in the dining room and shot the man he suspected of cuckolding him. The victim fell down with a bullet hole in his forehead and an exit wound at the back of his head. Just a few minutes later he got up, very much alive; the bullet had glanced off his frontal bone, traversed around the skull beneath the skin and popped out opposite where it entered. Despite – or perhaps because of – such ribaldry, the Bull & Mouth was one of the Bourke Street businesses that survived the post–gold rush slump and other later economic fluctuations. By the early 1900s this part of the city remained a lively if seedy entertainment district, where thirty bars operated until late at night and criminal gangs like Squizzy Taylor's Bourke Street Rats flourished. Though Squizzy was shot and wounded just a block away from the Bull & Mouth in October 1922, Bourke Street was becoming better known for its shopping and movie theatres by the time the Maguires took over the hotel.

Everyone now knew Hélène as 'Peggy'. The nickname suited her – she was an angelic and energetic dark-eyed child just like tiny American movie tyke Baby Peggy Montgomery. This little star's films, with titles like *Peggy, Behave!*, *Little Miss Mischief*, *Helen's Babies*, *Little Miss Hollywood* and *Peg o' the Movies*, packed cinemas all along Bourke Street. Two of these theatres were right next door to the Bull & Mouth: the Britannia, the city's first purpose-built cinema, and the Melba, also a busy motion-picture house. On the other side of the Melba on the corner of Swanston Street rose The Leviathan, offering five storeys of shopping in one of the

city's first department stores. The Bull & Mouth's east-side neighbour was the sprawling Cole's Book Arcade, which stocked some
two million volumes, justifying its claim to be 'the largest book-
store in the world'. For Patricia, Peggy and little Joan, the Bull
& Mouth stood at the centre of a wonderland. The Britannia and
Melba each ran one or two new films weekly. There they could
marvel at the movies of not only Baby Peggy but also Charlie
Chaplin, Mary Pickford, Douglas Fairbanks, Gloria Swanson,
Marion Davies, Charles Farrell and Janet Gaynor. When nothing
at the pictures appealed, Cole's famous motto promised 'Read as
Long as You Like – Nobody Asked to Buy'. But the Maguires
didn't even have to leave home for entertainment. From the Bull
& Mouth's first-storey balcony they could watch all of Melbourne
pass by, which was particularly exciting on Anzac Day and other
special occasions that saw Bourke Street lined with tens of thousands of people. Each St Patrick's Day, Mick put their grandmother
Ellen in a chair out there with a beer and cigarette so she could
watch the parade.

For Mick and Bina, the Bull & Mouth's central location made
it a money-spinner – even if that very popularity sometimes put
them in peril and in the public eye. 'Busy as Bourke Street at
rush hour' was as true then as it is now: the thoroughfare teemed
with pedestrians, cable trams and motor vehicles. But the busiest
pockets were the public bars between knock-off and early closing.
Every workday the Bull & Mouth attracted a 'thirsty multitude'
for a frenzy of drinking that recalled the pub's riotous gold rush
era – and it was up to Mick to get them out the door by six
o'clock six days a week. In early December 1922 he failed and
faced court. Mick's lawyer explained his client's daily dilemma:
he risked prosecution if he refused men service at 5.59 p.m., and
a fine if he didn't have them all out and the doors closed a minute
later. The magistrate expressed sympathy at the task of 'emptying

half-muddled and cantankerous men from the bar on the stroke of six o'clock' but said the law was the law and fined Mick £7.

Bina made a more sensational court appearance in relation to the Bull & Mouth in February 1923 when she testified in the murder case that was the talk of Melbourne. The previous November, Bertha Coughlan, a 28-year-old woman from country Victoria, had come to stay at the hotel while supposedly seeking medical treatment for an ear complaint. Bina made her acquaintance and twice noticed her in the company of a tall man. One morning, she found Bertha crying in one of the hotel's lounges. Bina was gently rebuffed when she asked after the woman's health, offered to help and tried to cheer her up. Bertha then walked out of the Bull & Mouth and seemed to drop off the face of the earth. She remained missing until 2 February 1923, when police found her badly decomposed body – and decapitated head – in a sack in the Yarra River. Police charged Hannah Mitchell, a backyard abortionist, with the murder. Trial proceedings indicated the tall man Bina had seen was Bertha's lover and that he had sent her off to have her pregnancy terminated. That resulted in her death, a cover-up, the grisly disposal of the corpse and Hannah Mitchell then attempting to murder her ex-husband when he threatened to expose the crime. Remarkably, she beat the charges – just as she would later walk free again in similar cases.

Mick next fronted court in September 1923, testifying against a man whom he had ejected from the Bull & Mouth. The bloke had then come back with three or four mates and bashed Mick.

All of that paled in comparison with what happened at the end of October. After police went on strike, unrest spread and violent skirmishes broke out around picket lines. But disorder exploded into a riot as young men spilled from city pubs at six o'clock on Saturday, 3 November. On Bourke Street a group of sailors tried to stop the crowd from looting The Leviathan. They were beaten by the mob, who smashed the shop windows and helped themselves to goods. The rioters then swarmed along Bourke Street. A terrified box-office girl at the Britannia grabbed the takings and fled into the Bull & Mouth. Cinema staff locked the theatre's entrance doors behind her, and in the auditorium moviegoers huddled in fear as they listened to shouting and smashing outside. The mob burst in, surged through the cinema, and then rushed out and on to more mayhem. While neighbouring businesses suffered serious damage, the Bull & Mouth was passed over, suggesting Mick's boxing prowess deterred the thugs. Anarchy spread through the city, with rioters attacking any police still on duty, commandeering trams and targeting jewellery stores. One hundred thousand people came from the suburbs to watch the spectacle. Great War hero General Sir John Monash organised a volunteer militia of thousands of men to take back the streets with baton charges in scenes that called to mind the Russian Revolution. Sunday morning saw Bourke Street shopfronts barricaded. By Monday morning the rioters had retreated in the face of heavy rain and streets patrolled by soldiers armed with rifles. The madness had left three people dead and four hundred injured.

In mid-June 1924 Mick could have been forgiven for thinking it might be about to happen again after he confronted a drunk who entered the Bull & Mouth at 7.00 p.m. and demanded a drink. When the man let fly a string of obscenities, Mick kept his cool and called the cops. As he helped two constables take the resisting lout to the city watch house, a mob gathered and followed them. 'At the intersection of Swanston and Lonsdale Streets, many persons joined the others,' reported The Argus. 'The crowd began hooting, and several policemen were sent from headquarters.' Fortunately the mob dispersed.

Less than a week later Mick and Bina had another close call when they were in a head-on collision while motoring back to Melbourne from a short holiday. Their Studebaker was destroyed, but the couple emerged from the wreckage miraculously uninjured. A passenger in the other vehicle wasn't so lucky, suffering head and face wounds that required surgery and resulted in permanent disfigurement. The victim sued for £499, claiming that Mick was the negligent driver. Mick's defence – that the trouble had started because the plaintiff's driver had been on the wrong side of the road – appeared to be partially accepted by the judge, who nevertheless ordered him to pay £125 in damages. Bina fared better when she was next in court, in October 1926, defending a charge of assault brought by a Bull & Mouth waitress. The former employee presented photographs of bruises to support her claim for £49 in damages, saying Bina had manhandled her before physically throwing her from the hotel. The judge tossed out the case.

Peggy was too young to know much of these events, though a massive murderous mob on her doorstep might have imprinted itself indelibly. Regardless of what she remembered, Bina and Mick's triumphs, trials and tribulations meant that she and her four sisters – Carmel was born in 1924; baby Mary, nicknamed 'Lupe', followed in 1925 – grew up with a rich family lore. In their stories, her parents were always central to the action and always justified, whether on country roads and footy fields, in boxing rings and courts of law, in their very own historic hotel or out on the mean streets of Melbourne. The lesson – supported by scrapbooks filled with newspaper reports, sports articles and even Mick's football trading cards – was that her parents weren't ordinary and that the Maguire girls weren't going to be either.

3.

Bina was determined her daughters would all marry millionaires. Just how she would introduce her girls to such gentlemen wasn't clear. The Maguires were well off but not wealthy, and the Bull & Mouth was hardly an upper-class venue like the Menzies or the Windsor. But Bina could at least increase her daughters' chances of making such marriages by ensuring they were schooled as gentlewomen.

In 1924 Peggy joined Patricia as a student at the Academy of Mary Immaculate, which had been founded by the Sisters of Mercy back in 1857. In this imposing bluestone edifice on Nicholson Street opposite the Royal Exhibition Building – where Australia's federation was born – Peggy began her 'chalk and talk' rote education in English, French, history, geography, art, music and mathematics. The nuns also ensured rigorous religious instruction and took students to weekly benediction and monthly confession at St Patrick's Cathedral. Peggy learnt how to be a proper young lady, attending classes in deportment and elocution, the nuns making sure she and every other student was sick of hearing mantras like: 'Knees together, feet together, hands joined and dresses over knees!' When she wasn't at school, she was taking ballet and violin lessons, and would soon add piano and singing to her repertoire.

Peggy made her performing debut in October 1924 at the 'Princess Carnival', a highlight of the Academy school year. At this night-time concert, held in front of the city's Catholic hierarchy, she contributed a rendition of 'Baa–Baa Black Sheep' while Patricia did a 'Red Riding Hood' rhyme. Then came the elaborate ceremony to reveal who would be crowned 'Princess of Princesses' for raising the most money for a new school building. Alongside her four competitors, sumptuously gowned 'Princess Patricia' took to the stage – accompanied by prettily frocked maid of honour Peggy and tiny trainbearer Joan. The crowd held its breath for the big moment. The winner was . . . Princess Patricia! To deafening applause, she was crowned by Archbishop Daniel Mannix. Bina and Mick were elated for their girls and themselves, the family having raised £520 to their nearest rival's £470, with the entire event bringing in a whopping £1477 ($116 000 today). Melbourne's Catholic newspaper *The Advocate* published a photo of Patricia flanked by Peggy and Joan.

For the Maguire girls, this was a taste of fame and perhaps even a realisation they were competing for centrestage. They did, after all, come from a family of sibling rivalries, with frequent comparisons made between their dad's and uncle Andy's boxing careers, and most of their mum's brothers and sisters also running prominent Melbourne hotels.

Bina and Mick were thrilled with the 'Princess Carnival' newspaper story. They were also pleased to have friends in high places, given how powerful Dr Mannix had become in Melbourne, and how close he was to his neighbour and Mick's old boxing backer, John Wren. Their family ties with Dr Mannix – and their standing in the Catholic community – were further strengthened when Mick's parents joined the Archbishop on the first Australian National Holy Year Pilgrimage to the Vatican in mid-1925. A year later, they were able to call in favours from major Melbourne figures when Mick's nineteen-year-old sister Marie raised money for a St Vincent's Hospital building appeal via a grown-up 'Queen' charity competition. The major event of her campaign was a special performance of *Give and Take* at the Athenaeum Theatre, starring world-famous American comedian Harry Green and Australian funnyman Roy 'Mo' Rene. They both gave their services free. Prominent showman E. J. Carroll – another business partner of John Wren and producer of two of Snowy Baker's movies before he went to Hollywood – also provided his venue at no cost.

Marie's 'Queen' campaign fell short, with her ranking fourth in a field of six, though the Maguires still raised a tidy £1963 ($150 000) for the hospital. But before the decade was out she would make a more lasting contribution to the church by taking the vow of silence required to become a cloistered and contemplative Carmelite nun. It was an inspiring time to join the order: Marie Françoise-Thérèse Martin, a young Carmelite nun who had died of tuberculosis, had been canonised Saint Thérèse by the Pope just before Dr Mannix and the Maguires arrived in the Vatican on pilgrimage. In time Marie Maguire became mother prioress of the order in Australia.

———

In March 1927, after nearly five years, the Maguires sold the Bull & Mouth's licence and took over the Melbourne Hotel, just up the way on the corner of Bourke and Exhibition streets. It was a quieter venue that helped them avoid headline and courtroom dramas. Peggy was by now a pretty and popular Academy student, if a bit average academically. What she wanted more than anything was to be on stage. The Academy gave her the chance to perform at the end-of-year prize-giving ceremonies. In 1928, aged nine, she did an Irish jig and took a role in a scene from *The Merchant of Venice*, while the following year she was a slave in a Christian persecution drama called *The Roses of St Dorothy*.

Peggy was also soaking up everything she saw at the cinema. Movies were then enjoying popularity never seen before or since in Australia, with most kids having the 'picture habit' of attending a double feature or two every weekend. Peggy was even more obsessed, called 'film crazy' by family, friends and teachers. Although she felt guilty, she would wag school to watch movies, with one such truancy resulting in her seeing her name on the silver screen for the very first time. There Peggy was, hiding in the dark in a Bourke Street theatre, waiting for the program to start, when to her horror a notice was projected on-screen telling her to come home. Peggy rushed from the cinema, arrived back at the hotel and confessed in a deluge of tears. Bina and Mick had called the school asking that she be sent home for some reason – only to be told by the nuns that Peggy wasn't present. Remembering that she had enthused about a new movie, they found out where it was showing and pulled their heart-stopping stunt. It was a lesson Peggy wouldn't forget – whenever she planned to wag in future, she was sure not to talk about the film she wanted to see in the presence of her parents.

Peggy had no shortage of cinemas in which to hide. In 1929 more than a dozen were within a few blocks of the Melbourne Hotel, including majestic picture palaces The Capitol, the State Theatre and The Regent. Peggy had wide tastes, adoring romance, drama and comedy, and saw the biggest hits of the day, all in sumptuous surroundings with live orchestral accompaniment. By now Baby Peggy Montgomery was all washed up at age eleven. Instead Peggy Maguire saw the likes of Greta Garbo in *Flesh and the Devil*; Clara Bow in *It*; Charlie Chaplin in *The Circus*; Buster Keaton in *The General*; and Janet Gaynor paired with Charles Farrell in *7th Heaven* and again in *Street Angel*. She also had the chance to see popular Australian productions, such as *The Kid Stakes*, *For the Term of His Natural Life*, and Charles Chauvel's *The Moth of Moonbi* and *Greenhide*. Yet being 'film crazy' meant more than just seeing movies: Peggy could learn about the lives, loves and careers of stars in newspapers, women's journals, local movie magazine *Everyones*, and imported American fan rags such as *Photoplay*, *Screenland* and *Moving Picture Stories*.

Peggy's film fervour intensified just before her tenth birthday, when talkies arrived in Melbourne on 2 February 1929. At the Athenaeum, *The Jazz Singer* offered Al Jolson speaking a few lines of dialogue and singing six of his songs. His wasn't the only sound feature starting that day. At The Auditorium, heartthrob Charles Farrell starred in *The Red Dance*, which had a magnificent synchronised musical soundtrack. More sound pictures followed, with Peggy enamoured of *The Four Feathers*, *The Return of Sherlock Holmes* and anything else starring British heartthrob Clive Brook. But she reserved her greatest enthusiasm for MGM's *The Broadway Melody*, which took her behind the scenes of a stage show. Not only was this Hollywood's first true musical, it also featured a Technicolor sequence. Peggy was a huge fan, seeing the movie every day until she had mastered the dance routines performed by its wise-cracking dames.

In June 1930 Peggy showed off her footwork and dramatic skills in *The Doll's House Tea Party* at the University of Melbourne's beautiful Melba Hall. A medley of songs and dances, the show was part of a matinee entertainment program for the Million Shillings Fund to establish a permanent Melbourne orchestra. The initiative had been made even more poignant by hundreds of musicians being put out of work as cinemas converted to sound, just when economic conditions were worsening in the wake of the previous year's Wall Street Crash. *The Age* and *The Argus* ran photos of the cast in costume, with Peggy distinctive in a maid's black blouse and banded hat, while little sisters Carmel and Lupe wore white dresses and bows as visiting dolls. A few months later, Peggy was among forty youngsters doing *The Toymaker's Dream* as a ballet on ice at the Glaciarium. In December, she had a lead role in *Fairy Princess*, a production of songs, dances and drama staged at Werribee's Corpus Christi College, with Joan playing in support. Peggy accidentally delighted the audience when the ascending curtain caught the train of her fairy-queen frock and she was lifted into the air over the stage.

By April 1931 the family had taken over the Hotel Metropole, also on Bourke Street and then attached to the swanky Metropole Arcade. Having lived in the heart of Melbourne for nearly a decade, the Maguires were a striking and familiar sight: the handsome former sportsman, his charming and beautiful wife, and their five pretty daughters who ranged in size like Russian dolls. In that year's September school holidays, Peggy made her modest professional debut in the pantomime *Jack and the Beanstalk*, staged as a supporting show meant to help lure increasingly cash-strapped audiences to Mary Pickford's new movie comedy *Kiki* at Melbourne's State Theatre. Headlined by a trio of well-known Australian adult actors, she was in the all-girl chorus, called on to sing, dance and crack the occasional joke, just like the heroines of *The Broadway Melody*. It wasn't a starring role for Peggy, but it was a starry experience because the State Theatre was one of Australia's five great 'atmospheric' picture palaces. Behind its grand oriental exterior were 3400 seats set amid ornate Florentine statuary and backlit temple façades, all beneath a sky-blue vaulted ceiling across which wispy clouds drifted. In this garden of dreams, Peggy played three shows a day for a week, giving her plenty of opportunity to watch and re-watch the featured film until its title card – 'Joseph M. Schenck presents Mary Pickford . . . in *Kiki*' – became as familiar as the dance routines by an up-and-coming choreographer named Busby Berkeley. It wouldn't be that long before she was on a first-name basis with all three of these Hollywood personalities.

4.

Yet if any Maguire girl was predicted to one day befriend such Hollywood luminaries, the smart money really would have been on Joan. A better elocutionist than her sisters, she landed the title role in *Red Riding Hood* at the Playhouse opposite two veteran adult actors in December 1931. *The Advocate* ran a photo of her. 'The gifted young player,' the caption read, 'who is only ten years of age, is the daughter of Mr and Mrs Mick Maguire, of the Metropole Hotel.' The accompanying review called her 'one of the most outstanding juveniles seen on the Melbourne stage for years'. Such praise delighted her parents – and had to have made Patricia and Peggy just a little jealous.

But by then the Maguire lasses were wondering if they might be *screen* rather than stage stars. In 1930 Frank Thring had resigned as chairman of the Bourke Street–based Hoyts cinema chain to set up Australia's first 'talkie studio'. His Efftee Films would have as its sound stage His Majesty's Theatre, whose interior had recently been badly fire damaged. It was at this studio in late 1931, just two blocks from the Maguires' hotel, that Thring made Australia's first feature-length talkie hit, *Diggers*, a comedy set on the Western Front of the Great War and based on its star Pat Hanna's wildly popular revue show. But Efftee had an even bigger drawcard in

George Wallace, beloved on Australia's vaudeville circuit, who the next year made *His Royal Highness* for the company. When George, who loved a drink and a good time, was filming his follow-up flick *Harmony Row*, he stayed with the Maguires at the Hotel Metropole. At a dinner Mick hosted for the South Melbourne football club, the comedian 'kept the gathering in roars of laughter at his witticisms', helped out by other guests: British actor Alfred Frith, who had played opposite Bela Lugosi in Broadway smash *Dracula*, and American burlesque performer June Mills, famous after a stupendous run in Melbourne as the star of *Show Boat*. Patricia, Peggy and Joan were surely part of that night's entertainment. 'They were delightful little girls but they always had the manner of adults,' a family friend recalled later. 'They loved "dressing up" and I can see them now strutting about in the jewels and furs of anybody who was willing to indulge them.' Whether that night or on another occasion, June Mills saw something in Peggy and recommended her to Pat Hanna for his next movie, *Diggers in Blighty*.

This sequel would have Pat Hanna, George Moon and Joe Valli's larrikin soldiers going from the Western Front to the safety of leave in London. There were several prominent supporting female roles, and Hanna, making his directorial debut, wanted Peggy for one of these. Frustratingly, Victoria's Education Department refused the girl who had wagged school so often to see movies an official leave of absence to appear in one. Hanna made it up to her with a bit part as a secretary. Thrillingly, at just thirteen, Peggy was going to be in an Australian talkie and share a scene with its three biggest stars.

Anyone entertaining visions of Hollywood glamour was in for a rude shock on walking into Efftee Studios in October 1932. His Majesty's Theatre's stage was intact and usable for sets, but the fire had ruined the orchestra pit and stalls. Pat Hanna had further messed them up with sand and mud to make a sludgy facsimile of the trenches. The makeshift studio was primitively soundproofed with rock-wool and heavy curtains, yet nothing could stop the twisted girders and steel seat frames left by the fire from acting as radio receivers to fill the cavernous space with static, ghostly voices and snatches of songs. Scenes were sometimes delayed for hours until there were a few minutes of blessed silence. 'The place is ridden with wireless music,' cursed little Scotsman Joe Valli.

On her big day, Peggy was made up in the gaudy yellow greasepaint actors then wore so their skin appeared normally on film. In a white blouse and dark skirt, black hair gleaming in a permanent wave, she took her place in the London office set of an uptight British army paymaster. Pat Hanna told her all she had to do was look and act secretarial by typing and filing in the background while her boss and his underling were mocked by the film's leading ladies and male stars. He showed her the script of the scene and where she was to utter a single subversive syllable – somewhere between a hiccup and a snort – to puncture her commanding officer's most pompous statement.

As is the case on film sets, downtime was filled with industry talk, giving Peggy a chance to learn much about her co-stars and how movies were really made. She also got a glimpse of the way screen fame could fade because Raymond Longford, pioneering director of the Australian silent era, was working on the film. Broken by the tuberculosis death of Lottie Lyell, his partner in love and movie-making, he had been reduced to associate director and playing a ham role as a German spy.

Pat Hanna called for action and the camera rolled on Peggy's long scene. She did what was asked of her and timed her interjection nicely.

As she made her way home, Peggy's head had to be spinning. She was one of the few Australians who could say they had seen the other side of the silver screen where talkie stars lived and worked. With Frank Thring's ambition promising that more movies would be made in Melbourne, bigger roles would surely come her way. Around this time, *Table Talk* correspondent Stanley Parker met Peggy at dance-and-dinner venue The Rex. As the youngster ate an ice-cream sundae, he asked about her ambitions. 'To be a film star by the time I'm eighteen,' she told him. 'To make pictures in Hollywood by the time I'm twenty. To be able to look after my family. To see my name in electric lights in London before I'm twenty-one.' Having accomplished all of that, she wanted to marry: 'After all, that is every woman's real ambition.'

Diggers in Blighty was a step towards realising those dreams. But Peggy's hopes of making more Melbourne movies were dashed when her parents announced their big news: the family was moving a thousand miles north to take over Brisbane's historic Belle Vue Hotel. The announcement had to be traumatic for all of the Maguire girls, soon to leave behind the only lives they had ever known at the centre of Melbourne.

Bina and Mick had a plan. The hotel trade was getting ever tougher in Melbourne as the Great Depression put nearly one in three men out of work. With conditions so grim, people travelled less and booked fewer hotel rooms. They also drank far less, and Australian beer consumption had nearly halved. Not helping matters was that the Licences Reduction Board had slashed the number of hotels in Victoria in the past quarter century, while increasing land values in Melbourne's city centre meant pubs were being demolished for redevelopment. But Brisbane – that was a different story. Queensland's agricultural economy and state government policy had slightly softened the Depression, keeping more men in jobs or at least on relief work with a few shillings in their pockets. And the government wasn't demolishing pubs.

Mick's brother Andy had also just moved there, buying a huge horse stud in the Darling Downs, though the two men had become estranged since their boxing days.

If it hadn't been the Belle Vue on offer, Bina and Mick probably wouldn't have moved. But this particular hotel provided more than just a good business opportunity and a chance to escape Melbourne's doldrums – it presented a rare opportunity in 1930s Australia. As proprietors of the Belle Vue, the Maguires might leave behind the middle class and enter the upper echelons of polite society.

Minds made up, Mick and Bina spent Christmas in Melbourne with both sides of the family. Then, in January 1933, they headed north with their girls.

5.

After Melbourne's million-person metropolis, Brisbane's population of just three hundred thousand must have made it seem a little like an overgrown country town to the Maguire girls. But Peggy and her sisters were now the young mistresses of a grand and historic landmark. Located at the crossroads of state power, the Belle Vue shared the intersection of George and Alice streets with Parliament House, the Queensland Club and the city's Botanic Gardens. Even before the state became a separate colony from New South Wales in 1859, this prime site was occupied by Belle Vue House, used for a time as a 'Seminary for Young Ladies'. The name – reflecting the sweeping views – was retained when the first Belle Vue Hotel was erected as a one-storey, shingle-roofed building in the mid-1860s. Two decades later a new owner set about raising a hotel whose grandeur complemented Parliament House and the Queensland Club. Opening in 1886, this new Belle Vue was a three-storey brick and stone architectural masterpiece with a deep street verandah to protect from the sun and an enclosed rear garden courtyard. There were single rooms, double rooms and private suites with hot and cold baths, and balconies offering privacy behind exquisite iron-lace railings. Lavishly appointed, the hotel had a private bar, billiard parlour, vast dining room, numerous lounges, and telephone connections to all the city's important public and private offices. A hotel waiter met arriving river steamers, and each morning a barber ensured guests looked their best. Over the past fifty years, it had been a place where the rich and powerful shaped the fate of the city and the state.

The Belle Vue was a huge step up for the Maguires and it aligned perfectly with Bina's grand plan for her daughters. 'If you want to marry money,' she was fond of saying, 'you've got to go where the money is. You simply have to go to the right places.' While the Bull & Mouth had been colourful, and the Metropole frequented by famous show people, few places in Australia were better than the Belle Vue to meet the right moneyed people. The visitor books proved it. Here were the signatures of Australian prime ministers, premiers, governors-general, high court judges, business tycoons and wealthy graziers, along with local and international celebrities such as Oscar Asche, Dame Nellie Melba, Sir Arthur Conan Doyle and – in 1920, 1924 and 1928 – the visiting English cricket teams. The Belle Vue had also enjoyed royal favour. The Prince of Wales (the future King Edward VIII) was fond of dropping in for a drink during his 1920 tour. As a measure of thanks he gave a table, specially made for his use in Parliament House and autographed on its underside, to the Belle Vue. In 1927, when his brother, the Duke of York (the future King George VI), visited Brisbane, he also drank in the private bar.

The Maguires took over the Belle Vue on Australia Day 1933.

Peggy, though not yet fourteen, had reached her adult height of five feet and already appeared to be a beautiful young lady. She had deep brown eyes, long chestnut curls and a healthy complexion from riding horses and playing golf and tennis. Her beauty was matched by a kind nature, soft voice, cheeky smile, quick sense of humour and the self-possession that came from growing up amid a passing parade of hotel patrons. She settled into her new home town quickly. Two days after her parents became the Belle Vue's hosts, she and older socialite Mercia Doran went to the Ascot races, with Peggy looking very sophisticated in a *Truth* photograph. Bina and Mick, too, were quickly in the good graces of Archbishop James Duhig, who had been head of Brisbane's Catholic Church since 1917 and was Queensland's answer to Melbourne's Dr Mannix.

The Monday following her day at the races, Peggy and Joan started day school at Loreto College at Coorparoo, south of the Brisbane River, while Carmel and Lupe were enrolled as boarders. With just forty or so pupils across all grades, Loreto was quaint after the Academy. Peggy remained a restless student, more so now she was just weeks away from the school-leaving age, and would have envied older sister Patricia, who had finished her studies back in Melbourne. But irritation about a new year at a new school was eclipsed by the excitement of famous visitors checking into the Belle Vue.

Captain Douglas Jardine and his English cricket team became guests of the Maguire family at the height of the Bodyline controversy. Under Jardine's orders, bowlers unleashed fast balls pitched short to bounce high at Australian batsmen. Popular fury rose at the tactic most believed to be far from the spirit of the game. Tensions boiled over in mid-January during the Third Test in Adelaide when Aussie Bert Oldfield's skull was fractured by a Harold Larwood bumper. While the offending ball hadn't actually been a Bodyline delivery, fifty thousand furious spectators didn't care, and only mounted police stopped them from invading the field. Australian cricket authorities sent cables of complaint to their counterparts in England, labelling Bodyline 'unsportsman-like' and saying it threatened to upset 'friendly relations' between the two countries. There was talk of Australia seceding from the

Empire, and the English team were said to genuinely fear for their lives. With the visitors leading 2–1 in the Ashes series, all eyes would be on the Fourth Test in Brisbane.

By the time the English team pulled up to the Belle Vue in a rattling charabanc, Jardine and Larwood were the most hated men in Australia. While the controversy saw the Queensland Club forbid official English team dinners on its premises, Jardine and his players were to find hospitality, friendship and protection at the Belle Vue across the road. Bodyline might have been testing Australia's national identity and Anglophile loyalties, but Mick and Bina had no doubts about whose side they were on – their own. The English cricketers presented a terrific publicity opportunity for the Maguires to announce they were now hosts of the Belle Vue. Mick booked a larger-than-usual ad in *The Telegraph* that said he was personally supervising these important visitors so they might have rest, quiet and service. Bina announced a charity dinner-dance that would have the English team as guests of honour.

Jardine's public persona was 'Pommy bastard' but privately he was capable of warmth, charm and humour. As his hosts for nearly two weeks, the Maguires had the chance to see this side of the man. And, with Patricia, Peggy and Joan each night dressing in their finery and eating together in the dining room, Jardine and his team couldn't miss the daughters of his hosts. How the girls got about at less formal times also caught the eye. Veteran Australian reporter Gilbert Mant travelled with the English team and wrote:

> We all became a happy family with the Maguires. One of the reasons for us liking the Belle Vue so much was the presence of the licensee, Mick Maguire, and his wife and their three beautiful teenaged daughters. The three girls were nubile beauties who used to race along the hotel verandahs in the early

morning rather scantily clad, shouting and giggling. It was said
that Jardine took a shine to one of them. The fact was that
we all took a shine to all of them.

The daughter Jardine liked most was Peggy, as Australian Test
cricketer Bill O'Reilly discovered when he accepted an invitation to the English team's communal Saturday night dinner at
the Belle Vue. What he saw in the dining room surprised him:
there at the head of the table, sitting beside the English captain,
was thirteen-year-old Peggy Maguire. Though there's nothing
to suggest this was anything more than friendship, Jardine took
such a liking to her that he gave her a gold watch. Peggy had to
feel flattered by the attention of the famous older man and much
later told an American gossip columnist she had been 'that way'
over a man named Doug in Brisbane. Her acquaintance with
Jardine also came with the strange dissonance of learning the
private charms of a publicly despised figure. The angry crowds,
political leaders and newspaper columnists: they just hadn't seen
him the same way she had. It was an experience she would later
repeat with another very different English captain.

During the team's stay, Peggy also knew something else few
others did. With Brisbane sweltering in a heatwave, the Belle
Vue's private bar was a haven for the thirsty English cricketers,
whose safety couldn't be ensured at other Brisbane pubs. Mick
could also lend a sympathetic ear as someone who knew what it
was like to be abused by a hateful crowd, having spent his youth
belting and being belted on the footy field and in the boxing
ring. Those very pugilistic skills protected the bonds of Empire
one night when Mick was entertaining English players Harold
Larwood, Bill Voce, Les Ames, George Duckworth and Tommy
Mitchell, along with Australian journalist Gilbert Mant. As they
enjoyed their beers, a huge, bearded local strode into the bar and

started hassling the diminutive Mitchell. Fired up with a few drinks, the little Englishman challenged the bushman to fist-icuffs. Mant later recalled:

> Suddenly the big stranger produced a large revolver from his pocket and brandished it in the air. I can't remember whether it went off but we did. Harold says he vamoosed. I went under the bar, while Mick flattened the stranger with a perfect right cross.

Without Mick's fist, newspaper headlines might have screamed 'English Cricketer Shot Dead in Brisbane Hotel', leaving a far darker historical understanding of the term 'Bodyline War'.

The English and Australian teams faced off on the first day of play at the Gabba on Friday, 10 February. The whole country held its breath to see if Bradman and his boys could mount a defence to save the Ashes. Peggy had another reason for nervous anticipation that day: *Diggers in Blighty* and Frank Thring's new George Wallace comedy *Harmony Row* were set to premiere as a double-feature the very next night – albeit in Melbourne. The following week, newspapers reported the films had elicited a 'cascade of mirth-made applause' from a 'thronged and enthusiastic audience'. One article claimed the films set such a standard that everyone should feel optimistic about the new talkie industry. 'We are endeav-ouring to make Australian films of a worthy standard,' Pat Hanna had told the premiere crowd, 'and judging by the applause we are succeeding.' Peggy was proud to have played her part – however small – but she would have to wait three long months for *Diggers in Blighty* to make its way to Brisbane.

Back at the Gabba, Bodyline was temporarily forgotten for a moment of cricketing heroism – in which Mick played a supporting role. On the second day of the test, English batsman Eddie Paynter took ill with a fever of 102 and was confined to hospital. On the Sunday rest day, Mick proved he truly was – as his advertisement had claimed – personally supervising the players when he delivered nourishing soups from the Belle Vue's kitchen to Paynter's hospital room. By Monday the Englishman had improved a little and was listening to the third day's play on the radio when he heard his side faltering. Rising from his sickbed, Paynter demanded to be driven to the Belle Vue. There, he grabbed his cricket flannels and rushed to the Gabba to take the crease. Despite his fever and the stifling heat, Paynter hit a whopping eighty-three that put England in the lead. Then, on 16 February, the sixth day's play, he hit the six that saw the English team win by six wickets and retain the Ashes. Viewed from an Australian perspective, Mick might have made those soups a little *less* nourishing.

Heavy rain drenched Brisbane that night but nothing could dampen spirits at the Belle Vue. While most Australians mourned the loss of the Ashes, Mick, Bina, Patricia and Peggy helped to host the charity gala that was now also an English victory celebration. Triumphant Douglas Jardine dined with his team and guests, and a bat autographed by the English side raised £21 at auction for a children's charity. Jimmy Bancks, creator of Ginger Meggs, and Arthur Mailey, the Aussie Test cricketer turned cartoonist, did lightning sketches of guests that were sold to raise money for the cause. The hotel's orchestra played for the sweaty dancers in the ballroom, parties enjoyed bridge in the lounge, and supper was served in the dining room spectacularly decorated with pink roses. Presiding over this glittering affair, Bina looked every bit the society matron, flanked by her beautiful young daughters Patricia and Peggy.

The next day Brisbane's newspapers politely reported a sophisticated event held for a charitable cause. In his definitive book *Bodyline Autopsy*, cricket writer David Frith paints a more familiar picture of sportsmen letting off steam after a big win: 'The Englishmen had a celebration dinner-dance that night, and there were schoolboy shenanigans back at the Belle Vue, with bed-clothing, shoes and whatnot strewn all over the hotel.'

The Maguires had arrived in Brisbane society. But they had even bigger and better plans for the Belle Vue, themselves and their daughters.

6.

As Peggy counted down the days to *Diggers in Blighty*'s local release, Bina and Mick set about restoring the Belle Vue to its status as *the* place to be in Brisbane. The renovations announced in March 1933 were to remodel the bar and offices; repair, repaper and refurbish the fifty-three guestrooms and suites; and, as a measure of what pubs were like in the days of the iceman, install a refrigeration plant and coldroom for the kitchen. Even more impressive were plans for the Belle Vue's public areas. The hotel would have two new lounges and a big new ballroom that was to double dancer capacity to four hundred and offering the latest in luxury technology: *air-conditioning*.

While her parents planned, Peggy plodded at Loreto, showing talent only for elocution, languages and history. Her favourite subjects came after school at the Belle Vue, where she continued tuition in singing, violin, piano and ballet. Apart from going to the pictures, Peggy's other passions were reading and religion. Growing up next to Cole's Book Arcade had made her an avid reader who devoured J. B. Priestley's *Angel Pavement*, John Galsworthy's *The Forsyte Saga*, and Georgette Heyer's Regency romances and detective thrillers. Growing up Catholic had made her believe she was called to be a Bride of Christ like her aunt

Marie. Moved by the spirit, Peggy begged Loreto's mother superior to let her take the veil. But she was told: 'Your vocation lies in the outside world.' Peggy's parents were thankful. Even as a staunch Catholic, Mick had been quietly horrified by his sister's decision to become a nun, and Bina certainly didn't want her pretty young daughter cloistered. Peggy's religious fervour was short-lived. Although she signed up as a founder of a new Catholic youth group at Loreto, she didn't attend its inaugural meeting – or any of their monthly devotional sessions.

Where Peggy worshipped most consistently was in the motion-picture cathedrals of her new home city, with the Belle Vue not far from the grandeur of the Regent, Tivoli and Wintergarden theatres. Moviegoing was much more exciting now that talkies had come into their own. Even though Peggy liked the ones she'd seen back in Melbourne, there was no getting around how many were stagey and stilted. She knew why – she had seen how big and cumbersome the sound equipment was on *Diggers in Blighty*. But actors and directors had grown used to the new medium, and now films were more natural. Dialogue sparkled, songs and dances were sublime, and the special effects ever more breathtaking. Her first year in Brisbane, Peggy had the chance to see *Grand Hotel, Shanghai Express, I Am a Fugitive from a Chain Gang, Red Dust, Trouble in Paradise, Duck Soup, Tarzan, King Kong, The Invisible Man* and *Little Women*. Back at the Belle Vue she could play at imitating a new breed of screen heroines – women like Maureen O'Sullivan, Jean Harlow, Kay Francis, Katharine Hepburn and Ginger Rogers – and try to nail the dance routines Busby Berkeley had perfected in the musicals *42nd Street, Footlight Parade* and *Gold Diggers of 1933*.

Peggy yearned to use these skills on screen. Yet there was little hope she'd ever do so in Brisbane. Pat Hanna was shooting a film called *Waltzing Matilda* in Melbourne. Sydney was taking off as a production centre, too, with Charles Chauvel making *In the Wake of the Bounty* and Ken Hall filming his romantic saga *The Squatter's Daughter*. No movies were being made in Queensland – not a single feature had been produced in the state since the silent days.

––––––––

Peggy was up there on the silver screen, larger than life, doing everything right but unable to stop her big moment from going wrong. She wouldn't have known whether to laugh or cry. Perhaps she did both. Her first chance to see *Diggers in Blighty* was the 10.00 a.m. session on its opening day at the Regent Theatre on Saturday, 13 May. Always keen to advance their daughters' interests, Bina and Mick surely let the cinema's manager, Edgar Betts, know he had a rising star in his presence. Peggy couldn't have hoped for a grander Brisbane venue to see her film debut: the Regent was the city's finest picture palace. As people-about-town, the Maguires would have opted for pricier balcony seats in an auditorium built for 2600 patrons. That meant passing through an entry hall whose ceiling was richly decorated with plaster moulds, traipsing along a grand foyer with Spanish gothic balconies, then climbing a dazzling white marble staircase to a mezzanine anteroom. From their seats, the view was even more impressive. A massive bronze chandelier cast a golden glow on the majestic proscenium framing gold silk-velvet curtains. Everywhere they looked, plaster decorations were bathed in soft cove lighting.

Peggy's nerves weren't helped by the long wait for *Diggers in Blighty* to start. After ushers in their smart uniforms showed the audience to their seats by torchlight, bandleader Ned Tyrell and his orchestra struck up 'God Save the King' and everyone stood to sing along. Then Edgar Betts took to the stage to read the cable he had received from Frank Thring, just back from showing the films to British distributors, who had acclaimed George Wallace and Pat Hanna as 'two of the world's funniest screen comedians'. Betts, a master of film publicity, wouldn't have missed the chance to hit a local angle by telling his audience that *Diggers in Blighty* showed the charms of Miss Peggy Maguire, daughter of the Belle Vue's new managers. If her reactions to later previews are anything to go by, she felt a mixture of pride and awkwardness at suddenly if briefly being the centre of attention. Cheers and applause subsiding, Ned Tyrell led his orchestra in a few tunes before ceding the stage to a noted bird mimic and whistler. Next: the Fox Movietone newsreel. That week's big stories included George Bernard Shaw's first American visit and the chilling prediction that new chancellor Adolf Hitler's grip on Germany would lead to a Nazi dictatorship.

Diggers in Blighty's opening shots showed Aussies being shelled by dastardly Germans on the Western Front. Peggy then saw funny sequences she'd heard about during filming. There were Pat Hanna, Joe Valli and George Moon flirting with nurses, getting ducks drunk, chasing rum and beer, and sticking it to their stuffy British superiors at every opportunity. Peggy's big moment approached when London city shots established that the Diggers had finally reached Blighty. Now all they wanted were their salaries from the paymaster, who was too busy boasting to the film's unimpressed leading ladies, Thelma Scott and Prudence Irving. Peggy, huge on the screen, or at least at the edge of it, pretended to go about secretarial duties and snuck a few amused glances over her shoulder at her co-stars.

'Hey!' Pat Hanna called from the off-screen waiting room. 'You haven't got a dozen eggs in there, have ya?'

'No, what the devil!' the sergeant blustered. 'Why?'

'We've been sitting here long enough to hatch them!' came the rejoinder.

'Have you been "over there", sergeant?' Thelma needled, just as an actor playing a corporal entered the scene – and blocked the camera's view of Peggy.

The actor didn't move, nor did the camera, as her funny bit got ever closer.

'Of course not,' the pompous sergeant snapped. 'Our services are indispensable here – aren't they, corporal?'

'Certainly,' his adjutant agreed.

'Hic!' Peggy objected.

Her character's mockery made her superiors whirl in shock at such impudence. The actors alone saw Peggy's reaction because the camera's view of her remained blocked. Not that the audience cared even if they noticed. But as they fell about laughing, Peggy had every right to feel crushed. Pat Hanna's careless direction had ruined her big moment. She had been heard but not seen – that's what radio was for.

But Peggy had to see the bright side. What did it matter if there had been a little kerfuffle? Everyone in the Regent had laughed. And they were still laughing as the rest of the scene played out with Pat, George and Joe now hassling the paymaster. Peggy was still on screen alongside three of the country's biggest stars. How many people could say they had been in a talkie? There had only been a handful made in Australia. The action moved to an English country house in order to tie up the film's romantic and espionage subplots. Then, after intermission, the Maguire family watched their mate George Wallace bumble his way through *Harmony Row* as Melbourne's most hopeless policeman.

Exiting the Regent, Peggy saw that the queue for the next session went right out onto the street. She must have realised she might be in for minor recognition during the coming weeks; at the very least, she would be a schoolyard celebrity at Loreto.

Pleasing as these prospects were, they didn't put her any closer to real stardom. While *Diggers in Blighty* did good business, Brisbane audiences also flocked to other movies that same week. Charles Chauvel's first talkie, *In the Wake of the Bounty*, was on at the Majestic, starring new Australian discovery Errol Flynn. At the Savoy Astor, handsome Charles Farrell and beautiful Janet Gaynor were in love yet again in the remake of Mary Pickford's silent *Tess of the Storm Country*. Film-crazy Peggy surely saw both. But even in her wildest fantasies, she didn't dare imagine newspapers would soon compare her with Janet Gaynor and Mary Pickford as she made movies with Charles Chauvel and Charles Farrell on her way to partying in Hollywood with Errol Flynn.

Yet it would all happen just like that.

7.

Bina and Mick put Peggy on that very path by renovating the Belle Vue. Although the hotel's full glories were still a year from being realised, the Maguires quickly restored its status as one of Brisbane's busiest VIP venues – which, in turn, increased their social standing, raised Patricia and Peggy's profiles, and put the family in all the 'right' circles. Not a week went by without the social pages reporting the comings and goings of notable citizens – including Governor Sir Leslie Orme Wilson and Premier William Forgan Smith – at dinners and balls. As the year progressed, Patricia and Peggy became members of Brisbane's 'youth set', their names starting to appear in these newspaper columns as they went to dances, and theatrical and musical performances. Their friends were similarly fashionable unmarried women in their teens, twenties and thirties. There was Ina Jones, daughter of a prominent state politician. Mercia Doran, who'd been photographed with Peggy at the races, and her close friend Marjorie Norval, a rising public servant in an era when few women worked in government. Sharing the Maguire girls' interest in the arts were: Moya Connolly, a talented young actress and aspiring film producer; Barbara Oelrichs, who tutored them in ballet, deportment and physical culture; and wonderfully named elocution teacher Una Vowles.

At just fourteen, Peggy was a junior member of this social circle and still playing second fiddle to Patricia, who, now nearly seventeen, could accompany Bina to more sophisticated events. Having always suspected Peggy to be their mother's favourite, Patricia made the most of these occasions. Though she would lose the competition for maternal affection, public attention and male favour, for the moment the sisters were on relatively equal footing. While Peggy had been befriended by Douglas Jardine and seen in *Diggers in Blighty*, Patricia had done better at school and was a far better singer, thanks to private tuition by Gladys Moncrieff, a performer so beloved by Australians she was known as 'Our Glad'. Patricia occasionally sang with the Belle Vue's orchestra and was good enough for *The Telegraph*'s music critic to publicly urge her to do professional shows. She was also now of marriageable age, presented as a 'strikingly pretty blonde' debutante to lieutenant-governor and state chief justice Sir James Blair at the Nudgee Old Boys' Ball in the presence of Australian Prime Minister Joseph Lyons. To mark the occasion, Patricia's elegant portrait appeared in *The Telegraph*. But this would be one of the last times for many years that she received newspaper coverage without being mentioned in the context of her younger sister.

On 1 November 1933 Bina, Patricia and Peggy were together in the dress circle at the Theatre Royal for the opening night of comedian Jim Gerald's new show. While the VIP audience included the governor, the crowd really went wild for Don Bradman, who received a huge round of applause as he took his seat with the New South Wales cricket team. By then Patricia and Peggy were attractions in their own right. 'After the show they all went backstage to see Jim Gerald and be introduced to the two colleens Maguire,' *Truth* reported of the cricketers, using

the Irish term for 'girl' to describe the young beauties. Peggy and
Patricia charmed Don Bradman and his teammates as surely as
they had enchanted their sworn enemies at the start of the year.
Bina worked her magic and invited everyone back to the Belle
Vue for supper. 'Cricket does not prevent Don Bradman making
an onslaught on the cream cakes,' *Truth* noted wryly.

Fun though this impromptu gathering was, Bina's next social
invitation seemed more calculated to connect Peggy and Patricia
with the 'right' people.

Jocelyn Howarth, heralded as Australia's 'first girl talkie star',
arrived in Brisbane by train from Sydney on 8 November. The
22-year-old beauty had enjoyed some stage success before director
Ken Hall cast her in Cinesound's *The Squatter's Daughter*. The
production had nearly ended in tragedy when a bushfire scene
went wrong, seriously burning two crew members, and scorching
the director and his cinematographer, Frank Hurley. Jocelyn had
been singed. That, along with her bravery in a scene where she
galloped on horseback past trees being dynamited, was publicity
gold and ensured she was big news throughout 1933. Much was
also made of her being the first Australian actress to fly in a plane
to a film set and that she was the 'living double' of Hollywood
goddess Constance Bennett. Jocelyn had come to Brisbane to do
interviews and make personal appearances before each screening
of her film at the Regent. Such was the excitement that school-
girls lined up at the railway station to watch her arrive, pressing
against the gates, autograph books held out hopefully.

Peggy wasn't among them – she didn't need to be. Jocelyn's
first social engagement was a tea party held for her at the Belle
Vue. On that warm spring afternoon, the actress was ushered into
the hotel lounge that Bina, Peggy and Patricia had decorated with
marigolds and roses. Their guest didn't disappoint: Jocelyn looked
every bit the movie star. She had blue eyes, a dazzling smile,

golden hair set in a wave and a petite figure draped in a grey crepe frock. But she endeared herself to the Maguire women with an unspoiled manner. Even more charmingly, she had brought her mother along. Jocelyn held court, now accustomed to recounting how she had come to film fame after Ken Hall had spotted her in an amateur play and subjected her to gruelling screen tests. Yet life on set wasn't as glamorous as the fan magazines would have readers believe. 'Everybody made up and on the set by 8 a.m.,' she had told an interviewer earlier that day. 'If you are lucky you may finish at 6 p.m. or 9 p.m., but if it's a ballroom scene that is being shot it may go on until 3.30 the next morning.' Despite such hours, to say nothing of the dangers posed by bushfires and exploding trees, Jocelyn admitted she was hooked on her new career. 'Film work gets into one's blood,' she said. 'There is the feeling that one simply must go on.' Jocelyn could also confirm she hoped to make films in Hollywood and London.

While Jocelyn was the guest of honour, the others present – Edgar Betts, Jim Gerald and his wife and actress Essie Jennings, famous pianist Edward Cahill and youth-set fashion trendsetter Joan Perry – ensured lively conversation. Edgar was hopeful *The Squatter's Daughter*'s strong box office in Sydney and Melbourne augured well for its Brisbane season. Jim and Essie could talk about Hollywood: he had made two-reeler comedies there in 1928, accompanied by his niece, the actress Phyllis Barry, who had since returned to America and just hit it big as leading lady to Buster Keaton in *What! No Beer?*. Phyllis's success had to make Jocelyn hopeful she could be a Hollywood star – and surely lit a fire in Peggy's and Patricia's eyes. The Maguire girls, never backwards in coming forwards, would have recounted their own musical, stage and screen experiences. Fred Derrick, one of Brisbane's leading publicity men, was also at that afternoon tea. A guest of the Belle Vue's Empire Day function six months earlier, he was well aware of the charms of the colleens Maguire, particularly the ever-prettier Peggy.

Shortly after that tea party, Peggy did a screen test for Cinesound in Brisbane, likely recommended by Jocelyn Howarth. Such try-outs were nerve-racking. On her big day, Peggy spent hours being prepped by a hairdresser and make-up artist while the director, cameraman and sound-and-lighting boys readied everything. Then came those stressful few minutes where she had to deliver her lines, expressions and movements. A photo from the test shows her sparkling eyes and brilliant smile, pretty face framed by long, coiffured curls. Peggy seemed to burst with charisma – but Cinesound didn't cast her in anything. She did, however, find a fan in Pendil Rayner, young pictorial editor at *The Telegraph*, who published a photo of her looking vivacious in a swimming costume at the end of January 1934, with the caption noting her *Diggers in Blighty* role and recent screen test. In early April, Rayner put a photo of Peggy on the front page of his newspaper, with her looking rather ladylike in a broad-brimmed hat.

She wasn't the only Maguire whose movements made the newspapers that month. Mick again proved a man of action, even though now nearly forty and running to fat. This new opportunity for heroics arose when a young crim broke into the Belle Vue. This 'pub barber' – the nickname for a sneak-thief who pilfered hotel rooms – crept in around midnight. Mick chased the intruder out into the street, collared him and called for the constabulary. Given how Mick had protected the English cricketers, the pub barber may well have been relieved to be taken into police custody.

All the right people were guests at the reopening of the Belle Vue on Thursday, 10 May 1934. But anyone with access to a radio was also invited, because the gala was broadcast live by 4BH. Depression-era listeners had to feel a mixture of awe and envy as they heard the fanfare of trumpets and descriptions of guests who entered according to their social rank. Governor Sir Leslie Orme Wilson, wearing his full dress uniform, was received in the hotel's foyer by Bina, splendid in a black velvet gown and flanked by the matrons whose charities were to share the proceeds from the night. Queensland's leading political, business and legal figures were welcomed, accompanied by society wives and daughters shimmering in satins and velvets. A battalion of waiters in blue dress suits looked like an imperial army as they tended to these VIPs.

The Belle Vue's new ballroom was a marvel, with walls panelled in maple and inset with large mirrors so guests could watch themselves waltz beneath the crystal chandeliers. The atmosphere was of richly appointed refinement. And everyone adored the air-conditioning, which would transform Brisbane society by allowing for dancing on even the most oppressive summer nights. The old ballroom had been converted into the elegant Green Lounge, its carpet, curtains and chairs offering soothing woodland hues beneath golden lights. Across the hallway was the refurbished Brown Lounge, with cream pillars, pile carpet, chairs in floral velvet and everything softly lit. In the new dining room, tables were set with a profusion of chrysanthemums, while the second and third dining rooms were also floral spectaculars. Guests swanned around exclaiming, 'How perfectly perfect!' and 'Too sweet for anything!'

Acting Premier Percy Pease officially opened the new ballroom, noting that it was the biggest in the state and proud it had been built using twenty different types of Queensland hardwood. His speech over, white-suited conductor Charles Webb tapped his baton to ready his tuxedo-wearing orchestra. Now Peggy Maguire, stunning in a Victorian-vintage *robe de style* of white

Spanish lace and gloved to the shoulder, had the first dance with
His Excellency the Governor. This wasn't her debut but it caused
a stir. 'She should be in talkies,' an observer remarked, 'she is so
lovely and vital!'

Fred Derrick was there to watch that dance. The publicity
expert had volunteered his services for the ball, and he was frequently at the Belle Vue in April and early May. But he was now
also working for filmmaker Charles Chauvel, soon to arrive in
Queensland to shoot exteriors for his historical epic *Heritage*, whose
£24000 ($2.3 million) budget made it the most expensive film
ever attempted in Australia. Fred Derrick had just that week been
location scouting at Canungra, a valley hamlet some fifty miles
south of Brisbane, which had inspired him to cook up a stunt to
ensure everyone in the city knew about the movie. Partnering
with *The Telegraph*, 4BH and the Railway Department, he got
Chauvel to announce a 'movie picnic' at Canungra that would
let ordinary folk see how a talkie was made.

What hadn't been publicly announced yet was that *Heritage*
was still in need of a leading lady. Soon after he saw Peggy whirl
gracefully around the Belle Vue ballroom with the splendidly
attired governor, the pair looking every bit like a beautiful vision
from colonial history, Derrick had a publicity and casting idea he
thought might be of interest to Chauvel.

———

Heritage was to chronicle the white settlement of Australia from
the First Fleet through to the modern day, with this sprawling
history following several generations of two families. Queensland
filming began near Canungra on Saturday, 19 May. That night, at
the little village's School of Arts, writer-producer-director Charles
Chauvel, a slight, dark-eyed fellow who talked a mile a minute,
and his wife, Elsa, a beautiful former actress turned script editor,

thanked the townspeople for their hospitality in a speech carried on 4BH. Charles revealed that, though he had cast Sydney stage actor Franklyn Bennett and Melbourne stage actress Margot Rhys in lead roles, he was still looking for the right actress to play the crucial character of Irish colleen Biddy O'Connor, whose scenes were soon to be filmed in Melbourne. Then he welcomed to the stage Joe Valli, who had a supporting comic part in *Heritage*, to introduce a special screening of *Diggers in Blighty*.

The movie picnic – now called 'Brisbane's Day Out' – was held on Sunday, 27 May. By late morning, four thousand out-of-towners had descended on Canungra, arriving in two specially chartered trains and a convoy of nearly four hundred cars. As a brass band played, city people and Canungra locals ate their packed lunches and took up positions above the creek crossing just outside of town. In the early afternoon, Charles Chauvel climbed a dais, voice amplified by speakers, to praise the region's natural beauty and tell the crowd that *Heritage* would celebrate Australia's pioneering spirit. He introduced his stars: Franklyn, Margot, Joe and an old bullock driver named Dave Ware whom he'd discovered when filming at the Clarence River over the border in New South Wales.

Then it was time to show Queenslanders how a movie was made. Down the hill from the crowd, a settler's covered wagon, pulled by bullocks and flanked by riflemen in period garb on horseback, made its way towards the creek. From the surrounding bush, forty Aboriginal warriors suddenly appeared and hurled spears at the white men. The settlers fought them off with a fusillade that sent the peppery smell of gunpowder floating across the valley. Excited shouts went up from the crowd at the realism of these stunts. The day's filming done, the spectators enjoyed a variety show, broadcast by 4BH, with much excitement generated by the Aboriginal gumleaf band and corroboree, and spear- and boomerang-throwing demonstrations.

How the Indigenous men felt about the day wasn't recorded. They certainly would have had a different perspective, given they were from Barambah Aboriginal Reserve, which housed hundreds of Aboriginal people who had been forcibly removed from their tribal homes. The forty men had been 'loaned' to Chauvel 'under authoritative control' by the Queensland Government for *Heritage*. Instead *The Telegraph* noted how rare such an opportunity was anywhere in the world: 'The Brisbane folk who went to Canungra on Sunday achieved something that many Hollywood residents have failed to do – go on location with a film company.' A lot of young girls also saw the picnic as a chance to be discovered. 'Some of the youth and beauty of Brisbane went down with the object of trying to break into the movies via Charles Chauvel's search for a girl to play the heroine,' *Truth* reported. 'Some nearly froze in shorts that were little more than V's to get the camera man's eye.'

Film-crazy Peggy wasn't one of them. Though she knew *Heritage* picnic organiser Fred Derrick, though she had already shared the silver screen with the film's co-star Joe Valli, though she was aware that Charles Chauvel needed an Irish colleen-type just like her, she of all people missed out on the opportunity.

Yet back at the Belle Vue, Peggy was bursting with excitement. Not that she could tell anyone why.

8.

Where Is Biddy O'Connor?
Girl to Play Irish Colleen
IMPORTANT ROLE IN "HERITAGE"

So read a headline in *The Telegraph* on 1 June 1934 as Charles Chauvel and Fred Derrick launched the next phase of their publicity strategy. Partnering with the Brisbane newspaper — where Peggy had a fan in pictorial editor Pendil Rayner — and 4BH — which was now broadcasting live from the Belle Vue ballroom four nights a week — they described the girl they hoped to find through a nationwide competition:

> Wanted . . . about one hundredweight of feminine charm and loveliness. This little bundle of mischief must be about 5 feet 2 inches in height and must be able to adapt her speech to a broad Irish accent and to well spoken English. If you, charming lady, can fulfil these qualifications you may be able to fulfil a few more which Mr Charles Chauvel will demand of you before he casts you as Biddy O'Connor in his new film "Heritage".

An outline of Biddy's story followed, from her arrival in Australia on the *Red Rover* bride ship in 1832 and romance with a teamster to her marriage to a pioneer, eventual tragic fate and resurrection of sorts in the persona of her great-granddaughter. Both roles were to be filled by the same 'petite, raven-haired colleen, beautiful to the eye, with a captivating smile'. The winner, Charles promised, would have 'screen celebrity within the year', though not *all* potential Biddies were to apply: 'It must be obvious that such a girl must not be too tall and not too . . . well, plump.'

Aspiring screen celebrities were asked to send a photo, physical description and details of stage or screen experience to *The Telegraph*'s pictorial editor. The best entrant portraits would be published daily until the competition closed on 14 June. The article ended with the exhortation: 'There is no time to lose in this matter.'

Peggy lost no time in this matter. The call for entries appeared on page five of the afternoon edition. By the late edition her photograph featured on page eleven. 'Two hours after *The Telegraph* announced that Australian Expeditionary Films were searching for an Irish colleen to play in the film *Heritage*, Miss Peggy Maguire submitted this photograph of herself for the competition,' read Pendil Rayner's caption. In the picture, Peggy was in the white lace dress she had worn when she danced with the governor. She sat side-on to the camera, a curve of pale shoulder showing, dark hair shorter than in the screen test, set in a permanent wave and adorned with a rose. Face turned to the lens, her dark eyes held a mischievous glint and she offered an elusive smile. Peggy ticked all the physical boxes.

In the coming days, the competition generated constant publicity, with *The Telegraph* publishing contestant photos, reprinting the call for entries, and devoting several full pages to pictorial features about *Heritage*'s now-completed Queensland shoot.

Then, on 16 June 1934, came *The Telegraph*'s big announcement.

STAR AT 15!
Biddy O'Connor for "Heritage"
MISS PEGGY MAGUIRE'S CHANCE

Most girls will envy Peggy Maguire, who, from many applicants in all states, has been chosen to play the part of Biddy O'Connor in the Australian film "Heritage" . . .

Peggy had won her chance at movie stardom fair and square in a national star search. It was a great story and one that followed her through her career. But she had to keep secret about how she really got her big chance.

———

On Sunday, 20 May, the Maguires had received a surprise visit from Charles Chauvel, which led to Peggy being offered a screen test more than a week before the competition was announced.

That afternoon, Bina and Mick were in foul moods because the Belle Vue had been raided the previous night for after-hours trading. This time the Maguires hadn't just stayed open a few extra minutes as Mick tried to clear the six o'clock swill crowd; they had been busted at 11.20 p.m. with a full house and a barmaid busily serving drinks. Bina and Mick suspected their planned defence – that the law was an ass and they were doing the state a favour by giving tourists what they wanted – wouldn't fly when it came time for the magistrate's hearing. So a visit from famous filmmaker Charles Chauvel – who, like Mick, had started out as a protégé of Snowy Baker – was a welcome distraction. Particularly when they heard why he had driven up from Canungra on his day off from shooting *Heritage*.

Charles explained that their mutual friend Fred Derrick had enthused about Peggy's suitability for the role of Biddy O'Connor. So had Joe Valli. Last night he had seen proof with his own eyes watching *Diggers in Blighty* with the good folks of Canungra. Was it possible to meet her? It was, and Charles was delighted. Peggy, nearly two years older than she'd been when she'd made Pat Hanna's film, was beautiful, charming, confident, slender, and both well spoken and capable of a reasonable Irish accent. Despite being only fifteen, she looked mature enough to convince as a colonial bride and modern woman. Charles asked if she could do a screen test in a few weeks in Melbourne. Bina and Mick gave their delighted consent; Peggy was wild with excitement. But Charles had an unusual request: they should keep this confidential and be ready to submit a photo for a casting competition he would soon announce.

While not the official story, it is possible to divine this scene from inconsistencies in *The Telegraph*'s coverage, conflicting reports in rival newspapers, and careless comments made by Charles, Elsa and Peggy.

Immediately upon Peggy's photo being published so soon after the competition announcement, whispers began that Charles had already chosen her as his Biddy. The very next morning, just before he boarded a train to Melbourne, he felt compelled to issue a denial. 'You can assure your readers that I have not promised anyone in Brisbane or elsewhere the part of Biddy O'Connor,' Charles told *The Telegraph*. But he also abruptly brought forward the competition closing date to 9 June, saying it was now even more urgent for him to start filming – without explaining what had so suddenly changed. Another comment hinted he had someone in mind: 'Any competitor in Australia who happens to be in Melbourne before the closing date, and who I consider justifies a test, will be given one . . . just as I have done with so many hundreds of others . . . so far without success.' Given that tests cost upwards of £25 each, and doing so many would have eaten up much of his budget, this exaggeration was meant to create the idea of a major talent search.

On that first weekend in June, Bina couldn't quite suppress her exhilaration. *Truth*'s society scribe, Ruby Eve, who would become close to the family, spilled what she knew in her gossip column on the Sunday. 'There was great excitement in the Maguire household when Peggy was chosen by Charles Chauvel to make a test in Melbourne for the leading feminine role in *Heritage*,' she wrote. 'She leaves this morning with her father . . .' Just thirty-six hours had elapsed from Peggy's photo being published to her departure on the train. Though the contest's official sponsor, *The Telegraph* neglected to report this important development. Then, after the official announcement of Peggy's casting, Charles's account of how he found her faltered in that very newspaper when he said she had been brought to his attention when he saw *Diggers in Blighty* in Canungra. Yet he still maintained it wasn't until after seeing her photo in *The Telegraph* that he interviewed her and offered the screen test. Except, of course, that Peggy's photo appeared on Friday evening and he left Brisbane early the next morning.

In later years Elsa Chauvel forgot the competition entirely. 'Before commencing production, and during a short visit to Brisbane, Charles had discovered Mary Maguire,' she wrote in her autobiography. 'This lovely child was brought to our notice by a Brisbane publicity man . . . One look at Mary, or Peggy as she was then called, told Charles that he had found his Biddy.' That aligns with a report in the *Courier-Mail* on 16 June: 'Mrs Maguire said that after her daughter had been mentioned as a possible Biddy O'Connor to Mr Chauvel, he drove from Canungra to Brisbane to see her. After their first meeting he said that Peggy was the Biddy for whom he was looking, and negotiations for the contract were begun.' The sequence of events also explained

Peggy's absence from the movie picnic. It wouldn't have been smart for a prominent 'youth set' beauty to be seen there if she was to be 'discovered' a few weeks later through an exciting national quest.

Hundreds of *Heritage* entrants would have been angry if they had known they never stood a chance. But it was understandable that Charles, who had done publicity for Douglas Fairbanks in Hollywood, resorted to such a ruse. American studios had a near-monopoly over the Australian movie market, so his best chance at securing distribution and a profit was to get as much free newspaper and radio coverage as possible. Charles knew that women, who bought 60 per cent of tickets and held great sway over what their menfolk saw, often decided if they wanted to see a movie based on such advance publicity. It made sense to make *Heritage* a hot topic with its main Queensland audience. Few things were more exciting than a star quest – and now many women would want to see the movie to decide if they – or their sister, friend, daughter or niece – would have made a better Biddy than Peggy Maguire.

Charles had even used the ploy before. Making his debut feature *Greenhide* in Queensland in 1926, he had known he wanted stage actress Elsa Sylvaney – soon to become his wife – for his leading lady but nevertheless staged a 'bathing beauty' quest for newsreel publicity. He also would later invent the story that he'd chosen his most famous leading man, Errol Flynn, for *In the Wake of the Bounty* after serendipitously seeing a newspaper story about him being shipwrecked and sending a man out to scour Sydney pubs until he found the young adventurer.

Just like Flynn's casting yarn, the story of Peggy's discovery stuck and she stuck to the story. With one exception – speaking to Grafton's *Daily Examiner* in September 1935, she let slip that she had been discovered when 'an emissary from

Expeditionary Films' visited the Belle Vue after receiving a 'tip' from a friend. 'He gave me the once over with his eyes,' she said, 'and sighed when I consented to a test at the company's studios in Melbourne.'

9.

Peggy and Mick stepped off the train and into the wintry cold of Melbourne's Spencer Street railway station on Tuesday, 5 June 1934. Father and daughter checked into the elegant Menzies Hotel, whose guests had included the likes of Mark Twain, Herbert Hoover and Sarah Bernhardt. After the long journey from Brisbane, the Maguires welcomed the chance to freshen up and rest awhile. Then it was time to visit with family, because Mick was turning forty the following day. Although still suffering the effects of the Depression, Melbourne was preparing for its own birthday as its centenary approached, with the city sprucing itself up before the Duke of Gloucester arrived to launch celebrations in October. The shabby Port Melbourne waterfront had been given a facelift with the Centenary Bridge, while Captain Cook's Cottage had been transported brick by brick from England to be reconstructed in Fitzroy Gardens. Most impressive was that the Shrine of Remembrance on St Kilda Road was nearing completion after seven years.

Another change that had taken place in Peggy's absence was less welcome: a new Woolworths store now stood on the site that the Bull & Mouth had occupied for eight decades. Realising the first home she could remember was gone forever had to be a sad moment for the sensitive youngster.

There wasn't too much time for contemplation. Despite Charles's certainty about her, Peggy needed to be screen-tested for *Heritage*. She went out to St Kilda's Wattle Path Palais – which had been one of the city's biggest dance venues last time she was in Melbourne – and saw how Australian talkie pioneer Frank Thring had transformed the place into his new Efftee HQ. Charles had rented what was now a truly professional film production facility for his epic. Walking through its doors, Peggy was a little over-whelmed. 'I felt really afraid when I found myself in the large studio,' she confessed. 'Bullocks were yoked in the studio, and there was a selection scene, with pigs and calves, and at the end of all this, the big ship scene in which I was to play my first part. Men were being chosen for sailors and soldiers for the sequence, and in rooms at one end of the studio, sixty Irish girls, who had been chosen from more than four hundred applicants, were being fitted for their costumes.' The sets, props and period outfits were based on months of research led by Ray Lindsay – son of the famous artist Norman Lindsay – who interviewed pioneer fam-ilies and sourced artifacts from museums, old homes and ancient second-hand shops. Such period realism stood in contrast to the latest in movie-making equipment: cameras encased in sound-proof blimps, microphones mounted on swinging booms and a wooden tower for capturing overhead shots. Everything was lit by huge arc lights mounted on gantries and powered by the stu-dio's own electrical substation.

Awed, Peggy was anxious to prove that she was the right girl to be at the centre of all this. She was welcomed by Charles, shown around, and introduced to key cast and crew. Seeing a couple of familiar faces from *Diggers in Blighty* – Joe Valli and cameraman Arthur Higgins – was comforting but she gravitated most to Elsa Chauvel. As an actress, Elsa knew the pressure Peggy was under. As the film's script editor, she understood Biddy's character and dialogue. As a woman, she offered her husband expertise in all things 'feminine' – including soothing the nerves of his hopeful leading lady.

Peggy was told her character had been renamed Biddy O'Shea, then given her screen-test script pages and some time to familiarise herself with them as she was coiffured, made up in yellow greasepaint and put into a period dress. Then it was time for her to go in front of the camera beneath the glare of the klieg lights. Under Charles's direction Peggy had to sit, stand, face this way and that, walk here and there, and deliver emotional lines with the right tearful conviction and Irish brogue. The searing heat of the lights that could quickly raise the studio temperature to fifty degrees Celsius didn't help her efforts. And, in between takes, as Charles told her what he wanted more and less of, concentration was difficult with all the studio activity and the cacophony caused by set construction. 'That film test was one of the worst ordeals of my life,' Peggy recalled. 'I felt like a sinner before the judgement seat, with the eyes of the world on me. The beating of my heart rang in my ears. I felt every nerve in my body jangling like a live electric wire.' Test complete, Charles had another ordeal in store. Efftee had processing facilities and a small theatrette, so Peggy was soon watching herself exactly as a cinema audience might. 'Seeing my own picture – seeing myself making nervous gestures, walking with such shocking self-consciousness, I gave up all hope,' she said. 'I knew I would never be selected from the hundreds of applicants to play the dual role in *Heritage*.' But Charles remained sure she was right for his Biddy.

By night at the Menzies Hotel, Peggy quietly celebrated her good fortune with numerous Melbourne friends who came to visit, and continued her French and German lessons with a tutor. By day at Efftee, she buckled down to rehearsals. 'They "gave me the works",' she explained. 'That is, knocked off all those nervous, self-conscious corners and made me act with polish and suavity, despite myself.'

———

Whatever polish and suavity Peggy achieved during a week of rehearsals were sorely tested by her first day of shooting. Her baptism by fire was *Heritage*'s biggest set piece: the arrival of the *Red Rover* in Sydney in 1832, the first ship to bring unmarried free Irish women to Australia to be wives and servants. The bride ship sequence was expensive and meant to feature heavily in publicity. Once filmed with Peggy, Charles couldn't change his mind about her because his budget couldn't be stretched to reshoot this complicated scene.

Peggy and the bride extras stood on the side of a section of sailing ship complete with sails, spars and rigging. She got to know another of the colleens, a young Melbourne stage actress named Janet Johnson, and they hit it off immediately. It was nice to have a friend, even if only for this scene. Together they faced a wharf and building-lined street set, filled with men recruited from the ranks of Melbourne's unemployed dressed as red-blooded colonials and red-coated marines. Damien Parer, who would become Australia's legendary newsreel cameraman within a decade, was getting his first professional experience on the film, working as a stills photographer and assistant to cameramen Arthur and Tasman Higgins. He was also in charge of the clapperboard, which he snapped when Charles called for action.

Lusty colonial men roared boisterously, barely held back by redcoats. Peggy's Biddy came down the gangway with Janet's colleen and other Irish girls. Standing apart from the mob, rakish teamster James Morrison, played by Franklyn Bennett, spied Biddy just as a settler broke from the crowd to force a kiss on her. This extra took the opportunity to grope Peggy's breast. If she noticed, she didn't break character, fighting him off and adjusting her hat as he was hauled away by the redcoats. 'By Gad's, she's mine!' James exclaimed, sweeping in with a more gentlemanly approach. 'Excuse me, miss, may I carry your bundle?' he asked.

'You will not! I'll carry me own bundle!' she shouted in a passable Irish brogue, rolling her eyes and stomping off.

James flanked her and took her bag. 'I'll carry it, miss.'

Biddy pummelled him, screaming, 'Give me my bundle!' She yanked his hat off, hurled it to the ground and kicked it away. 'You long, lankish bullpig!' she cursed. 'That'll teach you to play tricks on an Irish girl!'

Storming away, Biddy rejoined the march of Irish colleens into Sydney town as soldiers threw James to the ground.

Charles was using actors with little or no movie experience, choreographing hundreds of costumed extras on elaborate sets, and trying to film and record it all with cumbersome equipment. The sequence took days to get right. Standing for long hours in a period costume and poke bonnet under hot lights, Peggy quickly found that being a leading lady was every bit as tiring and time consuming as Jocelyn Howarth had said.

Peggy's subsequent scenes weren't as technically complex but each made her anxious in a different way. After waltzing with persistent suitor James, Biddy was swept off her feet and taken into a moonlit garden where he sweet-talked her into a passionate kiss. This was surely awkward for a fifteen-year-old girl who had never even had a boyfriend. What made it more difficult was that she and Franklyn had to rehearse in front of a large crew, retake the scene several times for Charles's camera and then recreate it for Damien Parer's stills camera.

Peggy was under continual stress making *Heritage*. 'I can hardly describe my feelings when Mr Chauvel put on the headphones and called for the siren,' she said later to the *Courier-Mail*.

When this screeches through the studio everyone downs tools, all the soundproof doors are closed, and everybody stands still without a word, except for the actor or actress whose scene is being recorded. There is a horrible silence. Everyone seems to be staring at one another with anxious eyes, wondering whether a word or a whole string of words will be forgotten, and hundreds of feet of film spoilt . . . The idea is always terrifying. When the camera wheels begin to whirl, there is no respite until they stop.

Even then there was no respite. Biddy could not be 'too plump', so Peggy needed to adhere to a strict exercise and diet regime. 'I had to keep in constant training like an athlete,' she explained. But what she found hardest were those early starts Jocelyn had mentioned, particularly if the previous night's filming had gone late and she'd had trouble sleeping. 'I used to go home and lie awake . . . thinking of the next day's scenes,' she said. Peggy took comfort from Elsa's reassurances and the supportive crew. 'Mrs Chauvel always cheered me up and helped me through any trying times,' she said. 'Being the youngest member of the cast has its advantages, and all the people I came into contact with were very kind and patient.'

Despite her best efforts, Peggy sometimes forgot her lines. But the delays she caused were nothing beside other production problems. Charles's horrible siren one day sent a large pig into a panic. Breaking free of its rope, the porker rampaged around the studio for twenty minutes, pursued by an army of extras and crew as it sent props and equipment flying and instigated a bestial riot. 'Cows and bullocks bellowed, dogs barked furiously, ducks quacked, and the fowls, the sheep, the goats, and the pigs added their respective choruses to the bedlam,' *The Argus* reported.

Another sequence – showing Biddy as a young mother married off to a settler – proved even more time consuming. A variety of babies were tried for these homestead scenes, but each tyke ruined takes by being too happy, too cranky or too sickly. Eventually the crew resorted to a baby they found in the pram of a woman passing by the studio. This one was just right, placid as shooting proceeded, only for an enraged grandmother to storm the set and refuse to let Charles use the baby the next day.

The pioneer sequence culminated in an Aboriginal attack killing Biddy's husband and leaving her dying of a spear wound in their burning homestead. When it came time to start this scene, Dave Ware, the old bullocky from up north, forgot himself and experienced an 'immense, natural wrath' at seeing Aboriginal men menacing Peggy. The old bloke rushed to the rescue, swearing loudly and profusely in a bullock shout that filled the studio and ruined the take. Then, shooting the scene, Peggy and her cast mates needed to don gasmasks between takes so they weren't over-powered by smoke chemically enhanced to photograph better. At least the baby Biddy hid under a floorboard wasn't bothered by the toxic fug – Charles used a bundled-up doll and later dubbed in crying sound effects.

Such troubles became the stuff of colourful news stories and interview anecdotes. But the production's true disaster barely made the newspapers. On the night of 25 June, Peggy was rehearsing Biddy's heartbreak scene, in which a matron character named Mother Carey revealed that James had married his betrothed. Above them on the gantry, crew adjusted lights for the next morning's shoot. Then came a cry from one of the electricians. 'Throw off the main switch!' he yelled. 'Quick, the main switch.' Up near the ceiling, an electrician named Cyril Stone had become caught on a live wire as he tried to focus a 5000-watt lamp. Men raced to the main switch. Peggy screamed and buried her face in the lap of Dora Mostyn, the old actress playing Mother Carey. The electricity turned off, Cyril released his grip on the live wire and toppled twelve feet to the concrete floor below, his head cracking, his body burned and broken. Crew raced to the man and called for the ambulance. Peggy was still screaming, so Elsa took her back to her hotel and summoned a doctor to give her a sedative. The next day, in a short article, *The Argus* reported that the injured man was in the Alfred Hospital, 'suffering from shock and cerebral agitation'. This 'agitation', according to the *Shepparton Advertiser*, translated as 'serious head injuries'.

As Cyril Stone lay fighting for life in hospital, *Heritage* resumed filming. Peggy knew that she had to press on; if she quit now the film would be ruined, and dozens of cast and crew would be without the wage they needed to feed themselves and their families. Proof of how vital Peggy was to *Heritage* was in the hands of every Melbourne paperboy the very next morning. The entire front page of the *Sun News-Pictorial* was given over to publicity photos from the film, with the most prominent showing Biddy leading the Irish colleens from the bride ship. Inside pages devoted further columns to the film's story and stars. For Charles, such coverage increased his chances of selling tickets and recouping his budget. For Peggy, it confirmed the show couldn't go on without her because she was now a movie star.

Cyril Stone would die fifteen months later of his injuries.

10.

Biddy died quite beautifully of her spear wound in the smoky pioneer hut. Then came her resurrection as her character's great-granddaughter, Sydney sophisticate Biddy Parry, engaged to Northern Territory station owner Frank Morrison, great-grandson of James, portrayed again by Franklyn Bennett. Peggy got to speak in her natural if clipped Australian accent as a cigarette-smoking, university-educated aviatrix modern enough to roll her eyes at her beau's assertion that 'a woman's life is her husband's life'. The sets were contemporary: a mansion's drawing room, a Northern Territory homestead and the chambers of Australia's Federal Parliament, where Frank gave a stirring speech as Biddy watched on adoringly.

Peggy had been receiving fan mail from the first week of filming, and now the letters poured in as more stories about *Heritage* were published. Her private life was also suddenly news-worthy. 'Peggy is offered everything for free,' Brisbane's *Telegraph* claimed, 'from a life-size portrait to settings for her natural curls.' She was also said to be spending a small fortune on long-distance phone calls to her mother and sisters every night. Bina, who had built relationships with columnists while promoting the Belle Vue, likely fed such 'insider' titbits to the newspapers. When she and Mick swapped chaperone roles in mid–July, she told *Truth* her daughter's diet and exercise regime had paid off and she was now a trim seven stone. 'There's hard work for you,' the paper noted approvingly. Peggy's salary was even more newsworthy: '£1,000 a Year for Girl of 15' read a headline in Adelaide's *Mail*, with variations on this story making front pages all over the country. This was an exaggeration – she was likely paid about £15 per week for the twenty weeks it took to shoot and promote *Heritage*. But hype about her earning a fortune gave Peggy that Hollywood aura Charles hoped would encourage women to see *Heritage*.

An even better way to get their attention was *The Australian Women's Weekly*. Launched a year earlier, it was selling 200 000 copies per issue and could claim: 'Larger Circulation Than Any Other Weekly Newspaper in Australia'. On 8 September, Peggy was featured in a big pictorial story under the headline 'Australia's Janet Gaynor?'. While previous news stories had given potted biographies of her, this article ran nearly one thousand words to exalt her as the homegrown version of the huge American star who in 1929 won the first Academy Award for Best Actress. The article told of Charles's star search, sketched Peggy's days in Melbourne and Brisbane, made mention of Mick's 'pugilistic fame' and noted that he had five daughters, 'all lovely, all gifted':

> All the good fairies must have been present at Peggy Maguire's christening. She is endowed with lovely features, a cloud of dark, silky hair, roguish Irish eyes, and a lissome figure, as well as a natural gift for acting, and that indefinable something that makes a lovely girl look as lovely as she really is on the screen. Add to that a rich, soft voice, and you have a mind picture of the lass who bids fair to become Australia's Janet Gaynor.

This was the story Charles wanted out there: the pretty, plucky and lucky youngster he was moulding into a star worthy of Hollywood.

Such fame might even open doors for her sisters. In August, Patricia was summoned to Melbourne for a screen test, with Charles considering her for a role in *Heritage*. 'She walked on the train as though walking on air,' reported *Truth*. 'Flowers and books and sweets were heaped on her as she was tearfully farewelled by the family.' Nothing came of her tryout, and instead she had to settle for the role of Peggy's chaperone while their mother returned to Brisbane. Patricia's Melbourne visit was the first time one of Peggy's siblings followed in her footsteps in the hope of film fame. It wouldn't be the last.

At the end of September, *Heritage* wrapped in Melbourne and the production headed to Canberra, where Peggy spent a weekend filming scenes, including exteriors on the steps of Parliament House. Upon her return to Sydney, she did her final takes wearing an aviatrix cap and goggles seated in a biplane as it bounced along a grassy paddock out at Mascot aerodrome.

Peggy had done it. After nearly four months of blood, sweat and tears, she had finished her first feature film. In the first week of October her mother joined her in Sydney, while Patricia was rewarded with the thrill of taking a flight back to Brisbane. Bina and Peggy stayed at the plush Wentworth Hotel and were guests of honour at a farewell afternoon tea hosted by Elsa at the Hotel Australia. Their little holiday coincided with another wave of publicity. Sydney *Truth* gushed:

> Piquant and pretty, she has a skin like rose leaves, with a typically Irish face full of laughter and the joy of being young and happy. She has brown eyes, charming brows – not plucked – a long wavy bob of dark brown hair, and the daintiest little nose in the world. Peggy is terribly keen on making a huge success of her first picture and ambitious to reach greater altitudes.

Under the headline 'Shure! She's the Swatest Colleen – Glamourous 15-Years-Old Heart-Capturer [sic]', Brisbane *Truth* repeated a claim that her youthful casting in the adult role of Biddy was probably a world record. The paper praised her work ethic for doing twelve-hour days on set, related her singing, dancing and horseriding talents, and impressed upon readers her suitability for the role: 'Australia should take the beauteous Peggy to its heart, for she is an Irish Australian of four generations.'

Just as Charles Chauvel had planned, Australia had already taken her to its heart before a frame of *Heritage* had been screened. Relentless publicity meant Peggy was recognised everywhere. Bina enjoyed sharing the limelight with her newly famous daughter, regularly approached by people who wanted to chat with a real-life movie star. Even a usually cynical *Smith's Weekly* scribe got caught up. 'Peggy wandered this week into a hair-dressing establishment that I patronise, and provided quite a sensation,' she wrote. 'I almost swallowed some of my dirt packing trying to get something more than a mud-lark's-eye view of this very, very youthful leading lady. Wherever she goes in the city, I'm told, it is the same – people crowd after her.'

11.

Leaving Bina in her wake, Peggy jumped off the Kyogle mail train when it pulled into South Brisbane station, ran along the platform, snatched off her rose-wreathed hat and threw herself into Mick's arms. She then hugged each of her sisters. Little Lupe looked up in undisguised awe at Peggy. The last time she'd seen her she was just an ordinary girl; now she was a movie star. It seemed every newspaperman and photographer in Brisbane had turned out. Flashbulbs popping, Peggy spoke to the press, describing the long on-set hours, the rigours of diet, exercise and early starts, her surprise at seeing livestock wandering at the studio, the strangeness of wearing a gasmask and her fears of the siren. Though all the city's newspapers covered her return, only the *Daily Standard* reported what she said about the production's tragedy:

> The huge lights were frightening at times, as they blazed at us from great heights, and the men who worked among them seemed like flies up in the heights above. One night a poor fellow, one of the electricians, dropped from the heights above, electrocuted. It was all very dreadful, and [I] wondered at the time whether all this was worthwhile for the making of a picture.

Yet Peggy's enthusiasm was undimmed. 'I have grown to love the work and love the part I had to play in the picture. It was a great adventure,' she said. 'At times Mr Chauvel used to remind me that I must do my best for Queensland. That I have tried to do and I do hope that my work will please the people.'

As wonderful as it had been, and as much as she hoped to make more films, Peggy was now looking forward to having a holiday at home. She wasn't just excited about relaxing with her family at the Belle Vue. The Maguires were then playing hosts to Olga Spessivtseva, the Russian prima ballerina who had just arrived in Brisbane to start her three-month Australian tour. Popularly known as Spessiva, she was the best ballerina in the world, renowned for her interpretation of *Giselle*'s mad scene and acclaimed as the successor to Anna Pavlova. For Peggy, who had long studied ballet, having this exquisite artist under her roof was another dream come true. She not only had the chance to see Spessiva perform at His Majesty's Theatre but she also received private instruction from her in the Belle Vue's ballroom. Despite their age difference – the ballerina was then nearly forty – the two became friends. Spessiva spoke very little English and was happy the youngster was conversant in French, and, as a nature lover, she enjoyed their day together cuddling koalas at Mount Coot-tha.

Did Peggy know her new friend was mentally ill? She may have suspected something was wrong but perhaps excused any odd remarks and persistent coughing as the eccentricities of a perfectionist performer who liked her cigarettes. But by the time the dancer met Peggy, life was tragically imitating art. Spessiva, who had suffered greatly during the Russian Revolution and grieved no longer being with the Paris Opéra Ballet, was succumbing to the mental illness she portrayed so stunningly in *Giselle*, writing terrified letters to her mother saying her legs were becoming paralysed and that members of the ballet company were spies planning to poison her or amputate her feet. She was also a long-time tuberculosis sufferer and was apparently starting to have a relapse. Spessiva's Brisbane performances went without incident but a few weeks later newspapers reported she had badly sprained her ankle in Sydney and wouldn't be able to continue her tour. The truth was that she had a mental breakdown. While the ballet went to Melbourne with another dancer taking her part, Spessiva remained in Sydney for a month, thought to have gone to a Blue Mountains sanatorium where the quiet might calm her mind as the cool air soothed her sickly lungs. But in 1943 further mental troubles culminated in a major breakdown in New York City, after which Spessiva was to be institutionalised for twenty years.

The day after visiting Mount Coot-tha with Spessiva, Peggy went out to Archerfield aerodrome to farewell Sir Charles Kingsford Smith before he took off in the *Lady Southern Cross* to attempt the first west-to-east flight across the Pacific from Australia to the United States. Planes in the Centenary Air Race from London to Melbourne had taken off that day, and Smithy's dangerous flight to America was partly to prove he wasn't a coward for pulling out of the competition. Daring aviators were then as celebrated as Hollywood matinee idols, so meeting one of the world's most famous pilots was another big thrill for Peggy. They were photographed shaking hands beside a plane, Smithy wearing his trademark pilot's skullcap and goggles, Peggy beaming in aviatrix headgear similar to what she'd worn in *Heritage*. They had a surprising crossover in their careers. She had just weeks earlier been acting as an aviatrix; he had just starred in a docudrama film, *The Old Bus*, about his adventures in his famous plane *The Southern Cross*. But the very real danger of what Smithy – and the Centenary Air Race pilots – were about to face had been brought home overnight by news that DH-86 biplane *Miss Hobart* was missing over Bass Strait. Grave fears were held for its two pilots and nine passengers, though Smithy hoped they had made a forced landing on a Victorian beach. They hadn't and the plane was never found. On 3 November, with Smithy having just landed safely in California after a harrowing flight, Peggy again brought film-star glamour to Archerfield, this time meeting the Dutch pilots who had come second in the Melbourne Centenary Air Race.

Queensland aviation's next big news story was tragic – on 15 November Qantas's new air-mail plane had fallen out of the sky at Longreach and killed the four people on board. Worryingly, it was another DH-86.

Peggy likely didn't pay the tragedy any special attention as she enjoyed Southport beach the following weekend. But *she* was news just by sunbaking. One reporter itemised her seaside style: her hat ('one of the biggest'), costume ('a pet of a black swim suit'), manicure ('lacquer red nails'), and even petite feet ('just out of the baby division in footwear'). Back at the Belle Vue that Monday, Patricia belatedly celebrated turning eighteen with a dinner party for forty guests. Prince Henry, the Duke of Gloucester, was soon to visit Brisbane, generating much excitement around the table because several of his staff were booked into rooms at the Belle Vue. A Maguire family friend at the party, Lieutenant Commander H. S. Platt, was to be even closer to the Duke. 'Platty' was president of the United Service Club and would be master of ceremonies at the ball it was holding for HRH. As midnight rolled around, the party's attention turned from Patricia to birthday girl Bina, with a three-foot-tall ice-cream cake and bottles of Champagne wheeled in to celebrate her turning forty-four.

Shortly before the Duke arrived, Brisbane hosted the visiting Italian warship *Armando Diaz*. The excitement about its crew was so intense that many of the city's young women tried giving themselves crash courses in Italian by translating opera lyrics. Patricia held a party at the Belle Vue for their friend Ina Jones and coaxed a group of officers up from the ship. Peggy charmed the men by speaking French and German; they impressed her, too, with manners as splendid as their white uniforms. That one was a bona-fide Count added a further exotic air to her first encounter with dashing aristocratic European fascists. After dancing in the ballroom, the men invited the girls back to see the ship, with Bina and another matron chaperoning.

But no Italian aristocrat could possibly compare with the son of the King of England. The Duke arrived in Brisbane on 4 December, splendid in the white tropical uniform of his regiment, the 10th Royal Hussars. He made his way through the city in an open-topped motor car, tens of thousands of people lining the streets in the biggest celebration the city had witnessed since the Armistice, and the Belle Vue was engulfed by a huge crowd gathered to see the royal motorcade enter Parliament House. From their upstairs balconies, the Maguires had a marvellous view.

That night Peggy got a closer look when she and Ina Jones, whose father the Lord Mayor had made the city's official welcome speech to the Duke, went to the Parliament House reception for the royal visitor. The young socialites were the envy of many Brisbane girls after they 'commandeered the two Imperial pressmen', Mr Percy Bayley, representative of the Australian Press Association, and Mr Leslie Birch, the official royal photographer. These two gents, who had sailed from England on the warship *Sussex* with His Royal Highness, were quite taken with the Australian beauties. 'The two girls sat on the lawn with the visiting scribes until the Duke went to bed and all the party made for home,' reported *Truth*. Leslie Birch met Peggy again during the royal visit; he

took a casual photo of her wearing a blouse, slacks and gum-
boots while patting a kangaroo, later published in *The Australian
Women's Weekly.*

Peggy was dressed far more glamorously the next night for
the United Service Ball, opting again for an early Victorian lace
frock. Before the big event, Bina and Mick threw a dinner party
at the Belle Vue for Australian air force and naval officers. Peggy
and Patricia – each escorted by a lucky gent – then motored with
their parents to New Farm on the north bank of the Brisbane
River. There they joined around a thousand guests awaiting the
arrival of the Duke in a huge wool store converted into a ballroom with a dance floor the size of a football field. The space
was decorated with palm groves and lit by hundreds of Chinese
lanterns. There was even a replica Norman fortress where the
orchestra played.

Just before 10.45 p.m., the band struck up 'God Save the King'
and a roar rose from the hundreds of people gathered outside as
His Royal Highness arrived. Escorted via elevator to the dance
floor, the Duke bowed as the guests cheered in welcome. With
Platty acting as master of ceremonies, the royal guest received
seventeen Brisbane debutantes. As dancing resumed he retired
to a special alcove for supper, accompanied by his entourage,
state and city dignitaries, and United Service Club committee
members. After the ball finished in the early hours, the Maguires
kept the festivities going at the Belle Vue by throwing a daybreak
breakfast party at the hotel opposite Parliament, where the Duke
of Gloucester slumbered in his apricot satin bed.

Peggy wouldn't forget the pomp, ceremony and splendour of
the Duke's time in Brisbane. His visit was commemorated in an
Itinerary Souvenir Program, whose full-colour cover showed him
resplendent in the medals, gold brocade and sashes that decorated
his captain's uniform of the 10th Royal Hussars.

Peggy had no idea that very same uniform would one day hang in the wardrobe of her home. Or that the Duke himself would hold her fate in his hands.

———

Just before Christmas, Charles Chauvel was editing *Heritage* in the hope of winning the Commonwealth Film Prize, which offered £2500 to the producer of the best Australian movie made in the past eighteen months. While he was busy trying to meet the competition's 31 December deadline, the Maguires enjoyed a summer holiday at Southport, where they rented one of the seaside resort's biggest houses for the family and a dozen friends. There was much to celebrate as New Year's Eve approached. Bina and Mick's gamble on moving the family to Brisbane and renovating the Belle Vue continued to pay off handsomely. Business was booming and the hotel's annual revenue had reached £15 300 ($1.5 million) for the year – and would double in the next twelve months.

The Belle Vue had helped Peggy get noticed and fulfil her dream of becoming a movie star. Now her sisters had the chance to follow in her footsteps. True, Patricia's screen test had not panned out and she was fonder of socialising than singing. But Joan was excelling under the tutelage of Barbara Oelrichs. She had recently received a great review for her emotional performance in a ballet called *The Captive*, and she featured in a *Truth* photo article demonstrating physical culture poses to help women banish 'thick thighs and heavy hips, knobby knees and shapeless ankles'. Meanwhile, Carmel and Lupe were attractive and charming youngsters also drawn to the spotlight.

The last days of 1934 wound down at Southport with long hours spent on the beach, Platty staging friendly competitions in the mansion's billiards room and Patricia arranging a big party to see out the year. As Peggy relaxed on the sand after a swim, her future was as vast and unknowable as the summer sky above. She and *Heritage* might bomb. But if the movie was a hit and she captured the public's heart, she might go all the way to . . . *Hollywood*. Such a thought no longer seemed far fetched. Not now that Charles's previous discovery Errol Flynn had signed a seven-year contract with Warner Bros.

12.

Heritage soon took Peggy high into those blue summer skies. Charles finished his movie in time for the Commonwealth prize and planned a special preview at the Mayfair Theatre in Sydney on Sunday, 20 January 1935. All the movers and shakers in the Australian film industry were invited. So was Peggy.

Determined to travel in style, the Maguires chartered Qantas's new plane *City of Brisbane* to fly Peggy, Patricia and Bina to Sydney on the day of the screening and whisk them back to Brisbane the next morning. The plane was another DH-86, and they would be its first passengers. Since the Longreach crash in mid-November, these models had been grounded while an inquiry and tests were carried out. With modifications made to correct control problems, the DH-86s had just been declared safe, stable and airworthy. Peggy wasn't nervous about the flight, though she had butterflies about the screening. Even if she had doubts about the plane – entirely natural given this model had recently killed fifteen people – there was every reason to trust the man who would be their chief pilot. George 'Scotty' Allan was a pioneering Australian aviator who had flown in the Great War, copiloted the first Sydney to Brisbane air-mail flights with Smithy in 1929, and made the record-breaking flight from England to Australia in 1933 with

Charles Ulm and P. G. Taylor. Scotty was a cautious flier; he knew the price of being cavalier. Just a month earlier, his best mate Charles Ulm had ditched and died in the Pacific Ocean, his fate thought to have been sealed by his decision not to carry the extra weight of inflatable life rafts.

Just before 8.00 a.m. that Sunday, Peggy smiled for the *Courier-Mail*'s photographer as she boarded the *City of Brisbane*. Wearing a polka-dot blouse and matching hat, she looked equal parts nervous and excited, one gloved hand steadying herself on the gangway's railing while she raised the other to point a finger at the heavens. At a time when few Australians had flown, this was another dizzying experience. Even more surreal was that while Peggy had been out to Archerfield to farewell other celebrities, this time *she* was the star the press boys had come to see off. Just over a year ago, Jocelyn Howarth had been compared to Constance Bennett and celebrated as the first Australian actress to fly to a set. Now Peggy was the nation's answer to Janet Gaynor and was being flown to a big preview screening.

The *City of Brisbane* took off at 8.10 a.m. Peering out the cabin's large windows, Peggy saw Archerfield's hangar and runway below and glimpsed Brisbane's modest skyline in the distance before the plane was engulfed in cloud and rain. The DH-86 climbed to an altitude of about one mile, managing to hit a cruising speed of 137 miles per hour despite a strong headwind. With the plane's wood, wire and fabric construction buffeted, the Maguires kept an eye on Scotty just a few feet ahead through the cockpit's open door. His calmness reassured them as he concentrated on making tests with a short-wave radio to see if he could maintain contact with Brisbane and Sydney throughout the entire flight.

They would have all been far less relaxed to know the DH-86 remained one of the most dangerous planes ever put into production. By the end of 1935 another crash would kill five people, while a further ten would be lucky to be alive after a miraculous forced landing. DH-86s also dropped out of the sky in Europe, forcing the British Air Ministry to hold an investigation, whose inconvenient findings were then buried. Nearly fifty years later – long after one-third of all DH-86s had crashed – the suppressed British report was made public. 'The aeroplane was only satisfactory to fly in calm air and for the gentlest manoeuvres,' it read. 'In bumpy weather and when executing normal manoeuvres for the class of aeroplane, it becomes nearly unmanageable.'

Luck and Scotty's skill were on the Maguires' side, and by the time the *City of Brisbane* was halfway to Sydney they were enjoying clearer weather with better visibility. Seeing the coast and hinterlands roll beneath the plane was breathtaking. So was the spectacle of the new Sydney Harbour Bridge under the summer sky as Scotty brought them down safely at Mascot just before midday. The *Daily Telegraph* was there to take a photo of the pilot and his three passengers.

'I hope this proves something worthwhile,' said Norman Lindsay as he took his seat for the *Heritage* screening that night. 'It should mean something to the new industry.' The artist was one of many VIPs in an audience that *Everyones* characterised as comprising 'members of Parliament, giants of the Press, the powers of local literature and arts and a smattering of those who can make and break most industries – Mr. and Mrs. General Public'. With thirteen hundred guests seated in the Mayfair Theatre, Charles Chauvel took to the stage to introduce his movie, his wife and his young leading lady, Peggy. He usually followed a stump speech when spruiking *Heritage*. The film they were about to see was proudly Australian. It was proof the nation could produce movies as ambitious as those made in Hollywood and London. If the

NSW government passed the film quota bill, then more like it would be made.

Patriotic fervour stirred and the house lights dimmed; *Heritage* began with scenes of colonial struggle and convict toil. After the final scene, in which Peggy and Franklyn Bennett embraced and dedicated themselves to populating Australia, the audience applauded heartily. But a fitful night lay ahead for the young film star as she awaited reviews in the morning's papers.

The Maguire women took off in the *City of Brisbane* at 8.00 a.m. on Monday. They had no shortage of reading material because the plane was carrying bundles of Sydney newspapers bound for the Outback. The *Sydney Morning Herald* liked what it had seen: 'Mr Charles Chauvel, working as director for Expeditionary Films Ltd, has made not only a good picture. He has made one which has elements of greatness about it.' *The Sun* said that *Heritage* 'soars away from all previous attempts' to portray Australian history, described Biddy as an 'ingenious and fascinating little Irish girl' and praised Peggy as a 'lovely addition to the players of any country'. The *Daily Telegraph* chimed in, saying she was 'pretty' in a picture 'wider in scope, richer in backgrounds and stronger in story than any previous Australian talkie'. It was also sweet that everyone else on the plane had been featured in the *Daily Telegraph*. Scotty's photo graced the front page, above an interview about the DH-86 and how radio could change aviation. Patricia and Bina appeared with Peggy and Scotty on the pictorial page; they were beneath a photo of Adolf Hitler giving a New Year Nazi salute to his Presidential Palace Guard.

A mile in the sky, Peggy was on a high. She still had her doubts about her appearance and performance, but these reviews were evidence that experts thought the film was good and she was good in it. By the time she landed at Archerfield, Peggy had come down to earth enough to charm waiting newspaper reporters with her self-deprecation. 'It was a great thrill to sit in the Mayfair Theatre and see and hear myself on the screen,' she told them. 'The screen certainly does some funny things with a girl. You seem so huge at times, and it shows up every mannerism you have and some you didn't know you had. For instance, I am inclined to wrinkle my forehead, and to me those wrinkles stood out like railway lines. Then my voice was much deeper than it is ordinarily.' Peggy knew she was being more critical than the rest of the audience. 'I heard that a number of people wept in one of the dramatic scenes, and Mr Charles Chauvel, the producer, said I was quite good at my first attempt, so I suppose the differences I noticed are not apparent to the general public. A lot of friends very kindly said that my performance was good, but I was any-thing but satisfied with myself in many of the scenes.'

More positive *Heritage* reviews came from influential weekly publications – though critics also noted Charles's desultory plot-ting and overwritten dialogue, and Franklyn Bennett's insipid performance. *Everyones* complained of his inability to 'put force and colour into his lines' but also said that both Peggy and Margot Rhys 'on looks and technique are able to hold their own in any company. Both girls do outstanding work.' *The Bulletin* gave the film tough love – 'the acting is stagy, on the whole; there is too much talk, and a lot of it is stilted and platitudinous' – but still called it 'by far the best film that has been made in Australia'.

Writing in *Smith's Weekly*, poet and journalist Kenneth Slessor said *Heritage* was 'a splendid and unexpected Australian achieve-ment' and reckoned it was 2-1 favourite to win the Commonwealth Film Prize. Peggy hoped he was right. *Heritage* was up against ten other films, many made by or starring people she knew. There was Pat Hanna's *Waltzing Matilda*; Frank Thring's *A Ticket in Tatt's*, starring George Wallace; and Ken Hall's *The Squatter's Daughter* and *The Silence of Dean Maitland*, both featuring Jocelyn Howarth.

With the prize to be announced in March and *Heritage* set for an April release in Sydney, there was nothing to do but wait for the verdict of the judging panel and Mr and Mrs General Public.

Peggy didn't return to Loreto at the start of the school year. Instead she continued her drama, music and language classes with private tutors, and studied dressmaking and domestic science at Queensland University. At the Belle Vue, the Maguires were charmed by one of the hotel's most interesting guests yet, Sir Neville Wilkinson. A member of the King's household, this blue-blooded eccentric was best known as the world's most famous 'tinycraft' architect, having spent eleven years building a miniature fairy castle called 'Titania's Palace', complete with hand-carved mahogany furniture and three thousand minuscule works of art on its walls.

Even more magical and unexpected was the news Peggy heard on Friday, 8 March. Charles had just received a telegram from Canberra: *Heritage* had won the Commonwealth Film Prize.

Reporters were soon at the Belle Vue. 'It is marvellous,' she told them. 'I am too thrilled for words.' She insisted Charles deserved all the praise for *Heritage*'s success and said that more Australian girls would have the wonderful opportunity she had enjoyed if the local film industry could develop sufficiently. Peggy wanted to appear on stage one day but declared that making movies was now her passion. 'I hope to have a film career,' she said. 'I would like it more than anything. Plans for the future? Well, that will depend a good deal on Mr Chauvel . . . I do not know just what he has in mind.' What Charles had in mind was revealed a week later when he arrived to spend a few days with Peggy on a publicity tour. *Heritage*'s success, he told her, had spurred him to plan two very different but equally ambitious films. One would be a romantic drama about a white woman's adventures with an Aboriginal tribe in Queensland's tropics. The other would depict the heroic struggle of Sydney's inner-city working class. Charles thought Peggy would be good in the latter.

With *Heritage*'s Brisbane release still a few months away, Peggy kept a low profile and kept busy. In early April she helped her dance teacher Barbara Oelrichs prepare for a charity concert and recital. Peggy didn't take the stage, ceding the spotlight to all of her sisters. Patricia and a partner danced 'The Continental', popularised by Ginger Rogers and Fred Astaire in *The Gay Divorcee*, while Joan did a classical recital to the music of Grieg. Carmel performed a gypsy dance, and little Lupe showed off her tap skills. Peggy was proud of her sisters. When a Sydney *Sun* reporter asked if all the Maguire girls were pretty, she shot back: 'The other four are.' Peggy was trying to deflect attention but she couldn't help being noticed. At His Majesty's Theatre with Patricia to see a show, the manager insisted they move from their stall seats to a box. For the rest of the night, audience members craned their necks to get a good view of Peggy in her red dress.

———

You didn't need to crane a neck in Sydney to see Peggy. Not with *Heritage*'s publicity blitz. One hundred massive billboards adorned the city, and five thousand posters were plastered on walls and fences. A genuine Cobb & Co coach packed with people in period costumes and bearing a *Heritage* banner rattled through the streets. Forty men dressed as red-coated soldiers marched around the city and manned the Sydney Harbour Bridge. A second wave of more detailed reviews accompanied *Heritage*'s opening in Sydney at the Lyceum on 6 April. Most mirrored Kenneth Slessor's conclusion in *Smith's Weekly*: 'Whatever its minor faults – and it would be a foolish kindness to dismiss them – I would like to say emphatically that *Heritage* is not only the best talking picture that I have so far known Australians to produce, but it is the first Australian film to give any solid hope for the establishment of a future world industry.' Peggy was often singled out in these notices – usually, though not always, favourably. *The Australian Women's Weekly* concluded that she was 'not very easy as a modern girl'. 'Peggy Maguire as Biddy O'Shea wins the hearts of everyone,' said Sydney's *Sun*. The *Sydney Mail*'s review was by far the best:

> In Peggy Maguire, who appears as Biddy O'Shea, Mr Chauvel has found incomparably the most promising juvenile actress who has been seen in an Australian film. Miss Maguire has warmth, vitality, and what the Americans call 'colour' or 'personality'.

Heritage also appealed to Mr and Mrs General Public, with the Lyceum's box office the best it had been for several months. As the movie's Brisbane premiere approached, local publicity ramped up. *The Queenslander* devoted a full page to film photos, while *Teleradio* magazine ran a special *Heritage* supplement. Just like a Hollywood star, Peggy's photos were used for endorsements. She was pictured buying her Mercolized Wax at Brisbane business Edwards The Chemist, while nearby Frances Salon boasted: 'Lovely Peggy Maguire entrusts her captivating beauty only to the highest skilled experts.' As Queensland's most talked-of celebrity, she supposedly drank Highfield, 'Queensland's Most Talked of Tea'.

Wherever she went, Peggy was the centre of attention. She was snapped by *The Telegraph* with Mercia Doran at Ascot's May Day race meeting and there again the next week by the city's newspapers as she patted the winning horse. 'Beauty and the Beast!' read the *Truth* headline, while *The Telegraph* detailed her floral frock worn with squirrel furs, a white camellia and a velvet halo.

The very next night Peggy had *the* classic film star experience. Out seeing a movie called *Regal Cavalcade*, which celebrated the British Empire leading up to the silver jubilee of King George V's

coronation, she was spotted and surrounded by a group of secondary school girls. Peggy was mightily amused to find herself
autographing dozens of handkerchiefs, scraps of exercise books
and bits of the film's souvenir program.

That fame continued to rub off on her family. Patricia was featured in a full-page *Truth* article showcasing Hollywood make-up
and diet tips. Mick was rediscovered in a *Referee* magazine article
that claimed he had forsaken the boxing ring at the height of
his career for marriage, family and the hotel trade, making him
'an object lesson to young and ambitious pugilists'. Bina made
the news in more distressing fashion when she was admitted to
Brisbane's Mater hospital with heart trouble. To cheer her up and
thank her nurses, Peggy and Charles put on a private preview
screening of *Heritage* at the hospital.

On Saturday, 18 May, the Regent's foyer bristled with Brisbane's
elite – and one hundred people from Canungra excited to see
their neck of the woods up on the silver screen. Commentary
about the arrival of the guests, along with music by Ned Tyrell's
Orchestra, was carried live on 4BC, as were interviews with
Peggy, and Charles and Elsa Chauvel. Bina wasn't going to miss
her daughter's big moment and secured temporary medical release.
Arriving at the Regent, she was helped to her seat and received
refreshments from Edgar Betts and flowers from the Chauvels.
She, Mick and their girls all beamed with pride as Charles introduced Peggy to the stage. Pretty in a pink frock with her hair
done in curls, she made a modest speech before *Heritage* played for
her home-town crowd. The film finished to sustained applause.
Leaving the Regent, Peggy was overwhelmed with floral bouquets and stunned that thousands of people had stayed to cheer
her. Once she'd given her thanks, she rushed home to Belle Vue
and her room, collapsing into bed, utterly exhausted by all the
excitement of the evening.

On Monday Peggy again followed in Jocelyn Howarth's footsteps, beginning twice-daily personal appearances to introduce *Heritage* at the Regent and hand out hundreds of autographed photos to women attending the matinee sessions. Her week-long season done, she had a short vacation with Charles and Elsa in the Gold Coast hinterland at Binna Burra, where they spent their days hiking before eating scones in front of a blazing fire.

Returning to Brisbane, Peggy threw herself into an even more gruelling week of personal appearances at *Heritage*'s afternoon and evening sessions at two Brisbane theatres. After another break, Peggy began a regional tour that saw her and a chaperone travelling by bus to theatres in northern New South Wales and southern Queensland. In each town she charmed the local ladies at afternoon teas held in her honour. 'Although surrounded by strangers, the young artist displayed no traces of shyness and took part readily in the conversation which touched on subjects as far apart as the probable extinction of the legitimate stage to the dust storms at Broken Hill!' reported the *Tweed Daily*.

During the interview with Grafton's *Daily Examiner* where she let slip the truth about her casting, Peggy, despite being so young, also fielded questions about her love life. The reporter reassured readers she has 'given little thought to the idea of marriage, and stoutly asserts that she does not intend to fall in love or to think of marriage until she has achieved her aim in the film world'.

Etiquette dictated Peggy watch the movie with her fans whenever possible, meaning she would have seen *Heritage* dozens of times. How torturous to watch her shortcomings over and over. But at least she knew what she would need to do better next time. *If* there was a next time.

13.

By early July 1935, Charles Chauvel had made up his mind about his next production, choosing to make the more obviously commercial adventure film. *Uncivilised* marked the only time he would try to pander to international markets, importing British actor Dennis Hoey to play the singing Tarzan-type white man who leads an Aboriginal tribe and woos the film's female author character. In addition to the film's blithe racism, bloodthirsty violence, opium-smoking hero and topless Indigenous women, the heroine was also required to do a skinny-dipping scene that showed her buttocks in mid-shot and full-frontal nudity in long-shot. It wasn't a role for Peggy. But *Heritage*'s Margot Rhys was willing to step up and strip off. Remarkably, the scene would get by the censors – and bring a publicity windfall.

With Charles preparing to shoot *Uncivilised* on Palm Island and in a new studio in Sydney, the prospects of Peggy making another movie anytime soon seemed to be receding. So far in 1935 only one film – *The Burgomeister*, starring Peggy's friend from the bride ship sequence Janet Johnson – had gone in front of the cameras. Charles said he still intended to make the other film he'd planned for Peggy. She had to hope he would.

Life at the Belle Vue went back to normal. Peggy continued her ballet studies, befriended visiting soprano Muriel Wilson when she stayed at their hotel, and attended various Brisbane balls. One of the more spectacular nights of the social season was the charity Halloween party put on at the Belle Vue by several prominent society women, including Lady Cilento. Not that these matrons did the organising, which was left to Marjorie Norval, now assistant to the premier's wife, assisted by Peggy, who oversaw the floral decorations and sold caps to raise money.

Australian movie production suddenly entered a new and exciting phase when the recently passed NSW film quota started to take effect. Almost overnight Sydney looked set to become the Hollywood of the Southern Hemisphere, where imported talent would make big movies with international box-office appeal. Cinesound trumpeted that its £25000 horseracing drama *Thoroughbred* would have bona-fide Hollywood beauty Helen Twelvetrees as its leading lady. Newly formed company National Productions announced that their debut movie *The Flying Doctor* would cost £34000 and be made by famed British actor and director Miles Mander. These, along with *Uncivilised*, were the biggest productions, but many more movies were also planned for the coming year. Even Frank Thring was talking about moving to Sydney to set up a studio.

Thin-faced and moustachioed, Miles Mander was well known to fans of British film. Born in 1888, he was the prodigal son of a family that had amassed a fortune from a hundred and fifty years as leading manufacturers of varnish. With both his parents dead by the time he was sixteen, Miles inherited more than £60000 and set about blowing it on a dizzying array of adventures. He bought and raced automobiles, horses, aeroplanes and hot air balloons, promoted prize fighters and worked as a sheep shearer in New Zealand before sailing back home from Australia with Ernest Shackleton. By 1914 he had married an Indian princess, developed an alcohol problem and was pretty much penniless.

The Great War saved him from himself. Signing up with the Royal Army Service Corps, Miles renounced the demon drink, survived both mustard gas and shell shock, and attained the rank of lieutenant by his demobilisation. In 1920 he started his film and theatrical career, playing in features and shorts, and starring in plays he'd written, even taking an acting troupe to Morocco, where they became stranded without funds. Having divorced the princess, in 1923 Miles married Sydney-born actress Kathleen French, and shortly afterwards his film career really took off when he became Alfred Hitchcock's first-ever murderer in the director's 1925 debut feature, *The Pleasure Garden*.

Miles was skilled behind the camera, too, pioneering the use of sound in British short films. His crowning achievement, though, was the 1928 silent classic *The First Born*. Miles directed and starred opposite his discovery Madeleine Carroll, the film based on his play and novel, with the script co-written with Hitch's wife, Alma Reville. Miles had an affair with Madeleine and directed her again in 1931 talkie *Fascination*, in which he also cast his latest discoveries, Merle Oberon and seven-year-old Freddie Bartholomew, in small roles. As an actor, he adapted to talkies and played character roles in British films like *The Private Life of Henry VIII* and *Adventures of Don Quixote*. Miles was also the bestselling author of *To My Son – In Confidence*, which set out his views on everything, not least what he saw as his urgent need for freedom from his now-estranged second wife. After nine months in Hollywood, where he had acted in *Here's to Romance* and *The Three Musketeers*, this Renaissance man arrived in Sydney on 12 November 1935.

Miles was big news, even on a day dominated by the ongoing search for Charles Kingsford Smith and his plane *Lady Southern Cross*, missing over the Bay of Bengal, with Maguire family pal Scotty Allan part of the frantic search. All the newspapers – along with Fox Movietone's newsreel unit – came out to see Miles and his British crew. 'A New Film Era for Australia' proclaimed *The Sun*. 'A film cannot make any substantial profit until it can penetrate the greatest market in the world, the 26 000 theatres of the United States,' Miles said at a press conference at the Hotel Australia. 'We have not come with the idea of making a picture for the local – for there are many here who could do that better than we can – but to make a picture for the wide world.' And so *The Flying Doctor*'s leading roles would be filled by Hollywood stars. But that was only half true. What Miles *didn't* say – probably to avoid being besieged by would-be starlets – was that his boss, Michael Balcon, head of the Gaumont-British Picture Corporation, set to distribute the film in the UK, had told him to find an *Australian* girl for his romantic heroine.

She found him. Miles settled in to the Hotel Australia. Early in his visit, after days spent preparing their film, he and screenwriter J. O. C. (Jock) Orton would dine at the Usher's Hotel restaurant across the road. One night, Miles spotted a dark-haired girl in the company of an older woman who looked like her mother. He and Jock couldn't keep their eyes of this young beauty, who occasionally caught them staring and appeared a little annoyed by the attention of the two strangers. Miles and his screenwriter conferred. Yes, *The Flying Doctor*'s script described its leading lady as about twenty-five, but they agreed it could be rewritten to star such a striking girl. Miles approached the table, introduced himself as the director of *The Flying Doctor* and asked whether this youngster might like to make a screen test for the role of its leading lady. To his surprise, he found he was talking to Peggy

Maguire, already well known in Australia as the star of *Heritage*. With the consent of her charming mother, Bina, Miles asked if Peggy would return to Sydney for the screen test, which he said would likely be made in late December.

Chances are this was no chance encounter. *The Flying Doctor* was based on a novel by one of Charles Chauvel's protégés, and Brisbane's *Telegraph* had reported in mid-October that Miles was coming to Sydney. A few weeks later Peggy and Bina decided it was high time for them to drive eleven hundred miles to visit family in Melbourne. Stopping in Sydney on the way back, they stayed at Usher's Hotel. It made sense that Bina and Peggy contrived to cross paths with Miles. He was a star-maker. She was guaranteed to turn heads. Peggy's later account also seemed disingenuous in depicting her annoyance at these rudely staring 'strangers'. She of all people would have recognised Miles from his many movies.

But in November 1935, newspapers knew nothing of Peggy meeting Miles. Returning to Brisbane, she waited for him to summon her back to Sydney. In the meantime, she found new admirers in an English cricket team who were staying at the Belle Vue while on a non-test tour meant to restore goodwill destroyed by Bodyline. When she and two girlfriends saw the players off at the railway station, the men hung from the train as it steamed away and serenaded the girls with 'Why Were They Born So Beautiful?' Peggy's wait for word resumed.

Then, nearly two weeks later, a letter arrived from Miles Mander. He wanted her in Sydney for the screen test just after Christmas.

A few days later, Brisbane's *Truth* had a front-page scoop. It had 'heard' that American star Charles Farrell had been cast in *The Flying Doctor*, which would make him the first male Hollywood idol to star in an Australian talkie. Every bit as thrilling was that local girl Peggy Maguire might play opposite him.

Interviewed yesterday, the Maguire family were like the famous politician – they would have nothing to say. But it is certain that Peggy Maguire and her sister are going down to Sydney during the week, and that something very exciting is in the air. What a 'dream come true' it would be for a Brisbane girl to play sweetheart on the screen to Janet Gaynor's old star.

But as Peggy prepared to make the trip, Miles got in contact again to say the screen test had to be postponed. Her nervous wait began afresh. Just after Christmas, newspapers everywhere confirmed *Truth*'s scoop: Charles Farrell was to arrive in Sydney at the end of January to headline *The Flying Doctor*. Although his star wattage had dimmed since he quit making movies with Janet Gaynor, as recently as 1932 he had been the number one male box-office attraction in the United States. Miles knew him well, having menaced the character played by Virginia Valli, now Charles's wife, in Hitchcock's *The Pleasure Garden*, and they had socialised recently in Hollywood. But the director was at pains to say he cast Charles because he was one of the handsomest screen heroes, enjoyed universal feminine appeal, was every inch a man's man, and was a sure box-office bet in the United Kingdom and the United States. 'He will be remembered for many outstanding films, the most successful of which were those in which he played opposite Janet Gaynor, such as *7th Heaven, Sunny Side Up, Tess of the Storm Country*,' Miles told the press.

At the Belle Vue, Peggy's anxiety increased. Had Miles cast another girl? Then a cable arrived on New Year's Day: Miles needed her in Sydney on Sunday. It was now Wednesday. Driving would take more than two days. Such short notice made it impossible to charter a plane or get a sleeping berth on the train. So on Friday morning Peggy and Bina crammed into a crowded train carriage, sitting upright with their cushions and suitcases.

Twenty long hours later, they reached Sydney's Central Station. Peggy was tired and crumpled in her flannel slacks, home-made cardigan and beret. Miles's immaculately dressed representative met them, handed Peggy a floral bouquet and escorted them to Usher's Hotel. Peggy had time to rest, prepare and try to calm herself. Having barely eaten anything, she had shed nearly three kilograms since Miles first made contact. Being nervous had its advantages.

Peggy awoke to a deluge as a severe storm swept Sydney. The car that took her to her screen test was one of the few on the roads. Even in such conditions National Studios was a fine sight – a brand-new production facility rising from Pagewood's sandy wasteland south-east of the city. The complex was a direct copy of Gaumont-British's production complex in London, with a huge sound stage, dressing and make-up rooms, a screening theatrette and negative-processing lab, wardrobe department, carpenter's shop, offices for producers and writers, and suites for musicians, sound technicians and special-effects men. There was even a kitchen and restaurant to keep everyone on site well fed. Surrounding the studio were twenty-five acres of empty land where exteriors could be filmed and huge sets erected. Built at a cost of £73 000 ($6.8 million) by National Productions, whose chairman was Sydney newspaper and radio mogul Sir Hugh Denison and whose fellow board members were similarly titled and/or notable, *this* was Australia's filmmaking future. And again Peggy had the chance to be at the centre of it.

But she wasn't the only girl up for the role of pastoralist's daughter Jenny Rutherford, who's wooed by the roustabout Sandy, to be played by Charles Farrell. Peggy was amazed to find Janet Johnson, her friend from *Heritage*, also testing that day, having been brought up from Melbourne. While it could have been awkward, the girls wished the best for each other.

Miles showed them around the studio, giving Peggy the chance to marvel at the modern facilities and at the ghoulish sets that Charles Chauvel had constructed to represent *Uncivilised*'s Aboriginal village. While she was nervous, Miles's charm put her at ease, and she'd also learnt much about calming herself from *Heritage* and the publicity tour. With *The Flying Doctor*'s costumes still to be decided, Peggy screen-tested in an evening gown and a couple of simple frocks Miles had asked her to bring. She even remembered not to wrinkle her forehead.

Returning to Usher's Hotel, Peggy began her wait for Miles's verdict, her mood as unsettled as Sydney's weather, which stayed stormy all week. Miles had a tricky decision to make. He loved Peggy's test – it was nearly perfect. But he also loved Janet's. In an unpublished publicity document, Miles wrote that he had found Peggy soon after arriving in Sydney, but he devoted many more words to Janet, noting he had brought her up from Melbourne after seeing her photo in a newspaper. His response to her test was ecstatic: 'Here was a winner!'

As Peggy's anxious wait continued, Miles cast Margaret Vyner in a supporting role. Arguably Australia's first supermodel – fifty years before the term was popularised – the statuesque 22-year-old beauty had caused a sensation just over a year before when she became the first Australian woman to strut Paris's catwalks for French fashion designer Jean Patou. Such was her beauty that Cole Porter had recently added her name to the list of wonderful things about the world in a version of his song 'You're the Top' from his hit musical *Anything Goes*. Miles putting her in *The Flying Doctor* guaranteed ongoing publicity. So did his casting of expat British-actors-turned-Sydney-radio-personalities James Raglan and Eric Colman, along with popular pro-wrestler Tom Lurich and everyone's favourite comic sidekick Joe Valli.

Miles announced his big casting decision on Friday. Peggy burst into tears when she heard the news – out of happiness for herself and concern for Janet. But her friend was thrilled for her, sending a congratulatory telegram and big bunch of flowers. Peggy even got a congratulatory phone call from family friend Archbishop Duhig, who had seemingly forgotten his warning just two years earlier that cinema was a 'crowning factor in the perversion of the young'. His young friend's beaming portrait appeared beside news of her casting in Sydney's *Telegraph*. Except Peggy was no longer to be Peggy: from now on her screen name would be Mary Maguire.

Peggy-turned-Mary told *Truth* she had chosen to change her name. It was said to be in honour of Bina's birth name, though it could also have paid tribute to her maternal grandmother, the eldest sister she had never known, and her baby sister Lupe who was also officially a Mary. Her new director surely had a big say in the matter, arguing that alliterative names worked better on marquees – just look at Claudette Colbert, Greta Garbo, Sylvia Sidney, Helen Hayes, Rosalind Russell, Virginia Valli or, for that matter, Miles Mander.

That Mary had just beaten Janet had much to do with Miles's commercial objectives. Janet was a rising stage actress yet almost unknown to the film-going public, with *The Burgomeister* having turned out so badly it was booked by few theatres and barely seen by audiences. Meanwhile, Mary had *Heritage* to her name *and* publicity proclaiming her as Australia's answer to Janet Gaynor. Who better to team with Charles Farrell? But Miles's enthusiasm for Janet Johnson saw him advise her to get her teeth fixed, then go to London and see his boss, Michael Balcon, with his letter of recommendation, in which he'd concluded: 'She's a BET in my opinion.' Janet followed the advice – and it changed her life as surely as landing the lead role in *The Flying Doctor* forever altered Mary's.

Charles Farrell! Mary had grown up watching his movies. Now she was to share love scenes with him in a big-budget film seen all around the world thanks to Gaumont-British's distribution clout. A Sydney journalist reporting for the Launceston *Examiner* reckoned she was living a beautiful dream when he met her at Usher's Hotel. 'Hollywood's most romantic success story has found its equal, or better, in the announcement of the signing of Mary,' the article began.

> Wide-eyed with wonderment that she above all others has been chosen for this important role, and still very much in the clouds over her good fortune, was Mary when she was interviewed following her signing of the contract that will give her the biggest opportunity ever afforded any other Australian actress – that of becoming famous as a motion picture star throughout the world. I was surprised to find her so youthful of appearance, so devoid of sophistication – and above all without make-up. She came dancing into the lounge, a petite figure clad in navy slacks and beret, her dark hair and dancing eyes offset by the scarlet shirt, which gave an added colour to her peach bloom complexion – natural, too. No trace of eyebrow pencil or lipstick here – how refreshing! I asked her what it felt like to be the most famous girl in Australia. She said that she still couldn't realise her good fortune; for the past few weeks have been very trying for one so young. Coming down from Brisbane for a screen test, which, if successful would alter the course of her whole life, is a big event in the life of a sixteen-year-old, and the suspense of waiting for the verdict of director Miles Mander would be unnerving to even the most seasoned veteran . . . She is full of confidence that, under the direction of Mander, her talent will be fully developed and that he will

draw from her the best of her acting ability. Naturally, she is very thrilled at the opportunity of appearing opposite such a popular and famous motion picture star as Charles Farrell, and anticipates that she will learn much more from watching him than she would in a year's dramatic tuition.

Miles's decision led to criticism that Mary wasn't experienced or good enough for *The Flying Doctor*. 'I don't want a great actress,' he said. 'I want a girl who will be obedient enough to let me make her a world success. I may do that. I have an ambition to team her with Fred Astaire in dancing numbers and musical hits – it is not impossible.'

Mary was enthusiastic – but also realistic. 'I have always been stage crazy,' she told *Truth*. 'When I am not working I cannot keep away from grease paint and frequently I make up at home for the sheer love of it.' While she wanted to make many films, Mary didn't think she would be an actress forever. 'If I have ten years of success,' she said, 'I think I shall be very lucky.'

14.

Mary's new name came with an *astronomical* new pay packet. Brisbane *Truth* had the scoop:

> Behind it all is the story of the part played in negotiations by the young star's mother, a part which had much to do with the final signing of a British Gaumont [sic] Pictures contract at £100 a week. For an Australian, in Australia, that contract allows for unheard-of things in the way of luxuries. Anything that the new star wants, providing it is within movie reason, will be charged to the making of *The Flying Doctor*. It covers a breath-taking number of items, from the hire of an aeroplane to a stocking to replace one that has sprung a ladder.

Other 'perquisites of a most comforting description' included fresh flowers, hair, make-up and massage services, dance lessons, and taxis to the city and studio. She had a nice dressing-room, too: 'art moderne and portable, wheels on to the set, and folds up if necessary. Furnishings are in chromium, eau de Nil and cream-cream carpets and green divans.' Without Bina by her side, Mary 'may not, to be a little slangy, have got such a good "break". Flanked by legal men, the star's mother spent many days considering the contract.'

Mary was actually paid £10 a week for pre-production and £20 weekly for two months of filming. The source of the hype appeared to be Bina, giving herself a big pat on the back by vastly exaggerating the deal she made for her daughter. Mary was paid more than veteran Joe Valli, who got £18 a week to play comic sidekick Dodger Green, but far less than Margaret Vyner, James Raglan and Tom Lurich, who all scored £20 per *day* for their supporting roles. Yet all their combined salaries were a small fraction of the £5600 commanded by Charles Farrell, then by far the highest fee paid to any movie actor in Australia.

———

Mary – along with Bina and Patricia, who would also live in Sydney during the shoot – rented a spacious apartment in 'Chesterton', an Art Deco block just east of the city in Double Bay. Near the corner of New South Head Road, their new abode was an easy stroll to the village and beach, and just a short cab ride to the city and to National Studios. Mary and Patricia were taken 'under the wing' of Sydney bon vivant Oswald Cheeke, who introduced his 'pretty protégées' to his society friends, and the girls also hit hotspot Romano's with Miles and Jock Orton.

It wasn't all play, though. Mary had to learn her part by studying her script and look the part by submitting to costume fittings at the David Jones' department store. Patricia was also put to work – appointed by Mary as her 'secretary' to manage all the fan mail pouring in.

The first weeks of 1936 saw Sydney swept by more storms that left streets flooded. Far more devastating was the death on 20 January of King George V, six months shy of the silver jubilee of his coronation. Despite the sadness of his passing, it wasn't lost on the Maguires that, with Edward VIII now on the throne, the Belle Vue had a table literally fit for a king.

That week was dominated by royal affairs, but Miles casting Don Bradman to cameo as himself in *The Flying Doctor* still made news everywhere. On Friday, 24 January, The Don starred in the first scenes shot for the film at the Sydney Cricket Ground. Not much was asked of the world's best batsman: he smashed a few balls, allowed himself to be bowled, walked off the field and then poked his shirtless self from a dressing-room window to ask, 'Hello, what's John been up to?' in reaction to a brawl to be filmed later. For cricket fan Mary, it was a chance to reacquaint herself with Don and watch one ball he hit nearly destroy a camera. Disaster averted by a matter of inches, *The Flying Doctor*'s first scenes were in the can.

Charles Farrell saw Sydney at its best on the Australia Day public holiday as the *Monterey* sailed through the Heads on Monday, 27 January. Beneath a blazing sun, the harbour's beaches were thronged with bathers and its sparkling waters busy with hundreds of small boats. Equally dazzling was the dark-haired beauty dressed in white, waving from the motorboat coming out to meet the liner off Watson's Bay. This was his co-star, Mary Maguire, flanked by Miles Mander, movie executives, reporters, photographers and a Fox Movietone newsreel crew.

Meeting Charles Farrell was surreal for Mary. Here in three-dimensional colour was the movie idol she had grown up with in two-dimensional black and white. Charles had a brilliant smile in a deeply tanned face and green eyes that flashed beneath unruly brown hair with grey streaks. Wide shoulered and tall at six foot two, he was even more handsome than in his movies. Charles evidently knew little about Mary except that she was young and small. 'Hello there, how are you?' he said, adding a crack: 'I thought you were going to be a little girl.' Mary gave as good as she got. 'He thought I was going to be about ten,' she joked to reporters. When they posed for cameras, there was barely a sliver of daylight between them.

From his first moments in Sydney, Charles charmed everyone. Chatting to reporters, he joked that he had thought Australia and China were so close he could have sailed from one to the other overnight. He explained that on his stopover in Pago Pago he'd given some choice American slang – 'Hi Toots', 'Bye Toots' – to the native chiefs. 'They thought,' he said, 'it was our official language.' Asked what he thought of Sydney Harbour, he quipped, 'It's great – but where are the sharks? I've been looking for them but I haven't seen one.' Though a joker, Charles was serious about his profession, aware that he had to give his all. 'An actor is only as good as his last picture,' he told the newsmen. But when work was done he wanted to have fun, hopeful he'd get to try surfing and rustle up a game of his beloved polo. Easygoing, hard-working, a keen sportsman with a sense of humour: this was an American so down to earth he might be an Aussie. *Table Talk* spoke for many: 'Farrell is one of the most perfect specimens of manhood it would be possible to find.' When the *Monterey* docked at Darling Harbour, hundreds of excited women waved handkerchiefs and, in a strange display of affection, dozens used pocket mirrors to reflect the sun into the visiting star's eyes. A squad of policemen held back this crowd of admirers as Mary walked down the gangway on Charles's arm.

National Productions held a luncheon for Charles at the Hotel Australia. Between speeches Mary got to know her co-star a little better. Of Irish stock, he had been a talented boxer at college before breaking into movies as a lowly extra. When not working, he loved tennis, swimming and horseriding. Like her dad and Charles Chauvel, he was another pal and protégé of Snowy Baker, who had taught him how to play polo in Hollywood. As for Janet Gaynor? Charles Farrell's public stance was that he had quit the partnership to pursue a solo film career with more manly roles. He had also wanted to end the persistent gossip about him and Janet having an affair, because it threatened his marriage to Virginia Valli. Not that he would have told Mary that in reality he and Janet had been madly in love during the making of their most beloved silent films; Charles had even proposed marriage. But Janet had rejected him because of his womanising. Respective unhappy marriages – she to a businessman in 1929, he to Virginia in 1931 – saw them reconnect in 1932. After starring in 1934's *Change of Heart*, they had a final split when his wife got wise. Charles moved to London for six months, forcing Fox to scrap their next film together. Since returning to Hollywood, he had devoted his energies to expanding the Racquet Club, which he'd co-founded in Palm Springs, and taking his yacht out on long voyages with young beauties who weren't his wife. Adding to his rootlessness, Charles and Virginia's house had burned down in California's October 1935 wildfires. Now here he was, with 'Australia's Janet Gaynor'.

———

In his Hotel Australia room that night, Charles settled in to learn his lines – something he took very seriously as an actor who'd made the transition to talkies. *The Flying Doctor* script introduced his roustabout character Sandy riding atop a freight train with his trusty dog Tiger. Jumping off in the Blue Mountains, he befriends scallywag Dodger Green, scams his way into working for a squatter and woos his new boss's beautiful daughter Jenny, who'd be played by Mary. On their wedding night, Sandy gets so spooked by the thought of settling down that he fakes his own death and hops on the next train to Sydney to work on the Harbour Bridge and reinvent himself as wrestler 'The Kalgoorlie Skipper'. Next, he lights out for the Outback. After striking gold, he decides he should return to Jenny. Before Sandy has the chance to do the right thing, he's shot by the town thug. His life is saved by his

Sydney friend John, now working for the Royal Flying Doctor Service, but the wounds leave him blind and with a weakened heart. Having become a saintly benefactor to the Flying Doctor, Sandy is mortified when John brings his new bride to town: Jenny. After fraught scenes in which Sandy threatens to spill the beans, he instead heads into the Outback, knowing the exertion will kill him, yet happy because he has willed his fortune to the Flying Doctor.

What puzzled Charles was that he had just travelled halfway around the world to take the lead in a picture whose title referred to a *supporting* character. Otherwise the script put him in a familiar role, right down to the blindness twist cribbed from *7th Heaven*. Sandy was a flawed romantic with a big heart, quick wit and streak of soulful sadness.

The next morning Charles signed the lease on a harbourside Elizabeth Bay apartment and set out to explore Sydney. His sartorial style — suede shoes, white trousers, coloured polo shirt, check tweed coat and hat at a jaunty angle — caused a stir on dull city streets dominated by men in drab blue and grey suits. Charles paid his respects at the Cenotaph in Martin Place, leaving a wreath and card — the latter promptly stolen by an admirer. If the sacrifices of the Great War moved him, he was chilled by what happened to Sydney that day at noon. 'A spell falls upon her million, the spell of a mighty moment of memory,' wrote a reporter for the *Daily Telegraph* about the two-minute silence to mark the passing of the King. 'It is eerie. Throngs that have hurried, jostled, and scrambled, stand petrified, as immobile as men and women of marble. The voice of the city, raucous and insistent, dies in a trice. There is no gradual tuning down. It is instantaneous . . . It might be a corner of Pompeii.'

Once the city restarted, Charles went to Pagewood and toured National Studios with Mary and Miles. The sets were impressive:

here was a section of Harbour Bridge; there was the interior of Sandy's riverside shack. Everywhere he looked he saw the latest in movie-making equipment. Charles declared it on par with Hollywood. Mary and Miles took him to afternoon tea in the canteen, where he gave his verdict on the script. 'It's just the sort of play I like,' he said. 'I like the scenery to be something out of the ordinary, and it will be in this. I also like a role where a fellow has to do things, not just hang around. This is a great story, and if we can put it over the right way it will sure be a big success.' Sipping tea, he answered a question from a hovering reporter about what he liked in a leading lady. 'If you work with a girl who enjoys acting with you, you get along fine. If she doesn't, it's an effort to drag yourself to the studio. Yes, I did like working with Janet Gaynor, of course, but Mary and I are going to get along fine, too.'

Charles's first few days in front of the cameras saw him doing scenes that didn't require Mary. On his Sunday off, he and Margaret Vyner cruised the harbour aboard a private yacht, with the *Daily Telegraph*'s photo caption suggesting she was shy about being seen out with a married man. But readers of that day's Sydney *Sun* could have been forgiven for concluding that a different romance was in the air when they saw a photo of Charles with his arm around Mary as they laughed and walked in lock-step at Pagewood.

Mary started working with Charles the next day when the production headed to the Blue Mountains. Charles walked with his swag against the big sky at Mitchell's Pass and had a wilderness wash at Leura Cascades. At Wentworth Falls he had to plunge off a rope bridge into a river. Then Mary, coat wrapped around her wedding dress, stood by the 600-foot drop, grief-stricken because she believed her new husband had fallen to his death.

The day's biggest drama came that evening on the return journey to Sydney. Police in a high-powered 'Bluebird' vehicle clocked Jock Orton zooming along busy Parramatta Road in Auburn at fifty miles per hour. They started pursuit, only for Miles to burn past both vehicles, Mary waving from his passenger seat and yelling, 'How yer, paaaaal?!' to the screenwriter. Jock accelerated; so did Miles. The cars hit seventy miles per hour as they reached Homebush, the cops chasing with siren wailing. As the police prepared to overtake, a sulky driver ahead of Miles held out his whip to indicate he was turning. The director swerved sharply into the centre of the road. A couple of car-lengths behind, the police veered to avoid a collision and their Bluebird nearly flipped before it smashed into the opposite kerb and came to a stop with serious damage. Miles's red eyes made the police suspect he was drunk, though they couldn't smell alcohol on his breath. 'I have had a few drinks – what has that got to do with you?' he snapped. Both Miles and Jock were charged with dangerous driving and ordered to appear in court.

Shooting continued at Pagewood that week. Sandy and Jenny met cute when he fell through a hole in a barn roof as she milked a cow. Later, he wooed her beside a brook, and then melted her heart with sweet-talk in his riverside shack. They made a beautiful on-screen couple, and Damien Parer's publicity photographs soon made their way into *Everyones* magazine. 'With all my knowledge of Hollywood and England, I don't know any girl of Mary Maguire's type,' Miles said. 'Here is a girl who is not only strikingly beautiful, but is fresh and unspoilt, blessed not only with that great asset, sincerity, but with the rare qualities of simplicity and innocence. Moreover she is an intuitive actress . . . There is a big place awaiting her on the screens of the world. If she is careful as to selection of roles and uses judgment with regard both to subjects and directors, she is almost certain to be world famous within the next two or three years.'

The Flying Doctor involved long hours. 'Working a dark one' was how the crew described pulling an all-nighter, and a 'Don Bradman' referred to doing a hundred-hour week. Mary was glad she didn't have to do these sorts of shifts; working six days a week was hard enough, especially when she got to the studio before 8.00 a.m. and finished twelve or more hours later. Still, she tried to enjoy Sydney's social life when she had the chance. Mary joined Miles and Charles at the premiere of *Anything Goes*, and they – sometimes joined by Margaret Vyner – attended tennis, pool and dinner parties put on by Australian film bigwigs.

Mary and Charles also saw each other informally. He would stroll over to the Chesterton apartment to chat and share meals with her and Patricia and Bina – and reciprocate by hosting them at his Elizabeth Bay flat. Joan, after a visit to Sydney, told Brisbane *Truth* that 'Charlie' was now part of the family, the paper reporting he was 'knocked cold' by Australian girls and admired 'Sydney belles from seventeen on!'.

Mary turned seventeen on 22 February. She had wanted to fly home to Brisbane but wound up having to work at Pagewood that Saturday. Once shooting was finished, the cast and crew presented her with a birthday cake and held an impromptu dinner. The next day, Charles threw a party at her apartment, though the day's best present was from Miles, who gave her a wire fox terrier for which he had paid a fabulous sum. On the Monday, Bina returned to Brisbane on the train, taking the puppy with her and leaving her daughters to their own devices for a fortnight. Patricia, meanwhile, did occasional talks on radio, recounting bits of movie-world gossip, and started collecting the shirts of the famous men she met through her sister.

Later that week, blessed with a sunny day during that stormy summer, Mary's co-star James Raglan took the controls of a Puss Moth aeroplane. With her in the copilot's seat, he flew over Pagewood before landing among the sand dunes. For a scene at Sydney's yet-to-open Trocadero nightclub, the ballroom was re-created in the studio, with dozens of the city's social butterflies arriving early in the morning to experience the thrill of being talkie extras. 'I've got out of my evening clothes at this hour but never before have I got into them at ten o'clock in the morning!' quipped one gent. It was all terribly exciting – but, as the day wore on, with Miles ordering take after take, the novelty wore off. Even seeing Mary Maguire pouting in a nurse's uniform and James Raglan dancing with Margaret Vyner couldn't compensate for all this sweating and sweltering under hot lights behind the big soundproof doors. 'Any of you who are altogether fed up can go now,' said Miles at 6.00 p.m. More than half of the Sydney socialites left; those who stayed were stuck there late into the night.

Miles was again caught speeding with Mary as his passenger. On 10 March, driving to the rural homestead 'Glen Lorne' on Sydney's south-western outskirts, he was spotted doing fifty-five to seventy-five miles per hour over a long stretch of Liverpool Road, allegedly even roaring by a school at 8.45 a.m. when a large number of children were in the vicinity. Stopped and charged, his response was typically arrogant: 'You people are always exaggerating.' If Mary was upset by the confrontation, it didn't show in home-movie footage captured that day. Far from it: she seemed perfectly at home taking a look through the camera's viewfinder with Damien Parer and being garlanded by the crew with celluloid offcuts. Mary had reason to be happy: Jocelyn Howarth was heading to Hollywood because Paramount had expressed interest in her. If the past few years were any guide, that would be the next step in Mary's journey to stardom.

The Flying Doctor had to wrap before Miles sailed for America on 1 April. But in late March the production was delayed when he and Jock fronted court to face the driving charges. Mary, summoned as a witness, attended all three days of the trial, the courtroom's public gallery packed by movie fans. Sydney *Truth* had the most fun with the proceedings; its big article headlined: 'No Slow Motion for Film Men – Sizzling Pace Through the Suburbs – Girl Actress as Piquant Witness'. Both men denied speeding and claimed they didn't even know they were being pursued. Miles also denied he'd been drinking. 'When I was asked how many drinks I had,' he told the court, 'I said, "Several" or "Plenty" . . . because I don't like being spoken to like that. I had not had anything alcoholic that day . . . I had plenty of ginger beer to drink . . . I have not had an alcoholic drink for 20 years.' But the court came alive when Mary took the stand. She remembered passing Orton's car and calling out, but reckoned the speedometer had then been at thirty-eight miles per hour and the first she had known of a police car was when it came alongside Mander's car and then crashed into a post. Told that the Bluebird had done no such thing, she begged to differ: 'It would surprise me very much to know that the police car did not hit a post at all.' Continuing, Mary enlightened the court about the untrustworthiness of speedometers in general, saying car companies made them register faster to increase automobile sales. Her odd claims did nothing to convince the magistrate. Noting extraordinary contradictions in evidence, he fined Miles £12 and Jock £10, though he didn't make them pay for damage to the police vehicle, the cops coming in for criticism for their reckless pursuit. Days later, Miles, preparing to sail for America, was absent from court when the second dangerous driving charge was heard. But Mary was there and played to the court as the police gave evidence about Miles speeding near a school. 'No, no!' she cried. 'We did not pass one child on the road!' The magistrate's review of her performance wasn't kind. 'It is ridiculous to say that no children were about at fifteen minutes to nine,' he said. 'It is school hour.' He fined Miles another £12.

On Saturday, 28 March, a fleet of cars delivered hundreds of people – including Bina and Mick, Charles and Elsa Chauvel, real-life Flying Doctor the Reverend John Flynn and his wife – to National Studios to watch the film's final shots and to enjoy a wrap party. 'Well, folks,' said Charles Farrell, kicking off proceedings, broadcast on 2GB, 'here we are at Pagewood. I came six thousand miles out here to take part in *The Flying Doctor*, and when I arrived I found Jimmy Raglan was the Flying Doctor, and all they did to me was knock me about and end up by killing me!' He introduced James, Mary, Margaret and Joe Valli. Miles made a speech. 'I feel sure it will be a picture which will be acclaimed,' he said. 'If it fails I am solely responsible, for I was given complete charge.' In reality the film's £35 000 budget had blown out to £45 000, and Miles was privately blaming the inexperience of his Australian cast.

Speeches made, it was time to roll cameras on Jenny handing out pay packets to shearers from a farm's shed window – and saying what she thinks is a sad farewell to Sandy. 'Oh, it's you,' Mary said. 'Yes,' replied Charles. 'It's time to say goodbye.' They did. Miles called 'Cut!' Everyone cheered. A supper party was held as the Trocadero Orchestra played the film's theme song and later sent everyone home to the strains of 'Auld Lang Syne'.

That week Sydney was a city of old acquaintances promising not to forget. Charles gave a cocktail party at his flat for *The Flying*

Doctor's cast and crew and his many friends. With her parents already back in Brisbane, Mary on 31 March held an even bigger soiree at Chesterton to say goodbye to Miles, sailing to Hollywood the next morning on the *Monterey*. The young hostess poured cocktails for a seventy-strong guest list filled with VIPs from Australia's film and newspaper industries. Later than night, they all kicked on to swanky Romano's, where they partied the night away – and crossed paths with a farewell for Jocelyn Howarth, also off to Hollywood on the *Monterey*.

When April Fool's Day dawned, the joke was on poor Jock Orton, who had been left to make sense of *The Flying Doctor* rushes. The scriptwriter had never edited a film before, and he turned up to the *Monterey* just before it sailed with a list of last-minute questions for Miles Mander. Further complicating the job, the director was departing before sound dubbing and musical arrangement were done. He had also neglected to shoot insert shots – little moments like a hand reaching for a door or a close-up of a gun – that helped stitch a movie together. Filming these was left to Damien Parer and cameraman Derek Williams. But the chief problem was that Miles had rehearsed too little and shot far too much. He had also filmed complex and expensive scenes – like James Raglan and Mary zipping through the air above Pagewood, and James dancing with Margaret Vyner amid dozens of extras – that just didn't further the story. Jock would tell one reporter he faced eighty miles of footage, five times what Hollywood editors usually had to whittle down into an average feature.

———

Did Mary Maguire have an affair with Charles Farrell? According to Sarah Baker's Gaynor–Farrell biography *Lucky Stars*, the answer is yes. Baker cited the 19 August 1936 issue of *The Movie Fan*, which said Charles and Virginia Valli had finally separated. Arriving back in Hollywood, he had immediately departed to make a film in England and was said to be in love with an Australian screen actress. Baker reported that Charles's sister Ruth confirmed the actor visited his family en route to England – and told them he had asked Valli for a divorce but she had refused. This *may* have been related to Mary; she and Charles got on well, and they had plenty of opportunity for off-screen romance. Certainly some candid behind-the-scene photos showed them very comfortable with each other. But when a *Truth* reporter asked Mary if she would have fallen in love with Charles if he wasn't already married, she came back with: 'Oh, never! Charles is a darling, but he's everybody's sweetheart.' It was a curious response, seeming to acknowledge his womanising and perhaps hinting that they had enjoyed a flirtation. Beyond that there was little to suggest a relationship.

Margaret Vyner was a different story. She and Charles went out frequently during the shoot, and both delayed leaving Sydney for Los Angeles by weeks, during which time they were photographed out on the town repeatedly. Even the usually tame Sydney press felt emboldened to ask her about the rumours. She denied anything more than friendship, saying such gossip was ridiculous because he was married. Charles and Margaret arrived in Hollywood within days of each other. Soon after, he asked his wife for a divorce. She refused. Charles headed for London; Margaret followed him. He got her the female lead opposite him in the prescient thriller *Bombs Over London*. But if they had an affair, it seemed to sour fast. When the production broke for Christmas, Charles decamped to Paris. Given he was married, a *Variety* item headlined 'Who Is She?' was particularly racy:

Charles Farrell announced here that he has lost all interest in the pic biz. 'I don't think I'll go on playing in pics,' he said. 'I love traveling too much and I hate studios: too many selfish, cold-blooded women who think of nothing but personal glory and for whom nothing counts, not even love . . .' After which one of the sympathetic listeners showed him over to Montmartre.

If Mary was romantically involved with anyone during production of *The Flying Doctor*, it was likely with Miles Mander. A *Smith's Weekly* piece that noted Margaret was Charles's 'favourite partner' in Sydney also reported: 'While on the subject of film stars little Mary Maguire seemed most perturbed when Miles left by the *Monterey*, for the two have been inseparable ever since they met.' There were other such hints. Both times Miles was caught speeding, Mary was in the passenger seat – though driving a star to set was hardly a director's job. In addition to a pricey puppy for her birthday, he gave her an expensive portable gramophone wireless set as a parting gift. Home-movie footage from their day on location at Glen Lorne shows how simpatico Mary and Miles seemed. He hugged her; they shared a laugh and were filmed seemingly unawares as they stretched out on the lawn together. Later, Miles appeared to be the one behind the home-movie camera as Mary goofed off in her bridal veil, going cross-eyed, sticking her tongue out and laughing at her own silliness.

There was a big age difference: he was forty-eight, older than her father. But such considerations wouldn't prove a factor in Mary's choice of partners. And whether they were lovers or merely friends, Miles's influence on her life had only just begun.

15.

It was a very different Mary who stepped off the train at South Brisbane railway station on Friday, 3 April. She didn't just have a new name, she'd had her curls cut short, looked chic in a grey frock and exuded the confidence of a Hollywood movie star. Reporters who had known her for years were impressed by what a witty and assured speaker she had become. 'This is the first time I've worn a dress for months,' she exaggerated. 'But I thought in honour of my homecoming I should really don a dress.' Mary told them how lucky she had been to work with Miles and Charles, and that despite the extremely long hours, she truly loved being a screen actress. The conquering heroine, flanked by Jock Orton, whom she'd invited to Brisbane for a short holiday, posed for photographs with her family amid a profusion of floral arrangements. The most spectacular was a model aeroplane of red and white flowers with 'Welcome Mary' spelt out across the wingspan. The day's only sad news was that her wire-haired terrier had run away.

Mary threw herself into charity work. At Easter, she spent a day on a truck driving around Brisbane, handing out twelve thousand Easter eggs to children at hospitals, kindergartens, orphanages, women's shelters, and homes for the deaf, blind and disabled.

A few weeks later, Mary was a guest of honour at a Belle Vue function for a children's charity, sharing the spotlight with actress Elaine Hamill, winner of an *Australian Women's Weekly* 'Screen Personality Quest' that led to her debut in Cinesound's *Grandad Rudd*. In addition to good work, Mary had a good time. She went to the races and took her sisters to movie previews. She hung out with some of the cast and crew of *White Death*, the shark movie starring American author Zane Grey, when they passed through Brisbane on the way north to the Great Barrier Reef. She met Mrs Louise Norton – mother of Darryl F. Zanuck, production chief for newly formed 20th Century Fox – when she was in town for a few hours. This white-haired movie matriarch declared that Mary had a 'striking beauty of the wistful type' and promised an introduction to her son if she ever got to Hollywood. Mary's beauty and fame brought male admirers, some proposing marriage. 'There was a well-known aviator,' *Truth* later reported, 'a young aristocrat from England sent out to get experience on a sheep station; the son of an Australian statesman; and a Victorian squatter of charm and substance.'

At the end of May, Jock, who had spent six weeks in Sydney feverishly editing *The Flying Doctor*, came back to Brisbane to say goodbye to Mary before sailing for England. She hosted a farewell cocktail party for him, with the Belle Vue's chef making pastries in the shapes of aeroplanes and kangaroos. During the festivities, she got a phone call from National Productions saying she had to catch the plane to Sydney the next morning for a trade screening of *The Flying Doctor*. 'What a breathless life these stars live!' Ruby Eve wrote in *Truth*.

In Sydney, Mary was photographed grinning in the cinema as she and Charles Farrell filled the screen. Shortly she had another reason to smile when a cable arrived from Miles Mander, who was now back in England to visit his estranged wife and son. He said a leading British studio wanted to sign her. More cables would follow to confirm arrangements, but it was likely she would need to sail in August or maybe even earlier. Mary was going to make movies in London!

But the next cable brought bad news – Miles told her not to come after all. The reason wasn't reported – and perhaps wasn't included in the message. What seems likely, given how easily Janet Johnson had found work in England, was that it was less related to Mary's prospects in British film and more related to Miles's personal desire and professional plan to get away from his wife and return to Hollywood.

Returning to Brisbane, down in the dumps about her disappointment, Mary stayed busy with the Mary Maguire Ball, which was to raise money to build St Vincent de Paul a new headquarters. She was also tickled to meet former prime minister Billy Hughes, whom she had missed when he visited *The Flying Doctor* set; he was recovering at the Belle Vue after breaking his collarbone when his plane made a miraculous forced landing at Beaudesert. At a special midnight charity screening, Mary also got to see how *Thoroughbred* had turned out. On 11 June, the Mary Maguire Ball attracted seven hundred guests – including the Lord Mayor and Archbishop Duhig – and raised more than £300. But the youngster didn't only do good when it was glamorous – at another big St Vincent de Paul fundraiser at the Belle Vue a few weeks later she was found in an apron in the kitchen, 'washing up thousands of pieces of cutlery'.

Towards the end of June another cable arrived from Miles Mander. This one asked her to come to . . . Hollywood. He would be there in early July and hinted he had her in mind for a film role. It was maddeningly vague. Cautious after being disappointed a month earlier, Mary replied saying she would come if there was real reason to go to Hollywood.

By now she had reason to stay in Brisbane. She had recently become friendly with a 25-year-old pilot named Beverley Shepherd. Young aviators were then called 'Adonises of the Air' and were such heartthrobs that women flooded airline offices with love letters and pestered staff for information on where their favourites were taking off and landing. Even among such a cadre, Beverley was a catch. The son of a prominent surgeon and a Sydney socialite, he was handsome, favoured Savile Row suits, drove a sports car and had recently spent a weekend at Windsor Castle visiting numerous cousins attached to the royal household. Even more heart-meltingly, his souvenir from that trip to England was Sam, the first-ever golden retriever imported into Australia, who just loved sitting in the copilot's seat in the Puss Moth plane as his master flew them high into the clouds. Beverley was brave, too. In mid-1935, just months after getting his pilot's licence, he took his plane on explorer Donald Mackay's aerial survey of central Australia. A year later, working as an instructor for Adastra Airways, Beverley had a miraculous escape at Mascot when a plane cut across his path as he was taking off in one of the company's Fox Moths. Both machines hurtled to the ground, smashing and toppling, their wings ripping off. Remarkably, everyone walked away with little more than cuts and bruises.

Mary and Beverley had plenty of opportunities to meet. He was learning to fly at Mascot when Mary flew to Sydney for her *Heritage* screening in January 1935, and he was working from there a year later when she went to the aerodrome for *The Flying Doctor*. By mid-1936 Beverley had joined Airlines of Australia and was flying the Sydney-to-Brisbane route daily. His brother Tony, also a playboy, was a regular at the Belle Vue. Beverley was likely the 'flying man' who escorted Mary to the Loreto Ball in early June. Soon *Truth*'s Ruby Eve felt emboldened to report:

'Beverley Shepherd and Brisbane's little film star are great friends. See them together at the film previews when Bev is not on his usual plane run.' But Beverley had a secret that could have turned that innocuous report into a scandal. He was secretly engaged to Jean Batten, the world-famous New Zealand aviatrix, though he hadn't seen her for more than a year while she chased aviation records on the other side of the world.

———

Mary received a follow-up telegram from Miles in mid-July. He was in Hollywood and going to bat for her. Whoever Miles talked to there about Mary had only his word to go on. *Heritage* hadn't been released in America, *The Flying Doctor* was still in post-production in Australia, and he didn't even have her screen-test footage with him. Yet cables kept coming, saying there were definite prospects, that studios were interested in her.

Finally, on Wednesday, 29 July, came the telegram Mary had hoped for. Miles said that not one but *two* studios had made definite offers. She burst into tears of joy, surrounded by her equally ecstatic family. Mary was going to Hollywood.

Miles told Mary to bring her *Flying Doctor* test footage, which he said would be sufficient for American casting directors to make up their minds about whether to give her a contract. What she didn't know was that this was nonsense; American studios demanded their own tests. Miles knew that. He was making them now as he struggled to land any sort of role. While a genuinely recognised talent in England, Miles was barely on Hollywood's radar. It was true he had played a few supporting parts in studio films in 1934 and 1935, but he had failed to land a contract despite having, as one American newspaper put it, 'laid siege' to the studios. And he had never directed a film there. No wonder his talk of offers was vague. The *Sydney Morning Herald* got a sense of this when it reported, 'No definite plans will be made regarding her work until she arrives.'

Mary was willing to take the chance. So was her family. She would go to Hollywood with Mick as chaperone and manager and test the waters. If things didn't work out they would continue on to New York and sail to London to see if Mary could get film roles there. Father and daughter got passports but ignored consular advice to apply for American work visas in advance. They were to sail on the *Mariposa*, leaving on 19 August from Sydney, two days before *The Flying Doctor*'s world premiere at The Regent. Denied its star's presence for the opening and public appearances, local distributor 20th Century Fox had little choice but to use its leading lady's upcoming Hollywood adventure as a publicity angle.

In the first week of August, the Maguires had another honoured guest in Lord Gowrie, Australia's new governor-general, when he came for a civic reception at the Belle Vue, with luncheon to be served on the table made for the man who was now King Edward VIII. Mary helped arrange settings of flowers and fruit, and when Lord Gowrie arrived she retreated to peek through a screen. But her Hollywood news had reached even the King's representative, and he summoned Mary to wish her his best. 'Queensland should be proud to have sent the first young Australian girl star to Hollywood,' Lord Gowrie told her as press flashbulbs popped.

Mary carefully selected eight new frocks to take with her to Hollywood, and the week leading up to her departure was a whirlwind of farewells and charity functions. She was feted at afternoon teas and midnight parties, civic receptions and radio broadcasts, receiving more gifts than a bride-to-be, including fourteen handbags, many stuffed with cash, and a stuffed toy koala mascot that she simply adored. 'As for stockings,' commented

Ruby Eve, 'she would need to be a centipede to wear out all of her hosiery gifts in two years.' Patricia put on a big cocktail party for her sister at the Belle Vue, with the Green Lounge packed with 'press, pulpit, and petticoat and motion picture executives'. Beverley Shepherd was there, along with his brother Tony. The farewells weren't only about Mary, with a surprise cocktail party held for Mick, the old lug sobbing as he tried to give a speech to family and friends.

On Saturday, 15 August, as part of *The Flying Doctor* promotion, Mary and Beverley made a public appearance together at the Queensland Aero Club's pageant, where thousands of spectators thrilled to stunt flying, bombing-run simulations, a parachuting display and the first Queensland demonstration of a helicopter. A biplane with *The Flying Doctor* prominently painted on the underside of its lower wing dropped thousands of promotional leaflets on the crowd. The event's biggest spectacle was the aerial derby, where aviators competed for a trophy put up by radio station 4BC. Beverley took Mary as his passenger in the competition. 'Like an H. G. Wells vision of things to come, planes of every type swooped down on the aerodrome . . . Tri-motor Fokkers, speedy Stinson transport planes, twin-engine Monospars, light monoplanes, and Moth biplanes whirled over the heads of several thousand spectators in the spectacular merry-go-round,' reported the *Sunday Mail*. As was often the case with aviation at this time, tragedy always seemed a heartbeat away. That day two Puss Moths bumped into each other a hundred feet above the ground after taking off in the derby, with one plane's wing fabric so damaged it was forced to land. But Mary was game, she trusted Beverley and he kept her safe.

Newspapers plugged *The Flying Doctor* and its departing star. The *Courier-Mail* found Mary at the Belle Vue, curled up in a big chair, looking 'more like a homesick schoolgirl than a promising film star'. The article began with her conflicting emotions: 'I'm very thrilled but now the time has come,' she said, 'I hate leaving my family.' Asked about her childhood dreams of acting, Mary told the reporter: 'I just didn't think it could be possible. I thought actresses must be beautiful and I was quite the ugliest child you can imagine.' The writer didn't believe her for a second; what was easier to believe was that she had genuine dramatic ambitions beyond simple stardom. Mary's favourite actresses weren't popular bombshells but Helen Hayes, Elisabeth Bergner and Luise Rainer, then ranked among the most talented female players working in films. When it came to movie men, Mary admitted she would like to meet Robert Taylor. 'They say he is really the most good-looking star,' she said. Otherwise she was more thrilled by the prospect of meeting acclaimed gents twice or thrice her age: William Powell, Lionel Barrymore and Wallace Beery. Still, her nerves dominated. 'I think one always appreciates home more when it is time to leave. I suppose it will be great fun after a while, but I feel sure I shall die of fright in the beginning. Anyhow, perhaps they may not find me suitable, and I shall just have to come back.'

Interview over, Mary went to Archerfield to greet Fred Daniell of National Productions, their meeting yet another photo opportunity for *The Flying Doctor*. There was real aerial–medical drama when his Airlines of Australia flight touched down and the plane was refuelled quickly so Beverley could fly three passengers to Rockhampton on the first leg of a mercy dash to see a dying relative in Townsville. Beverley flew back that night, landing in darkness at Archerfield, another test of his skill, planes still lacking radio navigation technology and airfields yet to have landing lights.

Trunks packed and her heart racing, Mary farewelled the staff of the Belle Vue the next morning. A fleet of cars took the

Maguire family to South Brisbane Station, where a band played 'Advance Australia Fair', 'Auld Lang Syne' and 'Home Sweet Home' for hundreds of friends and well-wishers on a platform festooned with flags and flowers. Mary's departure was broadcast live as a special 45-minute presentation on 4BH, with her admirers from the cinematic, theatrical and charity worlds making speeches as they handed over yet more floral bouquets and fruit baskets. Finally, Mary stepped up to the microphone to say her goodbyes. 'Dear Queenslanders, I love you all —' was as far as she got before she broke down and threw herself into Bina's arms. Holding it together, Mick told the press: 'There won't be any beg pardons about my girl. She's a Maguire.' Just before departure time, Mary composed herself sufficiently to say a few words of thanks. Then she and Mick boarded their carriage, the band struck up another sentimental song, and it was Patricia's turn to weep as the train pulled away.

Arriving back at the Belle Vue, Bina's emotions were strained further when she discovered Mary had left behind the case that contained her passport. She called Fred Daniell, who saved the day, organising to have the bag rushed by plane to Sydney. It seems this mercy mission fell to Beverley Shepherd. Certainly, he was in Sydney the next morning to meet Mary when she and Mick got off the train. Beverley took the Maguires to The Annery, his family's colonial-era clifftop mansion in Darling Point. They breakfasted with Beverley and his mother, Angel, a fixture on Sydney's social scene since the turn of the century. They also met Sam, the famous flying golden retriever, and Buddy, Jean Batten's mascot cat, entrusted to Beverley. Then it was time for last goodbyes.

At Darling Harbour's Wharf 1A, Mary and Mick braved the crowds to walk up the gangway onto the *Mariposa*. A cocktail party awaited her in the ballroom, attended by hundreds of Sydneysiders whom Mary had befriended. They toasted her with glasses of punch from a huge silver bowl as a band played yet more sentimental songs. When Brisbane's *The Telegraph*'s photographer captured this farewell, it was lovely little Joe Valli, who had been on screen with Mary from the start, who stood at her side, smiling with sad eyes.

PART TWO

America

16.

The Maguires sailed first-class on the *Mariposa* at a cost of around £130 ($A24 000 today). Mick had been in the hotel game for two decades and Mary had called hotels home her whole life, but nowhere they had lived compared with this floating pleasure palace. Built at the height of the Great Depression for $US8 million ($US145 million today), the *Mariposa* and her sister ships, owned by the Matson Lines of San Francisco, were among the most beautifully appointed in the world. 'One felt that the last word in maritime trimmings had been reached until someone puts a keel under the Louvre and floats it,' was how one American newspaper described them. The length of two football fields, the *Mariposa* carried seven hundred passengers attended by a crew of 350. Upon entering their stateroom, the Maguires were greeted by a Matson 'bon voyage' basket filled with fruit, cheese and wine. Their accommodations were attractive and spacious, decorated in a laurel green and gold colour scheme, with two large single beds, artfully designed furniture and sea views through porthole windows. A phone on the bedside bureau – 'your modern Aladdin's lamp', read the official guide for passengers – summoned bellboys and stewards at any hour with any request.

But why stay in one's room when there was so much ship to explore? The promenade deck was the perfect place to take a chair and the sea air. The first-class pool was replenished daily with fresh water. Feminine beauty products were provided at the Elizabeth Arden salon. There was a gymnasium, barber shop, photographic studio and night club. *The Polynesian* newspaper, printed daily on board, contained not just the world's news as received by radio, but also bulletins about activities and entertainment, from tennis, quoits, shuffleboard and clay pigeon shooting to the nightly dances and frequent screenings of recent Hollywood movies in the lounge. The most unusual diversion was the horseracing. Late each morning half a dozen knee-high wooden ponies, complete with toy jockeys, were set on a huge horseshoe-shaped green felt track laid over the ballroom floor. A ship's officer threw dice, whose combinations dictated which horse advanced how many spaces, while passengers laid bets and cheered their nags to victory.

The voyage from Sydney to Los Angeles would take eighteen days. That first night at sea, those who had their sea legs enjoyed the welcome dinner. The *Mariposa*'s menus, changed daily and printed as beautiful souvenirs, offered mouth-watering choices. A passenger might try hors d'oeuvres of crabmeat cocktail, move on to consommé brunoise, and then have a main of tenderloin in truffle sauce followed by dessert of almond puff pastry tartlet, all accompanied by fine liquor from the liner's well-stocked bar. The company was no less exotic, with first-class guests encouraged to get to know each other at dinners and dances. Celebrities and other VIPS were invited to share the table of the *Mariposa*'s Captain William Meyer, himself well known for his heroic role in the 1930 rescue of sinking ocean liner *Tahiti*, newsreel footage of which had been shown all around the world. World-renowned author Zane Grey was on board and sailing back to America. Having finished *White Death*, he was now telling anyone who would listen about his plan to come back to Australia to catch the eighty-foot-long sharks he was sure lurked in the depths of the Tasman Sea. Mary and Zane had plenty of friends in common, from Charles Farrell, who had under the author's instruction caught one of those Sydney Harbour sharks he'd wondered about upon arrival, to *White Death* supporting player Alfred Frith, who had been a guest at the Hotel Metropole back when Mary was first discovered in Melbourne. Then there was handsome, dark-haired Vernon Dorrell, one of America's foremost pilots, who had just spent one month teaching Australian aviators how to fly Lockheed's new Electra monoplane. Vernon had a movie connection, too, having been one of the many stunt pilots in 1930's *Hell's Angels* for that notoriously difficult multimillionaire director Howard Hughes. Another American aviator on board, Captain H. D. Bowyer, was returning home after overseeing delivery and testing of four Stinson Tri-motor planes to Airlines of Australia. He would have known Beverley, who was soon to start piloting these new aircraft for the company.

As guests became acquainted, conversation couldn't escape talk of war, not with new daily horrors unfolding in Spain as loyalists and fascists battled for control of the country. Another *Mariposa* passenger, retired US colonel Henry Sternberger, now a New York stockbroker – and husband of Estelle Sternberger, the world's leading female peace activist – had strong views on the war clouds gathering in Europe and Asia, and predicted that America wouldn't be able to remain aloof from any major conflict. Australian academic Dr Percival Cole, a giant of a man who spoke in a monotone, was even more pessimistic, fearing that war would totally destroy European civilisation. 'Modern weapons of war,' he'd say in that droning voice, 'bring annihilation within bounds of possibility.' Mary, like a lot of other people at this time, may not have been listening.

The *Mariposa* enjoyed smooth sailing and fine weather across the Tasman Sea only to arrive in Auckland just as major storms lashed the city and caused severe flooding. Sightseeing tours were cancelled but Mary had New Zealand's reporters to keep her busy. The press loved her every bit as much as they had in Australia. 'Petite, chic and charming,' said the *Auckland Star*, admiring her 'clear, bright, brown eyes which find it impossible to dim the slightest twinkle if there is a joke in the air'. Mary charmed with her wit when asked if she wanted to do character roles. 'Well, in *Heritage* I had a child and I was fifteen years of age when I took the part, and in *The Flying Doctor* I was a bigamist and am seventeen now. I think, perhaps, these must be "character" parts.'

Grand news arrived via telegram while the *Mariposa* was in Auckland. *The Flying Doctor* had broken all house records on its opening day at the Regent, advance bookings augured well for its continued success and the early reviews were favourable. As it was released around Australia, critics would hail *The Flying Doctor* as the best local film so far, praising its artistic and technical proficiency, though many thought its already weak story undermined by too many travelogue views. Charles Farrell's performance was considered as fine as anything he'd done in Hollywood, and everyone loved Joe Valli's comic stylings. Mary got mixed notices. Brisbane's *Sunday Mail* said she was 'deserving of high praise for her study of Jenny, the station owner's daughter. Only in the emotional moments does her acting weaken.' Sydney's *Daily Telegraph*: 'Little Mary Maguire, although pretty and appealing, has neither the dramatic training nor the understanding for the role.' ABC radio's critic said her emotional expression was limited to a 'faintly puckered brow' but allowed 'experienced directors have proved themselves able to make good screen actresses out of such material'. Kenneth Slessor of *Smith's Weekly* held a similar view: 'Mary Maguire is genuine screen-stuff: in the hands of the proper director, this Australian girl could be made a beauty of the order of Merle Oberon. As it is, she is still obviously lacking in polish and in firmness of technique. But a lot more will be heard of this young lady.' The *Sydney Morning Herald* had no problem with her performance – 'The progress of the courtship, gentle and hesitating on both sides, is delightfully portrayed by Mr. Farrell and Mary Maguire' – and Sydney's *Sun* also liked her: 'Mary is a delicious mouthful in the film, a little girl capable of tenderness.' The *Sydney Mail* was politely dismissive – 'looks sweet and pretty, but cannot cope with the varying shades of emotional expression demanded by her role' – while *The Argus* had knives out: 'seems little more than an insipid ornament'. *The Australian Women's Weekly* summed up the critical position best: 'Mary Maguire has a long, long way to go before she will make film history.' Luckily, she wasn't able to read those reviews, which might have seen her leave the *Mariposa* in Auckland and take the next boat back to Australia.

The prospect of trying to crack Hollywood was nerve-racking enough without also worrying about what critics back home were going to write. But as a bookworm Mary most likely sought distraction in the *Mariposa*'s elegant library, which was stocked with the latest bestsellers. That included Margaret Mitchell's *Gone with the Wind*, just published in America but yet to reach Australian bookstores. Speculation about who would play its Southern heroine in the film adaptation was already feverish, with everyone from Kay Francis to Katharine Hepburn mentioned for the role. It's not difficult to imagine Mary, heroine of her own period movie drama and lover of historical literary romances, curled up with this epic and dreaming that having already played spitfire Biddy O'Shea, she might somehow land the role of Scarlett O'Hara.

After a stop in Suva, where passengers toured palm-shaded villages and saw majestic blue lagoons, and then another day spent in even more remote and exotic Pago Pago, the *Mariposa* reached Hawaii. The *Honolulu Star-Bulletin* photographed Mary smiling with a lei and said she was 'Ballyhooed as Australia's No. 1 heart throb' and en route 'to seek world fame and fortune' in a Hollywood film directed by Miles Mander, in whom she had 'complete faith'. Mick took the opportunity to boast to the reporter of his Australian boxing career – and promote himself to 1912 world welterweight boxing champion.

Mary's anxiety intensified as the *Mariposa* steamed ever closer to Los Angeles. She lost a lot of weight during the voyage – one report said seven kilograms – wondering whether she would 'click' with the studios. Onboard newspaper *The Polynesian*'s feature article about the next port-of-call didn't help those nerves. 'Thousands of aspirants to fame are annually drawn to the movie arras; hordes of others come to see the widely publicized movie city do its stuff,' it reminded. 'But the way things are today, an outsider has little chance of getting into the studios. The gates are closely guarded.' Was Mary going to be able to get past those guards and show her screen-test footage to the men who mattered? Would Louise Norton actually introduce her to movie mogul son Darryl F. Zanuck? And, above all else, what did Miles Mander really have planned for her?

17.

The *Mariposa* reached Los Angeles just after dawn on Saturday, 5 September. Miles Mander sent his apologies – he was unable to meet Mary because he had been cast in 20th Century Fox's period drama *Lloyds of London* and was needed on set that day. But Miles ensured a *Los Angeles Times* photographer was there for Mary, and she posed this way and that against the liner's railings and on its gangway.

The Californian coastline, with the sun cresting the Santa Ana Mountains, had been spectacular from sea, but Mary's close-up impressions of Los Angeles were far less pleasant. San Pedro Harbor was a grinding place of cranes, canals and cargo ships. Inland, the city didn't improve – from her car window all Mary saw was mile upon mile of traffic. Everywhere she looked, steel derricks pumped oil from the earth, and the city's million cars funnelled brown exhaust into the sky. Even Hollywood was oppressive and alienating. 'It looks like an industrial city – ugly,' Mary said. 'All the shops big and ugly, and the studios as hard to get into as walled harems.' The Maguires checked into the Roosevelt Hotel, right on Hollywood Boulevard. Despite the glamour of its name, the thoroughfare was thronged not with film stars but wannabes and has-beens, drunks and drug fiends, pimps, prostitutes, con men and crazies. Mary found it rather frightening. Overwhelmed and homesick, she sobbed herself to sleep that night. 'My first few days in Hollywood were so lonely,' she confessed, 'that I wondered whether it wasn't better to be a big frog in a small waterhole than a tadpole in an aquarium.'

Even through teary eyes, this aquarium was more exotic than any other. The Roosevelt had a marvellous view of the Hollywoodland sign, spectacular when lit up at night by its four thousand incandescent bulbs. The hotel itself exuded Hollywood history. Built in 1927 by Louis B. Mayer, Mary Pickford, Douglas Fairbanks and Sid Grauman, its Blossom Ballroom was where Janet Gaynor two years later accepted her Oscar at the first Academy Awards. Right across from the Roosevelt stood Grauman's Chinese Theater, famous for its glittering premieres, where stars like Janet Gaynor, Gloria Swanson, Marion Davies, Wallace Beery, Jean Harlow, Shirley Temple and Miles's child-star discovery Freddie Bartholomew had left handprints, footprints and autographs in the concrete. Like any young actress, Mary would have wondered whether she might one day make her own mark.

Unlike thousands of hopeful nobodies who had daydreamed outside Grauman's, Mary grabbed Hollywood's attention within a day of arriving in town. When she awoke after her first sorrowful night, she was prominent in the *Los Angeles Times*. What studio moguls and their minions saw in their fat Sunday paper was a big photo of a pretty brunette perched on a ship's railing. 'Antipodes' Favorite' read the headline. A subhead explained 'Australian Film Actress Here – Mary McGuire [sic] Expects to Make Pictures For British Producer'. The photo caption said she was the 'reigning queen of Australian cinema' come to 'look over Hollywood before going on to London'. Mary, the article claimed, was 'under a contract but not knowing what her next move will be. The contract is held by Miles Mander, British producer.' What Mary thought of this falsehood isn't known – she wasn't quoted, though Mick, now billed as 'welterweight ring champion of Australia 1914–15', had told the reporter his daughter could swim, ride, tap dance and do everything athletic. The article noted that *The Flying Doctor* had been directed by Miles and co-starred Charles Farrell, and that it had 'beaten all opening records in the Antipodes'. As an announcement that Mary had arrived in Hollywood, she couldn't have hoped for anything better. But the article was as much a calling card for Miles, who had clearly briefed the writer to his advantage. Previously barely mentioned by the *Los Angeles Times*, the newspaper now presented him as a commercially successful filmmaker in control of the hot property from Down Under.

Miles did get Mary access to Hollywood studios. Not by casting her, because he wouldn't direct again after *The Flying Doctor*, and not via the two supposed studio offers, which weren't mentioned in the press again. Mary's big break instead resulted from that day's biggest movie-world news: after a long courtship John Farrow, Australian screenwriter, and Maureen O'Sullivan, Jane in MGM's Tarzan movies, had finally set their wedding date just a week hence. As it turned out, Miles knew the couple well enough to throw a party for them at John's place at the Ronda Apartments – and he took Mary along to make her social debut in Hollywood. Mary's dark eyes went wide when she walked into the party. 'It was very thrilling to meet so many of the big stars,' she said. This particular guest list is lost to history, but other celebratory soirées for the couple around this time were attended by friends like Jean Harlow, Dolores del Río, Madeleine Carroll, *King Kong* creator Merian C. Cooper, and David O. Selznick, then prepping *A Star Is Born* for Janet Gaynor and still searching for his Scarlett in *Gone with the Wind*. Mary was most impressed by the happy couple. 'Maureen looked positively lovely – magnolia complexion and Irish eyes with a lot of fire in them,' she said. 'They are absurdly in love . . . and the congratulations they received seemed to come from all over the world.' More importantly, John and Maureen liked the young Australian immediately. She and the groom-in-waiting shared Irish–Australian Catholic heritage, but Mary had even more in common with the bride-to-be. Maureen knew *exactly* what she was experiencing. In 1929, also aged seventeen, she had been discovered in Dublin by director Frank Borzage, who had just made stars of Charles Farrell and Janet Gaynor in *7th Heaven*, and brought to Hollywood to star in a film called *Song o' My Heart*. Seven years later she still suffered homesickness to such an extent that for her recent birthday she had treated herself to a hugely expensive twenty-minute transatlantic phone call. By the end of that party John vowed to introduce Mary at Warner Bros., where he was hoping to direct his first feature, while Maureen seemingly made the same offer regarding MGM, where mogul Louis B. Mayer doted on her like a daughter.

Mary got down to business her first Monday in Hollywood. She met her new manager, Richard Monter, suggested by Miles, and took meetings, with Miles present to offer advice. His counsel was welcome, for how nailbiting it was to step through the gates of MGM, Hollywood's most glamorous dream factory, known by its motto 'Home to more stars than there are in the heavens'. There, Mary met casting director Billy Grady, who had made stars of W. C. Fields and Ruby Keeler, and discovered Jimmy Stewart and Joan Blondell; duly impressed, he offered a screen test. True to her word, Louise Norton got Mary in to see her son Darryl F. Zanuck at 20th Century Fox. This was the man who, while at Warner Bros., had produced *The Jazz Singer*, *Little Caesar* and *42nd Street*. Now, as Fox's production chief, Zanuck was reshaping the studio to give it more star power. He also offered a screen test. But Mary was yet to step before the cameras for MGM or Fox when she headed to Warner Bros. at Burbank on Wednesday, 9 September.

Warners was an exciting and dynamic place to be in 1936. After some flat years early in the Depression, the studio had rebounded and recently erected big new sound stages and backlot streets so it could produce sixty pictures per year. Welcoming Mary, John Farrow would have shown her around this hive of activity, where rising star Humphrey Bogart was shooting *Black Legion*, Dick Powell and Glenda Farrell were hoofing through *Gold Diggers of 1937*, and Errol Flynn was brooding as a maligned medico in *Green Light*. If Mary wanted to be a star like these studio players she needed to impress the young head of the casting department: Maxwell Arnow. But she didn't just impress him. Mary knocked his socks off. Wanting to get the jump on the competition, Arnow ordered a seven-year contract be drawn up and that a screen test be made within forty-eight hours. Mary could hardly believe her ears. This was her shot at stardom – and a more concrete offer than she had received from MGM and Fox. If Warners liked her screen test, they had until 15 September to sign her or risk losing her to these rivals.

Arnow knew she was a hot property and agreed to the salary her team demanded. If Mary signed, she would get $500 per week for a six-month provisional period. If the studio took up her option, she would officially begin the seven-year period, paid $500 ($US9150 today) a week for the first year, increasing by $250 annually before a final jump to weekly pay of $2250 in the seventh year. It was big money. A talented young player named Jane Bryan had recently started on just $100 a week; Olivia de Havilland, already a star thanks to *Captain Blood* and *Anthony Adverse*, was still on $500. The catch was that Warners got to decide after six months whether to take up Mary's option – and if it did, this nerve-racking process would then be repeated each year. But Warners signing Mary *guaranteed* she would earn *$10 000* in the next six months. That was enough to buy two average-priced houses outright. And put a brand-new Studebaker in each garage. Staying the course with Warners, Mary would be on $90 000 ($1.3 million) a year and world famous by 1943. Everything depended on the screen test. Here Mary won an important concession from Arnow: Miles Mander was given permission to direct her tryout. It'd be comforting to have a familiar voice behind the glare of the studio lights.

Mary liked Hollywood better already. It felt more like home now she and Mick found an apartment in the handsome Mayfair building on North Wilcox, just a few blocks from the Roosevelt. 'When I arrived in Hollywood I think I was the most home-sick little girl in the wide world, but everyone has been more than charming and all have gone out of their way to make me feel happy,' she wrote to her mother.

Friday, 11 September arrived. Mary and Miles drove over to Warners for her big try-out. 'To my surprise they tested me in singing, too,' she said. 'I sang *The Object of My Affection*, which I learned to please my two young sisters. They seemed very pleased with my facial test.' While Mary thought it had gone well, the clock was now ticking. Warners had four days to decide.

Mary and Mick tried to get used to the Mayfair apartment, which had murphy beds and other things that disappeared into the walls. After the Belle Vue, it was on the small side and still pricey at $80 a month. In those first days, dad cooked and daughter kept house. Before long they were adapted to Hollywood's way. 'One never has a dinner in the home; everybody eats out in cafes and they are the last word in efficiency,' Mary wrote in a letter to Brisbane's *Truth*. 'Cheaper than cafes are the drug stores.' Domestic help was cheap, too, and the Maguires hired an African-American maid named Alice for $15 per month.

With Monday came the summons from Warners. On the eve of the deadline, Mary, Mick, Miles and Richard Monter talked through contract terms at the studio with Maxwell Arnow, production executive Bryan Foy and studio attorney Roy Obringer. There was much to discuss because the 21-page document was dense with clauses that gave the studio control. On and off set, Warners could direct her to do whatever they wanted, from publicity appearances to voice recordings. If she didn't turn up to set, she would be liable for all costs incurred. If she got sick, her pay would be suspended and her claims of illness subject to scrutiny. The studio reserved the right to loan her out to other producers and keep any profit from the arrangement. Clause 21 – the 'Morals Clause' – dictated that Mary conduct herself properly at all times according to public convention and do nothing to bring herself, her studio or the wider motion picture industry into disrepute. Clause 24 stipulated that if she refused a role she would go on suspension without pay for the time it took another actress to play the part – and the time of her suspension would be added to her contract. Clause 32 allowed the studio to change her name. Though standard practice – Carole Lombard was born Jane Peters; Mary Pickford had been Gladys Smith; Ginger Rogers started out as Virginia McMath and so on – Miles objected that it would ruin her marquee recognition in Australia while Mary was simply against another name change. The studio struck the clause from the contract. But there was no getting around the harshest of standard conditions: the provision for six unpaid weeks in her first six months with the studio. These layoffs were to be at the studio's discretion and announced at a moment's notice.

Pale and trembling, Mary signed just before midnight, with Mick adding his signature because his daughter was a minor.

Her age meant the contract still had to be confirmed by a judge, though this was a mere formality. The happy news was cabled to Bina at the Belle Vue.

Mary was going to be a Hollywood star.

18.

Mary's brightest night came after Hollywood's darkest day. Irving Thalberg, MGM's 37-year-old 'Boy Wonder' producer, died that morning of pneumonia. The news rippled out slowly and became a tsunami of grief and disbelief by the time Mary signed her name to the Warners contract. She awoke the next morning to newspapers filled with tributes from every star, director, producer and mogul worth a damn. The next day fifteen hundred of the movie colony's luminaries gathered to farewell Thalberg at Temple B'nai B'rith on Wilshire Boulevard. Police had to hold back ten thousand fans gawking at their favourite stars as though this was a film premiere rather than a film funeral. Hollywood art soon imitated Hollywood death when a similar sequence became the finale of *A Star Is Born*.

News of Mary's contract ricocheted, thanks to Harrison Carroll's gossip column in William Randolph Hearst's *Los Angeles Examiner*, which was syndicated to four dozen newspapers. 'Judging by the reports from Warner Brothers, the 17-year-old Australian star, Mary Maguire, is a definite find for Hollywood,' he wrote, adding, 'she is known as "the Mary Pickford of Australia".' Mary thought it an odd comparison: Mary Pickford was forty-four and had retired from acting.

Then it became clear. Mary Pickford had been known as 'America's Sweetheart' just as Mary Maguire occasionally got 'Australia's Sweetheart' back home.

———

Mary had landed a Hollywood contract within ten days of arriving in Hollywood. Could Patricia and Joan do the same? Mick wrote to Bina to ask for photos of the girls he might show around. Patricia immediately began dieting and selecting frocks to take to Hollywood. Joan concentrated on improving her acting in amateur films made by family friend Moya Connolly. Always far-sighted, Bina soon told reporters she was taking *all* her girls to Hollywood in 1937. News of Mary's contract, salary and rumoured debut opposite Errol Flynn in *The Prince and the Pauper* made all the Australian papers. 'I don't know definitely what my first work is to be, or with whom,' Mary told Brisbane's *Truth*. What she could confirm was that she had entered a different filmmaking realm. 'Work in Australia is child's play to the work here,' she wrote, 'for so much attention is paid to detail, and money is simply no object in turning out a good picture from a photographic point of view. For every retake they make in Australia, they might have 100 here, and then perhaps abandon the scene eventually.' Mary also downplayed her impressive salary as 'just pin money to some of the stars – even the young ones'. A few Australian news-papers became sceptical about her pay packet. The *West Australian* reckoned she was actually on $150 a week and a visiting Warner Bros. executive took it upon himself to publicly agree.

At the Belle Vue, Bina hosted a party for American movie star Victor Jory, in Australia to make Zane Grey adaptation *Rangle River*. Mrs Jory said she was surprised Mary had won a contract so quickly, because would-be starlets usually waited months. 'And sometimes forever!' chimed her husband. True cad Victor later also scoffed at Mary's reported salary during a radio interview. These were all fighting words to Miles, who would brandish his pen to defend Mary . . . and exalt himself. Writing to *Smith's Weekly* he set the record straight about her contract and salary, took credit for approving the terms, berated the Warner Bros. executive for not knowing his own company's business and intimated that Victor Jory was a jealous has-been. Miles's passionate letter led *Smith's Weekly* to mockingly characterise him as 'all hot under the collar' and having 'taken up the cudgels over a fancied slight . . . Nothing if not chivalrous, Mander now gallops to the aid of the beauteous Mary.' The newspaper would also report that Miles and Mary were constant companions and speculate that a romance was in the offing.

———

Mary started earning her salary on 1 October 1936, not by acting but by submitting herself to the cogs and gears of Hollywood's dream factory. Despite her achievements at home, she was still raw material to be processed and polished. Mary studied elocution, mime, gesture and dance at Warners, with classes conducted for her and other recently signed starlets on a small studio stage. Her hair was combed a dozen ways. Clothes were tried on and make-up styles applied. She was lit and photographed and filmed from every angle. Cameras rolled as she delivered lines to test her voice. She acted in scenes from comedies, romances and dramas. Mary would later say she had a hundred and fifty screen tests.

When not training and testing, she was in the hands of the publicity department. Days were spent posing, posing, posing for photographs. Here was Mary, teen waif in bobby socks ready for a round of tennis or washing the deck of her yacht in a short floral dress. Here was Mary, older than her years, sultry and bosomy in an off-the-shoulder satin gown or staring into the heavens with stars in her soulful eyes. When these photos were sent into the world they were accompanied by an official studio biography. Mary's background was relatively exotic, so hers contained fewer falsehoods than some others, but reporters and editors loved quirky details – true or otherwise – and a few such morsels were served up. To maintain her fresh-faced beauty Mary followed a simple regime of soap, water and sunshine. She had an aversion to layer cake with pink icing but was particularly fond of a special type of Australian pineapple. This biography was only the foundation stone of her persona. In 1936 the Hollywood studios combined produced some hundred thousand words of publicity hype *daily* to feed the town's five hundred or so correspondents. Thus readers around America and the world soon learnt that 'Antipodes', Mary's pet kangaroo, had been lost in transit from Australia and that, as a bronzed darling from Down Under, she regularly held surfing and boomerang-throwing classes for her studio pals. Those tiny feet, first reported on a Brisbane beach, were now declared the smallest in Hollywood, with Mary stealing the tiny tootsie title from Gloria Swanson. This trickle of trivia wasn't just to tickle readers from California to Connecticut – it was also meant to create Mary-awareness so she was famous before she made her first film.

But Mary hit the front page of the *Los Angeles Times* for an unplanned drama more related to her being Australian than imaginary pet kangaroos and boomerang lessons. Not familiar with driving on the right side of the road, she crashed the beautiful chrome-and-cream sedan she had just bought into another vehicle. Mary and the other driver, a woman named Viola Morse, were taken to hospital and treated for minor injuries. Hollywood insiders would have recognised the latter as comic superstar Oliver Hardy's long-time mistress. In-the-know movie folks would have also recognised that day's *other* Mary Maguire news as clever studio publicity – newspapers reported she was putting up 'the battle of the century' to stop Warners from changing her name to 'Margaret Lloyd'. 'My name used to be plain Peggy Maguire until six months ago,' she protested. 'Australians didn't seem to like it a bit when I changed to Mary, and if I change it again they'll probably disown me.' Given the story came with this convenient quote, Warners was using her name-change refusal to publicise her as headstrong. It was a theme they would return to and which Mary would come to embrace.

Mary belonged to a beachhead of Australian women then working in American film. Merle Oberon, given her break by Miles five years earlier, was the reigning antipodean queen of the screen (even if her claim to have been born in Tasmania would be posthumously proved a lie). May Robson, born in 1858 in Moama in country New South Wales, was the true queen. After decades on the New York stage, she had recently moved to Hollywood and become the first Oscar-nominated Australian for her performance in 1933's *Lady for a Day*. Young Melbourne beauty Mona Barrie, who had appeared with George Wallace in *His Royal Highness*, and Sydney's Marcia Ralston, a J. C. Williamson actress married to an American bandleader, had both recently signed with Warners. Jocelyn Howarth was with RKO – and had let them change her name to Constance Worth. Even Mary's friend Janet Johnson was newly in town and signed to 20th Century Fox after being discovered on the London stage by studio chairman Joe Schenck. Australian women could also be proud of their Hollywood heritage. In the past two decades Annette Kellerman, 'the million-dollar mermaid', had been a huge star for Fox, Louise Lovely had headlined dozens of pictures for Fox and Universal, and Enid Bennett had made even more movies as a popular leading lady married to pioneering director Fred Niblo. But success wasn't guaranteed. Just a few years ago Phyllis Barry, Jim Gerald's niece, had been on the rise, but by the time Mary reached Hollywood her star had fallen to the point where she was doing uncredited bit parts. That was nothing compared with silent beauty Lotus Thompson, who, wanting to be known for more than just her beautiful legs, had poured disfiguring acid on them so she would never be typecast again. As a career and publicity ploy, it got her a few B-movie supporting parts on the way to eking out a living as an extra.

———

On the night of 9 October, Mary witnessed Los Angeles blazing for the first time in electric light powered by the new Hoover Dam, with one million cheering citizens thronging downtown and bathed in rivers of new radiance.

This was also a brilliant time for Mary's circle. Miles got a seven-year acting contract with Fox, based on the good work he'd done in *Lloyds of London*. John Farrow scored his debut directing assignment at Warners with *Men in Exile*. Then Mary received the news she had been waiting a month to hear: she was to take the female lead in a light romantic drama called *Love Begins*.

19.

Love Begins was based on a short story 'Young Nowheres' by then-famous, now-forgotten Australian author Ida Wylie. One of Warners' cost-cutting strategies was to remake properties they already owned so the story, already adapted for the screen in 1929 and 1935, would hit cinemas again – this time with Mary in the lead. She was to play Nancy Lee, a down-on-her-luck Depression gal who seeks refuge in the basement of a fancy New York City hotel, where she's discovered by elevator operator Jimmy. He gets her a job as a hotel maid and they fall in love. But Nancy appears to be keeping a secret, with Jimmy suspecting she's sneaking off to see another guy. Truth is she's a single mother, trying to raise enough money to get her baby out of a home for waifs. Tragedy looms when Nancy flees back to the mean streets after accident-ally smashing what she thinks is a guest's priceless Ming vase. Jimmy discovers the truth about her baby and tracks Nancy down to a hospital where she has been ill and delirious for weeks. They share their first kiss while she's in her sickbed. Baby retrieved, everyone lives happily ever after.

Love Begins was to be produced by Bryan Foy's unit. While Foy had directed the world's first all-talking feature, *Lights of New York*, he was now nicknamed 'Keeper of the Bs' – meaning he oversaw the twenty-six B-pictures Warners made each year to feed their nationwide chain of cinemas. Bs were the steady revenue stream that underwrote riskier A-pictures for the studio. But Foy's fiefdom was also where Warners groomed their new players for stardom. Humphrey Bogart, for instance, had been toiling in them for years and had just gotten his big break as a charismatic hoodlum in prestige thriller *The Petrified Forest*.

Mary was riding high professionally but sinking lower emotionally. The *Courier-Mail*'s observations of her just two months earlier had been spot-on and now the *Los Angeles Times* reckoned she was suffering 'one of the worst cases of homesickness ever seen by Hollywood'. Her melancholy was made worse by hanging out with John Farrow and Maureen O'Sullivan when most of Maureen's family came from Ireland to visit. But Mary took a leaf from her friend's book. With Maureen, John, Miles and Mick by her side in the Mayfair apartment, she made a radio-telephone call home to Brisbane. The line crackled as the connections were made – via New York, London, China and Sydney, twenty-eight thousand miles of cable – and then Mary heard her mother's voice clearly. She promptly broke down in tears. Mick took the phone and told Bina their girl was just taking a few moments to compose herself. Miles got on the line next. 'You needn't worry about Mary,' he assured, 'she is sitting on top of the world.' Sufficiently recovered, Mary told her mother about *Love Begins* and how hectic the past month had been. Confessing she was very lonely, she wanted to send a boat fare so that Patricia and Joan could come and live with her as soon as possible. The reporter Ruby Eve, who happened to be at the Belle Vue, got thirty seconds on the line to hear Mary tell of rehearsals, her car and her maid Alice. The call was hugely expensive: $128 ($US2300) for six minutes. Frustratingly, though, Patricia and Joan couldn't get a boat to join their sister because soon the Pacific Coast of the United States was brought to a standstill by a marine strike.

At this time, Miles may have wanted to provide Mary with more than mere friendly comfort and career guidance. After signing his Fox contract, he told his wife Kathleen he needed a divorce on the grounds of incompatibility and because he now intended to settle in America. The urgency was curious – they had been publicly estranged and continents apart for years. Yet it made sense if he wanted to be free to marry another young Australian. Kathleen's response was swift and public. 'If my husband is serious, it is certainly a complete surprise to me,' she told the *Daily Mail*. 'If he tries to obtain a divorce on the ground of incompatibility, or for any other reason, I will do everything in my power to contest it.'

At Warners, Mary continued *Love Begins* rehearsals opposite a stand-in while the studio cast a leading man. When she had spare time, she slipped onto neighbouring sound stages to watch the stars at work. What better way to learn than to see Errol Flynn and Kay Francis sparring in *Another Dawn* or Pat O'Brien, Humphrey Bogart and Ann Sheridan talking tough in *San Quentin*. Most dizzying was taking lunch each day in the studio commissary right alongside these big names. Mary had to remind herself: these stars were her *co-workers*. Reality gradually sank in. 'Once I was able to forget what I had imagined Hollywood to be like and accept it as it really is I began to love it – and the people in it,' she said. 'They are a wonderful crowd.'

While *Love Begins* was a B-movie, her studio bosses assured Mary they wanted to build her up to an A-picture leading lady – just as they had done with Olivia de Havilland. Mary started house-hunting in the Hollywood Hills, looking for an abode large enough for her whole family. On Saturday, 5 November, Mary's contract was confirmed in court, prompting a *Los Angeles Times* columnist to call her salary 'startling' and remark: 'At seventeen I was getting $30 a month. How about you?'

Love Begins started filming the following Monday morning. An impressive set likely left over from an A-picture served as the main hotel, with exteriors filmed on the backlot's New York-style Brownstone Street and little garden and pond that doubled for Central Park. Typical for a Warners B-movie, it would shoot six days a week for three weeks. The film's laughs were courtesy of Hugh Herbert as the hotel's resident good-hearted drunk. The rubbery-faced comedian was then an audience favourite, known for his perpetually befuddled persona and catchphrase 'Hoo-hoo!', later 'borrowed' by Daffy Duck and Curly of the Three Stooges. As Mary's love interest, Jimmy, the studio had settled on Tom Brown, a young freelancer who had scored his breakout in 1934's hit *Anne of Green Gables*.

While Tom was her leading man, Mary's most ardent lover during the production was the camera. Starlet styling and studio lighting revealed a lustrous beauty, and her introduction in the hotel basement was breathtaking. Mary's performance was more confident, too, with easier natural charm and emotional expression. As the shoot progressed, she and Tom achieved a sweetly naïve on-screen chemistry, and she struck up a friendship with Hugh Herbert, introducing him to the concept of afternoon tea.

Filming proved as much or more of a physical trial as it had been in Australia. The cast sometimes arrived at the studio at six in the morning and worked until ten at night. Mary also suffered on-set misfortunes. First, she tripped and fell, spraining her ankle badly. Next, a cameraman dropped a light from above as she did a scene with the infant playing her baby. Protecting the child, she stumbled and fell. 'I'm carrying round a fine bump and a cut on the head,' she told a reporter. Syndicated American columnist Sheilah Graham – then more widely read than her rival Louella Parsons – ran an admiring quip from Tom Brown: 'That's just like a woman – a man would have saved himself and dropped the baby.' Mary's physical aches weren't a patch on the emotional pain caused by the shipping strike keeping Patricia and Joan in Australia. Yet for such sadness the studio publicity department had a sure-fire remedy: a column item with a rosy antipodean angle on how she had conquered such angst. 'I go out to the zoo and talk to the two wombats there,' Mary supposedly said. 'These little fellows are happy in their new environment. I'm a lot better off than they are, so why should I worry? Visiting them always cheers me up.' Reading such malarkey didn't help Mary's melancholy in the least.

Despite her blue mood, Warners wanted Mary out and about in Hollywood. She had to hit nightclubs like The Tropics, Trocadero and Cocoanut Grove, see and be seen, so photos could be taken and columnists might speculate on her love life and incidentally promote her upcoming debut. 'Film Assignment Starts Romance' read the headline of a gossip item in the *Los Angeles Times* on 24 November:

> Because he is so popular in her native country, Australia, Mary Maguire asked Warner Brothers to engage Tom Brown as her leading man in *Love Begins*. So Tom, receiving the assignment, called Miss Maguire and asked her out so that they might become acquainted. She accepted. One date led to another, and still another, and by the time they were ready to begin work in *Love Begins* maybe it already had.

Sheilah Graham reported their dalliance with piquant dialogue as Mary tried to lure Tom away from his duties as a boy-next-door heartthrob.

'He can't go,' Tom's mother told the 17-year-old Australian actress.

'Oh, please, Mrs Brown,' insisted Mary. But Mrs Brown remained adamant. 'Maybe you object to me?' queried the actress. That wasn't the reason. 'Tom can't go out until he has answered his fan mail,' stated Mrs Brown.

Any romance – real or concocted – was short-lived, and Tom was soon engaged to actress Natalie Draper. But that was fine because Mary was also getting married – at least in the pages of the *Los Angeles Times*. The lucky fella was Roy Randolph, a dance director twice her age, who had taken her out to the Blue Room Supper Club and a Roosevelt Hotel cocktail party. They were to be wed just as soon as Bina arrived from Australia. When Mary and her supposed fiancé arrived at the Knickerbocker Lounge and cracked a joke about this nonsense, the house band struck up the wedding march – and that led to a new story headlined 'Couple May Be Altar Bound' appearing in the *Los Angeles Times*. Mary wasn't linked to Roy again after that. Good thing, too. Six months later he was charged with the rape of a seventeen-year-old girl. He beat the rap with a victim-shaming defence and a judge whose verdict included this sentence: 'This is simply another case of a little girl coming out to find out about Hollywood.'

On Thanksgiving Eve, in the midst of these romance rumours, Mary went with Miles to the gala premiere of *Lloyds of London*. Newly powered by the Hoover Dam, Fox Carthay Circle Theater was a brilliant beacon and surrounded by searchlights sweeping the night sky. Two thousand film luminaries arrived in shining Duesenbergs and Daimlers, doors held open by liveried African-American valets. Mary and Miles strutted the 'peacock's walk' of red carpet as ten thousand fans pressed against the ropes and cheered from specially constructed grandstands. Here came Tyrone

Power, anointed a major star by his leading man role in *Lloyds*, with ice-skating goddess Sonja Henie, also now signed to Fox and soon briefly to be one of the world's highest-paid actresses. Robert Taylor turned up with Barbara Stanwyck, Mary Pickford with her handsome young boyfriend, Charles 'Buddy' Rogers. Everywhere Mary looked there were famous faces: Joan Crawford, Ginger Rogers, Fredric March, Claudette Colbert, Spencer Tracy, Harpo Marx, Dick Powell, Irene Dunne, Miriam Hopkins and Dolores del Río. And in the theatre's lobby were concentrated the men who made the movies: directors like Ernst Lubitsch, Michael Curtiz and George Cukor, and mogul-producers Louis B. Mayer, David O. Selznick and Darryl F. Zanuck. The most curious sight was Madeleine Carroll, Miles's discovery and luminous leading lady of *Lloyds*, arriving with a bald and jowly man old enough to be her jocular grandfather. This was Joe Schenck, chairman of 20th Century Fox. Curiously, the old mogul had history when it came to antipodeans that Miles Mander claimed as his discoveries. A few years earlier, Joe and Merle Oberon had been engaged for a few months; a few months earlier, he had brought Janet Johnson to Hollywood. Now Mary had Joe's attention, even if he wasn't in a position to do anything about it just yet.

20.

Mary sparked the interest of actress Marion Davies and her lover, the newspaper baron and film mogul William Randolph Hearst. Long one of the richest and most influential men in the United States, W. R. had since the early 1920s done everything in his considerable power to make Marion a star and pretty much built his Cosmopolitan Productions company around her. His distribution deal with MGM had fallen apart recently, and so he had taken Cosmopolitan and Marion to Warner Bros. To ensure his mistress's continued comfort, he had her fourteen-bedroom 'bungalow' removed from MGM on a ten-truck convoy and rebuilt on the Warners lot. Fearing that a musical number in Marion's 1936 film *Cain and Mabel* wouldn't be grand enough in the studio's already enormous Stage 7, W. R. paid $100000 to have the entire structure raised by thirty feet in an epic effort that recalled the slave labours of ancient Egypt.

Though they hadn't met, Mary picked up the phone to hear Marion Davies – an idol she had grown up watching – asking her up to 'The Ranch'. She had just been offered *the* most-coveted invitation in Hollywood. That was because The Ranch was actually W. R.'s fabled mansion, the 'Enchanted Hill', at San Simeon, halfway between Los Angeles and San Francisco. A white marble castle with twin cathedral-like towers, it was surrounded by more than a hundred acres of gardens. That included the outdoor Neptune Pool, with genuine ancient Roman temple façade, and America's largest private zoo, home to the world's most exotic beasts in grand enclosures or roaming free in parklands. W. R.'s castle, now best known for being satirised in Orson Welles's *Citizen Kane*, contained dozens and dozens of bedrooms, lounges and galleries, all bulging with priceless paintings, sculptures and artifacts. At the huge table in the dining hall each night, guests could expect to eat alongside the world's most famous people, from Winston Churchill and Franklin D. Roosevelt to Charlie Chaplin and the Marx Brothers. Pulling up to this castle, Mary thought she was in a fairy story. But she met W. R., they played tennis, and he and Marion took an instant liking to her. Mary was to become a regular guest, treated to their generosity and afforded an insight into their opulent if eccentric world. 'When I am called back to work, I do not travel by road and train, but by one of Mr. Hearst's private planes,' Mary said to the *Australian Women's Weekly*, continuing:

There is a lavish private theatre at San Simeon where previews are attended by the elite of Hollywood, and very imposing friends of the Hearst family from the East. There are secret underground passages and secret panels opening into the dining and morning rooms and into Mr. Hearst's study. Once, I was on my own in the morning room – where guests assemble after breakfast to chat with their host and arrange the day's fun – when I heard a faint 'slithery' sound. I swung round and Mr Hearst stepped from a dark opening in the wall. I almost fainted with shock. And do you know we dine off gold plates at dinner there, but use paper serviettes! The paper serviettes are perhaps the only suggestion that San Simeon is a ranch!

As *Love Begins* neared completion, Mary caught a cold, which she thought had been caused by having to stand under a rain machine for five hours on an earlier night shoot. She collapsed twice in the last two days of filming. The show had to go on. She struggled through and then went directly home to recuperate. Though she was in her sickbed, Mary's first Hollywood film was in the can, even if producer Hal Wallis had decided *Love Begins* would be released as *That Man's Here Again*.

Warners liked Mary and started the process that would send her to Mexico for a day so the American consul there could issue the work visa that she and Mick had neglected to get in Brisbane.

The studio announced Mary's next film as A-picture comedy *Call It a Day*, with her third-billed after Olivia de Havilland and Ian Hunter. In a letter published in the *Detroit Times*, de Havilland noted that her soon-to-be co-star 'doesn't look anything like Mary Pickford. But she's very pretty.' Around this time Maxwell Arnow's judgement in signing her so quickly was also vindicated when his talent scout Salvino 'Solly' Baiano returned to the office frustrated that he had spotted a knockout beauty on a Hollywood street but hadn't been able to talk to her before she disappeared into a bank building. Settling in to watch some recent studio footage with his boss, Baiano suddenly exclaimed, 'That's her!' Arnow had to laugh. 'That's Mary Maguire,' he said, 'we've had her under contract for months.'

Not yet needed at the studio, Mary drove north with Mick to see the sights in Monterey and Yosemite. The holiday was cut short when she was called back to test, not for *Call It a Day*, which ended up going to Anita Louise, but for a better picture, *Kid Galahad*. This boxing drama would star Edward G. Robinson, Bette Davis and Humphrey Bogart, and promote handsome newcomer Wayne

Morris in the title role. Mary was to test for the part of Marie, daughter to Robinson and love interest to Morris. It was a strong role, with plenty of dramatic scenes opposite the older stars. Mary and Morris spent an afternoon directed by the intense Michael Curtiz, acting highly emotional scenes in the bedroom and yard of a farmhouse set. The test went well. Mary, now phoning Bina weekly, felt confident enough to tell her mother she had the part.

Despite their calls, and the prospect of a good role in an A-picture, Mary was maudlin about her first Christmas away from her mother and sisters. She told H. H. Niemeyer of the *St. Louis Post-Dispatch* this was the lowest spot in her life. 'The family had always made much over Christmas and she had tried to catch a little of that spirit by buying herself a small tree which she decorated,' he wrote. 'Her father left the house and Mary was alone with the memories of other, gayer Christmases. But when he came back he had holly – there is some in Hollywood – and mistletoe and numerous packages.' Among the gifts was a lingerie set from Bina. Mary was also cheered by six plum puddings sent by fans in Australia. On Christmas Day, father and daughter diverted themselves by going to the Santa Anita Park racetrack, where the Christmas Stakes opened the season. Mary shared the stands with the Hollywood elite, and rated a mention in a *Chicago Tribune* fashion round-up with Bette Davis, Jean Harlow and Carole Lombard. Then there was the Christmas party with Jane Wyman and Glenda Farrell, and a young Warners player, Gordon Oliver, whom the gossips dutifully claimed that Mary was romancing.

The year 1937 dawned with more socialising. There was a party at The Tropics, with Mary on a guest list that included Jimmy Cagney and Gloria Swanson. On 3 January she was at the Brown Derby for lunch with Janet Johnson, another young starlet named Dixie Dunbar, and a pretty player still finding her feet in

Hollywood despite having knockout legs: Betty Grable. One subject the girls surely talked about: the *Los Angeles Times*'s big article that day about Australians invading Hollywood. 'Bronzed beauties from the Antipodes . . . outdoor gals who stress vigor rather than glamor and prefer one-piece bathing suits to trailing negligees . . . are "the type" in Hollywood today,' it claimed. Along with Jocelyn Howarth's story, Mary's rise was recounted and her success was said to be 'assured'. Poor Janet didn't rate a mention; in the three months she had been in Hollywood, Fox had done nothing with her.

The day after their lunch, Mary was back at work, testing yet again for *Kid Galahad*. Michael Curtiz also tried out Jane Wyman and Jane Bryan. Then came the now-familiar nerve-shredding wait for a decision. Mary wanted the role very badly but that desire came with the inherent knowledge that for her to succeed her friends had to fail – just as landing the part in *The Flying Doctor* had hindered Janet's chances of stardom. It was the nature of the business but it didn't feel good.

On 8 January, Mary got the news. She had the role! She'd be acting with Bette Davis, Edward G. Robinson and Humphrey Bogart.

With just ten days until the cameras rolled, Mary and Mick had to get their work visas and pronto. Warner Bros. attorney Roy Obringer wrote to the American consul in Mexico confirming the studio intended to star her in *Kid Galahad*. 'It is our opinion,' he wrote, 'based on the past record of Miss Maguire, and our contact with her in our studio, that she will be one of the outstanding stars of our studio, and we are planning to make many A pictures with her in important parts during the life of her contract.' Mary and Mick hopped in the car and drove down to Mexico, staying overnight, as required. They were back in Hollywood by 15 January with work visas in hand. Yet Mary had brought back something else from south of the border: a serious case of influenza. A day later Maxwell Arnow issued a curt memo to Jack Warner and Hal Wallis: 'I am sending a copy of this note to Mr Obringer to lay off Mary Maguire immediately and we will restore her to salary when she comes in for wardrobe tests for her next picture.' *Kid Galahad* started filming cameras three days later, with Jane Bryan taking the role that Mary had missed out on.

Winning and losing such a good role in this way was heartbreaking. If Mary and Mick had listened to the advice given back in Brisbane she would now be starring in *Kid Galahad* rather than sick and useless in the Mayfair apartment. Mary's illness was bad enough to rate a mention in the *Los Angeles Times*, her second newsworthy respiratory condition within five weeks.

21.

Mary was better by the end of January – and happier that Charles and Elsa Chauvel were in Hollywood. She was now up for A-picture *One Hour of Romance*, which would see release as *Confession*. The film was a remake of 1935 German movie *Mazurka*, which Warner Bros. had bought – and shelved – so they could remake it in English as a vehicle for Kay Francis. Now criminally forgotten, willowy brunette Kay was then queen of Warner Bros., its highest-paid star on an annual salary of $227 500, and the most fashionable film actress in the world. She was to play Vera, a singer who shoots dead a famous pianist after spotting him in the audience of her show with a young girl named Lisa. During the trial it's revealed that nearly twenty years earlier this man took advantage of Vera and that led to her losing custody of her daughter: Lisa.

Joe May would direct *Confession*. A German émigré, he spoke little English and used a translator to direct Mary in her screen test as Lisa, described in the script as 'seventeen, and trembling on the borderline between girlhood and womanhood'. In a scene set in a waiting room, he had her play opposite Linda Perry, another recent Warner Bros. acquisition, testing for the role of Hildegard, Lisa's impulsive best friend. Mary did the scenes with her natural hair – and then in two blonde wigs. Then she tested in a dramatic courtroom sequence. Two days later Mary played Hildegard to Anita Louise's Lisa in several more scenes. This game of musical chairs continued for a week as several more actresses were tested. Then the waiting game between friends began again.

Finally Hal Wallis and Joe May decided: Mary took the role of Hildegard while Lisa would be played by . . . Jane Bryan. It was bittersweet. Mary had scored an A-picture, but she was subordinate to the girl who had taken her role in *Kid Galahad*. The consolation: she would receive her full salary for ten weeks from the first day of shooting. She was still being paid five times what Jane was. And her modest role offered valuable experience with Kay Francis and Basil Rathbone, who had been cast as the perfidious pianist. 'I'll be able to learn a great deal working with such seasoned players as these,' she told the Adelaide *Advertiser*.

A week later came the news Mary had been desperate to hear: her contract had officially been picked up – and at the personal direction of Jack Warner. She had cleared the obstacle that saw so many hopeful stars fade out after just six months. Mary was to remain on $500 per week – and be subject to sixteen unpaid layoff weeks over the coming year. It wasn't perfect but she was safe for twelve months. When renewal time came around again, Warners would be contractually obliged to increase her salary if they wanted to keep her. Presented with the paperwork, Mary Maguire, born as Hélène Teresa and previously known as Peggy, who sometimes gave autographs as Ellen, signed the document with yet another variant: 'Helen Teresa Maguire'.

As *Confession* was being prepared, Melbourne *Sun News-Pictorial* reporter Jennie Conolly met Mary at the Warner Bros. commissary and marvelled at all the stars in their yellow face paint. 'We moved across the room, Mary smiling and waving all the time,' she wrote. 'She seemed well known and popular with actors and production side alike.' Chatting over lunch, Mary said she wanted very much to visit New York and London. 'Have you been there?' she asked the reporter. 'What's it like? They won't let you get away from here for more than six weeks.' The conversation turned to her love life, with Mary claiming newspapers had her engaged three times since she arrived in Hollywood. 'Did you like any of your fiancés?' [Conolly] asked. 'No,' said Mary.

She did like Bette Davis, one of the 'grand people' at Warners, though Errol Flynn, whom she had met at a few parties, was an enigma. 'No one knows what he does, though his wife is a great friend of Mrs. Warner's,' she said. 'But Errol is as mysterious as Garbo.' Mary described a happy and busy life but confessed to ongoing homesickness, and she hoped her sisters and mother would soon arrive. At least she had a faithful companion in Alice, who, after Mary had a second minor car accident, had seen her duties expand from maid to chauffeur. The reporter bristled at the African-American woman's presence, describing her in the subsequent article as a 'little, ugly, smiling mahogany-faced scrap'. But Mary had only praise for Alice.

> 'She's a grand bodyguard,' said Mary. 'When any of the boys want to take me out they have to go to Alice first, and she has a great time. She says she'll see if she can possibly fix it for them, and makes it very difficult for them. They call her "Mary's Little Lamb."'

The blithely racist reporter responded with a feeble 'joke': 'Her fleece is not as white as snow.' Mary didn't play along: 'No, she's got it all cut off short, like a boy's. She's priceless!' Lunch done, Mary was due at the publicity department to look at some photos. The journalist — writing in a year that saw the N-word used thousands of times in Australian newspaper articles – felt comfortable returning to her ugly theme. 'My final glimpse was of two beaming faces, one pretty and one plain, as Mary and her little lamb set off in Mary's car.'

Filming of *Confession* started on 22 February 1937, Mary's eighteenth birthday. A celebratory call to Bina would have revealed the shocking news that had everyone at home on tenterhooks: Beverley Shepherd was missing. Three days earlier he'd been copiloting the *City of Brisbane*, an Airlines of Australia Stinson, when it vanished on its afternoon flight from Brisbane to Sydney. Grave fears were held for him, the other pilot and five passengers. Desperate about her 'particularly close friend', aviatrix Jean Batten had immediately joined the huge aerial search. The plane's disappearance wasn't news in America, so Mary had to wait; she would need to phone home again to know if Beverley had survived another close call.

Mary kept on with Hollywood life. On 26 February she was in court again to have her new contract confirmed. 'My, my, that's a lot of money for an eighteen-year-old girl to be earning,' the judge said as he approved the $50 a week contract for Warner Bros. new hire Claudia Simmons. Next were Lorraine Krueger, on $75 a week, and Jane Bryan, still on $100 a week. Then came Mary's contract: $500 a week. The judge closed his eyes as if in disbelief. 'You see she's known as the Mary Pickford of Australia and has been a star in her native land for some time,' the Warner Bros. attorney explained.

Soon after the judge confirmed her contract, Mary's Hearst connections yielded her biggest press break yet when she was featured in a huge colour illustration on the front page of his flagship paper *San Francisco Examiner*'s 'City Life' section. The beautiful picture showed her reclining on a bed in profile in pink pyjamas, and its prominence for a player whose American debut was yet to hit screens was further proof she had Hearst's endorsement.

Ten days after the *City of Brisbane* vanished, Queensland bushman Bernard O'Reilly did what Jean Batten and other pilots involved in the search hadn't been able to do. Following a hunch based on his local knowledge and a study of the flight plan, he found the plane in the rugged mountains of Lamington National Park. There wasn't much left of the Stinson except for twisted, charred metal. Failing to clear a mountain, it had hit a tree and burst into flame as it fell to earth. Miraculously, two passengers were alive and evacuated in emaciated condition. A third survivor had perished when he fell from a waterfall after setting out to find help. But Beverley Shepherd, Chief Pilot Rex Bowden and two passengers had been killed on impact or incinerated in the terrible seconds that followed. Shortly after, as driving rain fell on that remote site, their remains were buried in lonely graves. It was a heartbreaking end for Mary's brave and handsome friend.

Mary filmed her first scenes for *Confession* on 9 March opposite Jane Bryan and Basil Rathbone. Behind-the-scenes publicity photos show the trio having nice chats over tea and listening happily to director Joe May, and Mary playfully using her hands as opera glasses in a scene where she and Jane sat in a theatre box. But it was a far from cheerful set. The director had decided to remake *Mazurka* shot for shot, timing every take with a stop-watch to match the original. Tensions were so high that Mary's first day coincided with consummate professional Kay Francis not showing up to set. 'Joe May driving us all crazy,' she wrote in her diary. 'For the first time in nine years refused to work!' Jack

Warner and Hal Wallis became increasingly furious at the film-maker, who demanded take after take even though rushes revealed that performances from one to the next were all but identical. His craziest decision was to make Basil Rathbone, rather than a stunt double, throw himself down a set of stairs ten times.

Mary fell victim to Joe May's madness when he ordered twelve takes of her first scene with Jane. Then six for the next one – and the one after that. The cast was even more stressed because he had a print of *Mazurka* on set and would screen the relevant scene to show everyone exactly how he wanted the performances and cinematography. Seeing this and witnessing the depth of her director's obsession, Mary would have realised how little chance she'd ever had of getting the Lisa role: the film's original actress was a blonde dead-ringer for Jane Bryan while her own dark looks made her a close fit for the original's Hildegard. Back on set the next week, Mary and Jane did café and concert hall scenes. They worked well together, nailing minute-long dialogue scenes in two or three takes even to the satisfaction of their overlord. Despite how stressed Joe May made everyone, Mary managed to turn in a cheeky and charming performance. Her last day on set saw her subjected to the director's full mania as he ordered six takes of a thirteen-second scene and ten of another lasting twenty-two seconds. Mary didn't publicly complain, then or later. Jane Bryan did. 'I was never directed in a more ridiculous fashion in my life,' she said later. 'We were all marching through the film like sleepwalkers.'

––––

Mary was feted at the Australians Dinner held at the Clark Hotel in mid-to-late March. Charles and Elsa were there, along with Janet Johnson, Jocelyn Howarth and Miles Mander. There was much mirth around the table, with Jocelyn ribbed as 'Squatter's

Daughter' and Mary 'kept in check' by her two directors. Charles posed for a photo with Mary and Janet, telling reporters he had discovered them both. Not so, said Miles, striking the same pose with the young beauties and claiming them as his.

Whoever had given Mary the biggest early boost, it was now Warners championing her debut in *That Man's Here Again*, with the studio's booklet for exhibitors including ready-made articles about its young starlet. 'Possessed of the qualities that made "Seventh Heaven" a "year's best" for Academy Awards and at the box-office, this romance of universal appeal is slated to be remembered as the film which sky-rocketed a new star into the film firmament,' read one. There were many pre-packaged publicity blurbs about Mary, the purse collector, and Mary, whose toy koala appeared in the film. All these little stories culminated with a plug for *That Man's Here Again*: 'the first National production now showing at the _____ Theatre'. Newspaper editors only had to add the name of their local bijou. Another studio article simultaneously hyped and downplayed her love life, portraying her as chased and chaste:

> Mary Maguire, young Australian movie player who has been linked romantically with an even dozen of Hollywood's eligible chappies by the writers of such subjects, has no intention of looking for romance until she is twenty one, she says. Seventeen years old now, Mary is devoting herself to fun instead of romance in spite of reports to the contrary. 'I'm much too young to think of marriage,' Mary says. 'Romance is the first step towards that so I'm avoiding anything that will get me involved before I'm ready to settle down. I've made up my mind not to worry about it before I'm twenty one. And even then I'm not going to set out purposefully to find love. I'll wait until it arrives.'

Mary was interviewed by syndicated correspondent Paul Harrison, with the resulting personality profile 'Australia's "Spoiled Child" Is Here to Win Film Fame – And May Do It' appearing in newspapers coast to coast in the coming months. The long article, usually published with the same two photos, one sultry, one sweet, comprised equal parts fact, fiction and false modesty. 'I must be a good type for a young mother because, in my pictures, I always seem to have a child or two,' Mary exaggerated. 'My first picture here at Warner Brothers gives me the youngest role I have had in years, but even in it I have a two-year-old brat – I mean baby. It was quite a sweet child, really, except when it got in front of the cameras. Also it would shriek at the sight of Hugh Herbert.' Harrison reckoned Mary's clipped accent was her biggest Hollywood handicap, and that her on-set injuries and illnesses were part and parcel of her overall culture shock. 'The strange and hard-boiled methods of Hollywood movie-makers bewildered her, for she had been pretty badly spoiled in Australia,' he wrote. 'She has been spoiled "Down Under" because she is a top-flight star there, known from Melbourne to the Northern Territory, and by rich men and bushmen, as "Australia's Sweetheart".' Harrison explained the Mary Pickford connection but told readers she looked more like Janet Gaynor, Mary Astor and recent French discovery Simone Simon.

Mary's profile ventured into titbits. She smoked but didn't diet or drink. She loved hamburgers and hot dogs. She was trying to acquire American slang but didn't swear like the rest of Hollywood. These were studio blurbs. More believable was her reaction to the endless romantic rumours. 'She was dismayed by the activities of gossip columnists who announced her engagement to every young man with who she went to a night club,' Harrison wrote. 'Not only dismayed, but a little frightened.' Since Christmas, she had only been out with her father. 'There are no romantic attachments.' But it was an unguarded moment that spoke most poignantly to Mary's ongoing melancholy:

> 'Sometimes I go down into the basement of our apartment house and dance by myself,' she said. 'It is one my sister likes to do, about an Austrian woman in a Russian prison. First she is chained, and then she breaks her chains. But after breaking her chains, she realises that she is still within stone and bars. So she gradually goes mad and throws herself again and again against the stones.'

Catching herself, Mary made light of her musings. 'What was that? Well, yes, I guess I do it mostly for exercise.'

That Man's Here Again hit theatres in late March. Mary was officially a Hollywood leading lady. Overall, she was well reviewed. *Variety* liked the film and her: 'Mary Maguire, the Australian girl who makes her debut, is revealed as possessing striking beauty and excellent talent.' A second *Variety* critic was also complimentary: 'Making her Yankee debut in flickers, Mary Maguire is a meltingly appealing brunet and does a conscientious job. She'll get by in future in feature roles.' *Hollywood Spectator* said she 'reveals a pleasant personality and a fair amount of talent, but does not seem to have the requisites for major stardom', while *Modern Screen* reckoned the role gave her 'little chance to prove anything about herself', and the *New York Post* opined that the film 'allowed Mary Maguire to give a poor performance'. But there were more bouquets than brickbats. *Film Daily* called her 'a charming girl with looks to match her personality', Washington, DC's *Evening Star* said she had 'that magnetic something for which nobody yet has thought up a word which would stick', while the *New Orleans States* said 'she has a rare appeal; she snuggles into one's heart immediately'. Most gushing of all was the *Kansas City Star*, which thought her 'face should be the toast of Hollywood before she makes more than two more pictures. Because Miss Maguire is s-o-o pretty! Gosh!'

Mary should have been on top of the world. She had a secure contract, a film in cinemas, an A-picture in the can, the favour of Marion Davies and William Randolph Hearst, and the friendship of the Chauvels, Miles Mander, Janet and Jocelyn, along with the companionship of her Hollywood pals. Best of all, the maritime strike had ended and, after a glittering round of Brisbane farewells, Patricia and Joan were sailing for California on the *Monterey*. But Mary looked wan and worried when she went to Easter Sunday mass. Days later she was in Cedars of Lebanon Hospital.

22.

In a photo in the *Los Angeles Times* Mary smiled from her hospital bed, a bow in her hair, a flower clasped to her breast. 'Her case of shattered nerves is as mystifying to Mary Maguire, the Australian starlet, as it is to her doctor,' its article read. 'Little Mary is in the hospital, with what is diagnosed as a breakdown. The truth probably is that she is homesick, and it's likely that Miss Maguire will snap out of it when her two sisters arrive from Sydney.' Other articles reported 'an illness informally diagnosed as "Hollywood excitement"', that she 'has worked so hard to achieve success that she has been forced to take a rest' or that she was 'suffering shock caused by a recent automobile accident'.

Mary's stressors were surely more complex. But in 1937 mental health issues were misunderstood, women who suffered them often marginalised and Hollywood was eighty years away from reckoning with its institutionalised misogyny. Worry about work was sure to be a factor in Mary's distress, the sensitive youngster now under constant scrutiny by temperamental men like Michael Curtiz, Joe May, Hal Wallis and Jack Warner. Public pressure was likely another. Every time she opened a newspaper she saw her appearance, talents and prospects discussed, and her love life chronicled or created out of thin air. Grief may have also played a part, given how recently Beverley Shepherd had met his horrible fate. Mary may also have been using pep pills to get through long hours and for weight control, and she was likely fending off unwanted sexual advances but expected to remain silent about such harassment. Then there were her documented homesickness, recent illnesses, injuries, and, it seems, a third minor car accident when Alice missed a traffic sign. It added up to a lot for an eighteen-year-old half a world away from home.

On 14 April, while Kay Francis was feted at a wrap party for *Confession*, Mary was preparing to go home from hospital. Five days later, Patricia and Joan arrived, with the *Los Angeles Times* running a photo of them waving, the article's headline reading 'Visitors Find Film Actress Recovering From Illness'. Using their sister's network of contacts, they would soon be out 'contract hunting'.

By the end of April Mary had recovered and was back at Warners awaiting her next assignment. She also returned to Hollywood's social scene, which meant a new crop of gossip. Mary and Warners publicity man Bernie Williams 'had it bad'. Agent Al Kingston was so lovestruck he could only remember her phone number. Gossip column queen Louella Parsons had Mary 'troccing' at Cafe Trocadero with Miles Mander, the interpretation of the verb left up to the reader. A potentially more damaging item coyly linked her to a Hollywood man nicknamed 'Buddy', surely interpreted by everyone to mean Mary Pickford's soon-to-be-husband, Charles 'Buddy' Rogers.

Louella, whose dish appeared in four hundred newspapers, was now taken with Mary, which was not surprising given that she took her cues from her boss Hearst. 'One of the cutest tricks this writer has met in months is Mary Maguire, Australia's little film princess,' she wrote at the end of April. 'About as big a minute, with enormous black eyes, Mary was a recent guest at one of Marion Davies' dinner parties and she not only captivated us with her beauty but also with her good sense. Bryan Foy, Warner producer, has great confidence in the little lady and is enthusiastic about her screen future. He plans to star her in *Alcatraz* and later in *The Pit and the Pendulum*.'

Mary had in a few short months crashed Hollywood's A-list. As proof of this she wore a lion tamer's outfit at *the* Hearst–Davies party that epitomised the glamour and extravagance of Hollywood's Golden Age. To celebrate her lover's seventy-fourth birthday, Marion invited four hundred friends to her Santa Monica 'Beach House', a sprawling ocean-front mansion built, furnished and decorated at a cost of $US7 million ($US120 million today). The party's theme was 'The Greatest Show on Earth', and it was staged under a big top erected on the estate's tennis courts. Mary entered over a little bridge, which 'prankster' W. R. had rigged with a wind machine to blow up women's skirts, their reactions caught by three 35mm movie cameras filming the event. Inside, she and the rest of the guests enjoyed the fun of a real circus, from crazy mirrors and fortune tellers to hot-dog stands, instant photo booths and a full-sized carousel borrowed from Warners. W. R. was – fittingly – garbed as a circus ringmaster while Marion appeared in an outfit of blue diamond design with ostrich feathers. Cary Grant tumbled into the party as part of a trapeze troupe. As a bearded lady, Bette Davis competed for laughs with elephant-poo-shovellers Errol Flynn and David Niven. Harold Lloyd, Louis B. Mayer, Tyrone Power, Sonja Henie and Henry Fonda came in various clown outfits. Tom Brown and fiancée Natalie Draper were cowboy and cowgirl, though overshadowed by Clark Gable and Carole Lombard in similar get-up and leading the Shetland pony that was a present for the animal-collecting birthday boy.

Other guests included Anita Louise, Claudette Colbert, Irene Dunne, Leslie Howard, Dolores del Río, Maureen O'Sullivan and John Farrow. Mary caught her breath at being surrounded by so many stars and amid such wealth – this was beyond Bina's wildest dreams of her meeting the 'right' people.

———

Mary had work to do before she was a star as big as the biggest stars beneath Hearst's Big Top. In May 1937 she was reportedly enrolled in Hollywood's first 'Glamour School', conducted at Warners, where her classmates included Jane Wyman and newly signed sixteen-year-old brunette Lana Turner. Around this time Mary formed a club called The Unmasquers with Jane Bryan, Jane Wyman, Lana Turner, Marie Wilson and Linda Perry to self-educate their way to greater stardom, pledging to see each other's previews, look at each other's still pictures and listen to any one of their group on the radio. 'They are all to take notes on each other's make-up, posture, mannerisms, way of wearing clothes, delivery, characterization and even the interviews they give out,' an article explained. Like some sort of starlet task force, each girl had a specialty: Maguire – make-up; Bryan – posture; Wyman – poise; Turner – fashion; Wilson – publicity; Perry – diction. Such starlet friendship and solidarity were pushed by studio publicity. Mary and the Janes were photographed as a beach-going, bike-riding trio for a cheesecake series. In another set of pictures, Mary and Jane Bryan sunned themselves, romped with dogs and prepared sandwiches. 'Rivals for screen roles at the studio,' read the accompanying article in *Screenland*, 'Jane Bryan and Mary Maguire are really chums . . . the girls work, and play together. Jane, typical American youngster, scored in *Kid Galahad* and is slated for stardom. Mary, from Australia, is one of Hollywood's most-dated girls, but so far her acting career has not kept pace with her friend's.' That Jane owed *Kid Galahad* to her friend's bad luck wasn't mentioned, though that insulted Mary less than the insinuation behind the description 'one of Hollywood's most-dated girls'.

Janet Johnson, meanwhile, parted company with 20th Century Fox and returned to London. 'I want to act and Hollywood makes you wait too long,' she told the *Daily Express*. 'They do your hair for weeks, then decide to put a tooth straight. Then they forget you. It's the boredom that beats you.' Janet said she had worked an hour a day while under contract – most of it on inane training. 'For people who are sincerely interested in dramatic art the prospect is heartbreaking . . . No-one with any ambition can endure that for long.' She told *Picturegoer* that Joe Schenck had been away on a yachting cruise for four months and no one else seemed to have had the authority to cast her. Then he returned. 'I asked him to let me off the rest of my contract,' Janet explained. 'He did, and I came home.' It was a mystifying outcome. Joe *hadn't* been absent from Hollywood for that long, and Janet *was* a talent who soon took over Vivien Leigh's role in *Bats in the Belfry* on the West End. Given the Fox chairman's reputation – and industry-wide 'casting couch' practices, which included hiring 'six-month girls' to sexually gratify studio executives – Janet may have been unwilling to do what Joe asked of her in order to get a role.

23.

Mary had Patricia and Joan to cheer her up – and was looking forward to her mother and youngest sisters arriving in July. She rented a twelve-room, older-style frame house with a swimming pool on Hillside Avenue near the fashionable Outpost Estates. Mary took a spacious second-floor bedroom, decorated in Wedgwood blue and white, with a view of the garden and the pleasing rise of the hills. Though just a few blocks from all the Hollywood action, this was also a quiet refuge that, when filled by her whole family, might even feel like a little slice of Australia.

Louella had been right about Mary's prison movie – as she should have been, because *Alcatraz Island*, as it had been renamed, would be produced by Hearst's Cosmopolitan for Warner Bros. In addition to remakes, the studio saw good profits from real-life subjects, and this was to be the first film set in the prison that had fascinated America since opening three years earlier. Mary would play Annabel, teenage daughter of Gat Brady, played by John Litel. A gentleman gangster too noble to commit murder, he's busted on a tax-evasion charge – just like Al Capone – and sent to Leavenworth prison. There Gat is set upon by a criminal enemy, and, after resorting to violence to defend himself, ends up in Alcatraz – where he's framed for murder. To free her father, Annabel teams up with Gat's girlfiend, Flo, played by Ann Sheridan, and a handsome young lawyer love interest.

Annabel wasn't a particularly complex part, but she was the first-listed female character in the script's cast page and had more to say and do than Flo. *Alcatraz Island*, following another busy three-week schedule, began shooting on 24 May. Mary started with interior hotel lobby scenes. Then they filmed on stages dressed as law offices, a boarding school, a steamship's exterior and customs building, the visitor's room and cells and gantries of Alcatraz. They shot on the studio's rear projection stage for a sequence where Annabel is kidnapped in a taxi, and outside at Griffith Park for the horseriding scene where she meets her lawyerly love interest. Mary's performance showed growing confidence and ease, particularly in the father–daughter scenes, and she usually gave director William McGann what he wanted in a couple of takes. But, like any actor, Mary flubbed her dialogue now and again. One such moment made it into the blooper reel shown at the annual Warners dinner that had everyone in fits of laughter at Humphrey Bogart, Bette Davis, Kay Francis and other stars letting fly with curses like 'Goddamnit!' and 'Oh, nuts!' at their movie mistakes. Mary, true to studio publicity that said she didn't swear, merely grinned at her mistake and said her messed-up line was 'screwy'.

───────

Australia was about to see what Hollywood had made of Mary. In Brisbane Edgar Betts put on a special preview of *That Man's Here Again* for those most desperate to find out: Bina, Carmel and Lupe. After watching the film on 4 June, mother Maguire held forth with her review in a special radio broadcast from the Belle Vue. She repeated her opinion for the *Courier-Mail*:

I consider the change a marked improvement. She is changed in her bearing, and her diction, too, is much improved. Her facial make-up also shows considerable improvement. It now appears to be more natural than it was in the film in which she appeared first.

Local critics agreed that Hollywood highlighted Mary's beauty, but there was no consensus about improvement in her acting. *The Queenslander* approved of 'trimness of figure she did not have locally' and thought her 'eyes are startlingly beautiful, and her voice is excellent, with now and again a distinctive trick which could be rolled into gold'. The *Courier-Mail* reckoned her 'so consistently good in a somewhat slender part that it will be welcomed by Brisbane admirers as a promise of greater things to come'. Further south, the *Sydney Morning Herald* was happy: 'Mary Maguire invests her part with much charm and sweet simplicity . . . and with more experience should prove immensely popular with American audiences.' *The Australian Women's Weekly* wasn't convinced: 'Unfortunately, her acting is very little changed . . . which is to say: she still has a very long way to go.'

Bina, Carmel and Lupe had a long way to go. This was really goodbye: to friends, to school, to the Belle Vue, to Brisbane, to Australia. They saw *That Man's Here Again* the same day the Maguires relinquished their licence and ended nearly twenty years in the hotel game. Lupe gave her huge cat, Wazir, to Archbishop Duhig for safekeeping, and their many friends farewelled them with flowers as they sailed south to Sydney on the *Canberra*. From there: Melbourne to visit family, and then the *Monterey* for Los Angeles.

Hollywood was again in mourning. On 7 June 1937, Jean Harlow died of kidney failure, aged just twenty-six, another star stepping too soon into immortality. A few days later Mary was found unconscious on the driveway of the Hillside house. She'd had a fall and was unable to work on *Alcatraz Island* that Friday. In Australia, Bina said her daughter was fine; Mary took the weekend to recover. She was back on set at 9.00 a.m. on Monday, working a thirteen-hour day. She and her co-stars shot twenty-four script scenes in twenty-five set-ups and posed for ten publicity stills. By late that night, Mary had wrapped her third Hollywood feature.

Boarding the *Monterey*, Bina was much annoyed that their Matson welcome basket was accompanied by a stack of telegrams from family, friends and strangers asking the same question: 'Is Mary married?' Shore-to-ship phone calls were coming in, too, with everyone wanting to know if her daughter had really wed the Trocadero bandleader in Hollywood. Half a world away, Mary had heard the gossip. 'I am not married, nor am I engaged to anybody,' she cabled to Bina. 'Still looking forward to and waiting for you to arrive. Love, Mary.' Turned out a suburban Melbourne newspaper had started the rumour.

Meanwhile, the American press used Mary's photos constantly in their women's pages. Here she was demonstrating how she cared for her pretty toes or buffed her creamy elbows. There she was exercising for that well-developed bosom or showing off perfect posture by balancing two books atop her head. Mary's outfits were also closely monitored, and detailed descriptions included in Hollywood fashion round-ups. Warner Bros. costumier and fellow Australian Orry-Kelly designed hats for her, which were in stores for $7.50 to $15 as part of the 'Studio Styles' collection, also featuring couture that he made for Ann Sheridan, Olivia de Havilland and Joan Blondell. Mary even had her own cigarette cards – just like her dad had back in Australia some twenty years earlier.

24.

Mary's horror movie, *The Pit and the Pendulum*, never eventuated but at the end of June her next film was confirmed as *Sergeant Murphy* – and she would be the female lead. Set at the Presidio cavalry base in Monterey and inspired by a true story, it had a young cavalry soldier named Dennis risking everything to save his army horse from the knackery and turn him into a racing champion. Mary was to play Mary Lou, daughter of the Presidio's gruff commander and love interest to Dennis. The script had been written for James Cagney but he refused the role after reading the script, probably less than impressed that the Sergeant Murphy of the title was the *horse*. With Cagney out, *Sergeant Murphy* became one of Bryan Foy's B-movies, and the male lead went to a studio newcomer named Ronald Reagan. Nicknamed 'Dutch', he was charming, funny, easy on the eyes and had already caused quite the stir with Warners women, including Mary's pals Betty Grable and Jane Wyman.

Unusually for a B-production, much of *Sergeant Murphy* was to be shot on location, at the real Presidio, using soldiers as unpaid extras, thanks to Warners winning the cooperation of the War Department. But Mary was outraged when she saw her call sheet. The studio wanted to drive her up to Monterey early in the

morning on Sunday, 11 July – the day before Bina, Carmel and
Lupe arrived on the *Monterey*. Mary's mood was further tested by
having to do twelve hours of reshoots and pick-ups for *Alcatraz
Island* on the Friday before she left.

The studio car collected her from the Hillside Avenue house
just after dawn for the drive to Monterey. Though cranky about
missing the arrival of her mum and younger sisters, the ten-
hour journey offered Mary the chance to chat with her co-stars.
Donald Crisp, whom she knew from *Confession* and who would
now play her father, was a fascinating Brit. He had served in
the 10th Royal Hussars in the Boer War, where he had become
friends with Winston Churchill, before moving to Hollywood
at the start of its movie industry and playing Ulysses S. Grant
in D. W. Griffith's *The Birth of a Nation*. At the very other end
of the career spectrum, Ronald Reagan was a fresh film recruit
from Iowa, where he'd been a sportscaster for radio WHO in
Des Moines. Signed by Maxwell Arnow for $250 per week, the
handsome 26-year-old had since made one picture, in which he
played a radio broadcaster. Now he was thrilled to be going on
location as a break from the studio life he had already decided was
monotonous. 'If I'd been standing on a spring board over a pool,
I'd have done a double back flip to show my joy,' he claimed in
one of the series of feature articles he penned for the *Des Moines
Register*. As a reserve cavalry officer, he was happy to again be
playing a character a little like himself. Spending the next two
weeks working with a 'dainty little dish' like Mary was also a
pleasant prospect.

The drive to Monterey was spectacular. They had breakfast
a hundred miles north of Los Angeles at El Paseo restaurant in
Santa Barbara, famous for being where young Judy Garland sang
that ode to marijuana, 'La Cucaracha', in an Oscar-nominated
short film. After lunch further north at San Luis Obispo, they

took an unpaved section of the new coast route. 'At first blush, you decide it was laid out by a guy with a snootful of Old Crow,' Dutch observed, 'but, after you've wound around sheer cliffs with the Pacific thousands of feet below and through narrow mountain gorges, you wonder at the nerve of the people who first staked this out as a possible thoroughfare.' Reaching Monterey at five that afternoon, their car pulled up to the San Carlos Hotel, a grand and golden Spanish-influenced edifice framed by breathtaking sunset views of the bay. But Mary couldn't believe her eyes at what else she saw. There were Bina, Mick, Patricia, Joan, and little darlings Carmel and Lupe! When the *Monterey* had docked, her resourceful dad had whisked them all to the airport and chartered a plane to fly them up for a surprise reunion. Once happy tears were dried, Bina, Carmel and Lupe told Mary all about their voyage across the Pacific. In Auckland they had been photographed for the newspapers. After they sailed from Suva, the *Monterey* was swept up in the ongoing drama of Amelia Earhart's disappearance in the area, with the ship's radio officers monitoring the airwaves around the clock for any sign of the missing aviatrix. Then, on arriving in Los Angeles, they had discovered the strangest coincidence: their fellow passengers had included the mothers of Mary's Warners pals Orry-Kelly *and* Marcia Ralston, yet somehow they hadn't found each other during the journey! Bina received a lovely welcome gift in the next day's Monterey *Peninsula Herald* when it described the Maguires as a 'socially prominent Australian family'.

Mary farewelled that family, who returned to Hollywood, and got to work on *Sergeant Murphy*. Her hair lightened and thinned so it would photograph better outdoors, she was expected to be on set and camera-ready by eight most mornings. Dutch found these early starts tough, though his spirits were lifted by her presence. 'Mary Maguire, who already has spent an hour with the hairdresser, arrives bright and cheery and full of pep and you begin to lose some of your early morning grouch,' he wrote in an article. They were working for director B. Reeves Eason, known to all as 'Breezy'; not just a natural contraction of his name, the moniker referred to his blithe attitude towards the humans and animals he used in his films. Breezy was most famous – infamous – as the second unit director who had used forty-two cameras to capture the chariot race in 1925's *Ben-Hur: A Tale of the Christ* – and whose methods killed numerous horses to get it all on film. More recently he had used trip-wires on 1936 epic *The Charge of the Light Brigade*, leading to the deaths of twenty-five horses and so much public outrage that the US Congress promised laws to prevent such cruelty in the future. To avoid any similar controversy on *Sergeant Murphy*, a representative of the Monterey County Society for the Prevention of Cruelty to Animals was on location every day.

This time Breezy took more interest in his equine star than his human players. The director rehearsed the horse ten or twenty times for a scene, the animal astounding Mary and Dutch with its ability to gallop wildly and stop on a dime right in front of the camera. 'This nag does everything but read lines, and I for one, wouldn't drop dead with surprise if he suddenly started to talk,' Dutch wisecracked in one of his articles. Conversely, Breezy would summon his leading lady and man by barking 'Gimme a couple of hams on set' before rehearsing them once or twice and rolling cameras. The actors called themselves his 'trained seals'. While Dutch liked the director's macho vibe, Mary was less happy with simplistic script instructions ordering her to deliver lines 'sweetly', 'frigidly', 'excitedly' or 'impulsively'.

Horse-loving Mary and Dutch were allowed to do some of their own riding, though anything dangerous would be handled by stunt doubles. This was just studio self-interest. 'We'd be in a swell spot, if you went out there and messed up your map by taking a header off a horse,' an assistant director said. 'We couldn't use you till your face healed up so you could look a camera in the eye again. That would mean delay and upset our schedule . . . So for the love of Pete, be careful.' But Dutch wasn't. Showing off between scenes, he tried to ride a notoriously unruly horse and found himself clinging to the galloping animal as base soldiers roared with laughter. Eventually thrown, he landed flat on his back, injuring his shoulder, his butt and his pride, and getting an overnight hospital stay as punishment.

The Presidio offered great production value, but shifting light conditions played havoc with the filming. Moving all the actors, crew, cameras, lights and generators to forty-two different loc-ations around the base in the space of twelve days also strained the tight schedule. A cruising aeroplane held up production for an entire afternoon. 'Anyone of us cheerfully would have tossed a live shell into a three-inch gun and let him have it,' Dutch joked. The Presidio's day-to-day operations − rifle fire from its range, a brass band parading each afternoon and the boom of a big artil-lery gun − further messed with sound recording. 'At these times we're completely stymied and can't do a thing but sit and gnaw our fingernails,' he complained.

Downtime wasn't all chewed fingernails. Mary and Dutch would sprawl on the grass, eat their box lunches, smoke and joke with each other. And after work there were dinners and parties, including one at the Hotel Del Monte, the first resort ever built in America and one that rivalled San Simeon for extra-vagance. According to several people who spoke to biographer Marc Eliot for his 2008 book *Reagan: The Hollywood Years*, Mary and Dutch's friendship blossomed into a romance during filming. Though Hollywood gossips had repeatedly linked her to other young actors, there weren't any columnists in Monterey to observe and speculate about these co-stars on and off set. But Dutch did send photos back to the *Des Moines Register* that showed him and Mary looking very easy with each other, including one casual snap where he sat on the ground pulling on a boot, leaning back against her legs. Nearly fifty years later President Reagan confirmed his playboy reputation at this time, telling Barbara Walters that he would fall in love with his female co-stars because he suffered from what he joked was 'Leading Lady-itis'. While Mary enjoyed Dutch's company, Jocelyn Howarth's recent experience had also demonstrated the potential pitfalls of falling too fast and too hard for a Hollywood hunk. She had been seduced into a quickie Mexican marriage by Warners lothario George Brent, who then changed his mind and demanded an annulment. Jocelyn's embarrassment was splashed across newspapers everywhere; she was dropped by RKO and, just like that, her promising career was on the skids.

Sergeant Murphy finished filming in Monterey on Saturday, 24 July, and the next day Mary was driven back to Los Angeles. Finally, she was with her whole family in Hollywood. She didn't just have them at her side: she was supporting them all in a big house with two cars and a butler, maid, cook and houseboy. Mary had ticked off another of the goals she'd told the *Table Talk* reporter back in Melbourne. All that was left was seeing her name up in lights in London and finding the right man to marry.

Patricia was yet to make much use of Mary's contacts, but Joan had done numerous screen tests and was looking to get stage work. Meanwhile, Carmel and Lupe were enrolled at Immaculate Heart College, which they found a culture shock – rushing from class to class in a big school was bewildering after the sedate pace of Loreto. But at least the American nuns were broadminded. 'They never tell you not to go out without your gloves,' Carmel said. 'In Australia that was a terrible sin!'

Mary was back making *Sergeant Murphy* at the studio on Monday morning. For the rest of that week, she and the cast traipsed all over the lot, shooting on as many as six sound stages a day, with Warners then juggling its facilities across nine movies in production. When Mary snatched lunch in the commissary, she might see Claudette Colbert bitching to Charles Boyer about her director on *Tovarich*, Olivia de Havilland trying not to mess up her eighteenth-century gown for *The Great Garrick*, and a handsomely suited Errol Flynn looking every inch the hero of *The Perfect Specimen*. That week the Maguires gave a dinner for a reporter from the Sydney *Sun*, with a French maid serving 'good old Australian fried brains and tea'. 'Don't Go to Hollywood Warns Mary Maguire' read the headline of the resulting article. 'Unless a girl has £10 a week of her own, she should not come here,' Mary told the reporter. 'It is a hopeless proposition, with sheer luck as the main factor.' As confirmation, the reporter noted Jocelyn Howarth's premature fade-out.

Mick had his problems with Hollywood, too. 'Four quid a week for a maid in this town,' he griped, going on to list their expenses somewhat ungraciously in a conversation that had already revealed his daughter was earning £5000 per year ($A450000 today) and would soon be making even more. 'That's the price of stardom,' he grumbled on. 'That's the racket. The things you have to do here –'

Mary cut him off:

Well, I earn it and you can afford it yourself, but what about the girls who come here to starve? Extras can't live on their five dollars a day when they are in work and they're Americans and know the town. What chance, then, for a girl without money coming from Australia?

The reporter asked if Mary had met some of these starry-eyed wretches. 'More than I can tell you,' she said. 'Thank Heaven I've been able to help some. We in the business know what it is to be filmstruck and broke in Australia, where people do help; but this is a different country. In Hollywood, when you're alone you really are alone.' The article continued with Mary saying she went to work before dawn, was in bed early each night and never attended parties. 'She's wise enough to never trust Hollywood,' the reporter concluded. 'That's why she wants to protect trusting Australian girls from the dangers she herself never had to face.'

Sergeant Murphy now filmed for two days at the Santa Barbara Horse Show, one of the most elite events in one of America's richest enclaves. Down-to-earth Dutch's nose was put out of joint by the snobbishness of a region he described as having 'more millionaires per square mile than Iowa has cornfields'. Back at Warners, Breezy, five days over schedule though a paradoxical $30 000 under budget, crammed everything he could into a final day's shooting, working his leads from eight that morning until eight that night. With sections of Griffith Park dressed to look like Aintree and the Presidio, Mary, Ronald and Donald Crisp sweltered in their heavy clothes as the temperature soared. 'Uncle Sam's olive drab shirts, woolen breeches and high laced boots are not what I'd pick out for a sunbath,' Dutch wrote, praising the make-up men who had mopped their sweaty brows. 'You'll see Mary Maguire . . . and I gaily chatting horses, jumps and her "old man" the Colonel, looking as cool as those underwear ads appear in the paper.' Then it was time for the final shot of the scheduled shoot, which also happened to be the film's fade-out scene. 'The race was over, the Colonel paid off his bet, I got the gal and we all went out for ice cream soda in celebration,' he wrote. 'Maybe it wasn't ice cream either, but it was something or other and soda.' It was a rare, if coy, acknowledgement of just how awash with alcohol Hollywood was at the time.

In the second half of July, Maxwell Arnow at Warners and his casting director counterparts at MGM, RKO, Columbia, 20th Century Fox, Universal, Cecil B. DeMille Productions, Selznick International and Samuel Goldwyn Studios were asked by the North American Newspaper Alliance (NANA) to study the screen tests and performances of 450 young actresses in order to arrive at a list of stars most likely to hit it big in 1938 to '39. This poll – an attempt to revive similar 'Baby Star' surveys of the 1920s and early 1930s that had anointed Joan Crawford, Clara Bow, Carole Lombard and others – was posited as above reproach because no star-maker was allowed to vote for girls from his own studio. When the NANA press release was sent to the newspapers, Mary topped the 'lucky thirteen', followed by Jane Bryan and Phyllis Brooks.

As exciting as such acclaim could be, Mary had learnt that Hollywood was a place with few guarantees. *Confession* had been released to good reviews if modest box-office numbers. Mary didn't merit a lot of notice, save for *Film Daily* saying she and Jane did 'pleasing work', a *Variety* writer calling her 'cute' and the *Los Angeles Times* noting she 'gives the impression of charm and skill in a small role'. But the film did mark a turning point for its leading lady Kay Francis. Tired of being made to do weepies and still angry at having to work with director Joe May, she

demanded Jack Warner give her the comic lead in *First Lady*. He
did, the film flopped and her career took a dive, contributing
to her soon being labelled 'box-office poison'. While Katharine
Hepburn, Marlene Dietrich and Joan Crawford recovered from
being tarred with that same brush, Kay Francis was effectively
finished in Hollywood. It was a lesson in how far and fast even
a big star might fall.

———

Sergeant Murphy wrapped in early August, and Mary was reported
as honing her dancing skills by helping Busby Berkeley train
the battalion of beautiful girls he used in his big choreographed
sequences. But her stint as assistant was short-lived: she was
sick again. Having caught a cold in Santa Barbara, she lost
her voice at the studio. Put on unpaid lay-off, Mary was sent
home, confined to bed with acute bronchitis. Brisbane's *Truth*
worried: 'The climate of Hollywood certainly does not suit
Mary Maguire — she has been ill six times in the year she has
been [there].'

The *Australian Women's Weekly* journalist Eve Gye went to the
Hillside house to interview Mary. She found her still sick and
living like a 'fairy princess', propped up by lacy pillows in her
cool, flower-filled bedroom. Over cups of tea and sponge sandwich, they chatted as the star cuddled her koala mascot.

'Doesn't he remind you of Australia?' Mary asked wistfully.
'Oh, you're going home. I wish I were going with you!'
   'Why, Mary!' I queried, 'don't you like Hollywood?'
   'Well, I don't mind it so much now that mother's here.
It's certainly more like home with her around,' she replied.
   'And, of course, you like your work?'
   'I love it,' she said, 'but it's hard.'

Mary detailed the frustrations behind the façade of fame.

Just think: it's not merely a matter of going back and forth to the studios and playing your part, waiting around for hours, or posing for pictures, standing countless hours for fittings, becoming word-perfect in your script, or meeting people or entertaining (which you must do). In addition to all this, you go on location and may travel thousands of miles for the making of one picture.

At least Mary had made some good friends in Hollywood, telling the reporter about her trips to San Simeon and how much she liked Marion Davies, Jane Bryan, Maureen O'Sullivan, Bette Davis and Pat O'Brien. 'They all have been charming to me, and have gone out of their way to help me,' she said.

At their homes I have met practically every star in Hollywood. Of course, I entertain, too. I must. Sometimes we go to the Trocadero, sometimes the Ambassadors. These places are regarded as Hollywood's most exclusive. Entertaining, as you may well imagine, is no inexpensive matter. The average dinner runs into two pounds per head, and I hesitate to tell you what a very special evening costs. When I build my own home, as I shall if I remain in Hollywood, I propose doing more real home entertaining. Home is, after all, the nicest place in which to entertain your guests.

Mary found it hard to shake her illness. For six weeks, she didn't go to work, and wasn't seen out at clubs and cafés with her Hollywood pals. Not that this stopped the studio publicity machine, which reckoned she was launching a range of koala and kangaroo toys, or the columnists who now speculated she was engaged to Warner Bros. publicity man Bernie Williams. By mid-September Mary had recovered and returned to the studio for two days of additional filming on *Sergeant Murphy*. She also hit the hotspots again, going to a club in a crowd that included Al Jolson, Fredric March and Ginger Rogers, and attending that season's night celebrity polo games.

———

Alcatraz Island looked set to be a bigger hit that any B-movie had a right to be. Jack Warner wrote to Bryan Foy saying how pleased he was with the film. He only regretted it hadn't been an A-picture with Edward G. Robinson playing Mary's gangster dad, Gat. But what the studio could do – with the help of their friendly production and press partner Hearst – was promote their B-flick as though it had been an A-film all along.

The publicity department wove some breathtaking magic. 'Secrets of Alcatraz Bared in New Film: Great Prison Reconstructed on Location' was how Hearst's *Evening Journal and New York American* headlined the story handed them by Warners. 'The biggest detective job ever undertaken in Hollywood was the task of uncovering the rock-bound secrets of Alcatraz Island for the Cosmopolitan production of the same name,' the article claimed, while Bryan Foy was quoted as saying, 'Our information was obtained from one of the few prisoners ever released from the grim gray house.' This, he claimed, gave them everything they needed to 'construct the big Alcatraz out in the valley'. But apparently the set wasn't just big – it was enormous, measuring seven hundred yards in length and up to a hundred and eighty feet in height. What's more, it was fully functional. Cells were fronted by steel-barred doors operated by an electronic locking system, corridors were guarded by working metal detectors and ceilings were studded with practical tear-gas ejectors, all within concrete walls three feet thick and behind barbed-wire fences fifteen feet high.

This was all nonsense: just $13 000 of the film's $134 000 budget had been spent on a few modest but convincing prison sets.

The *Alcatraz Island* hype was exciting because it could help the movie go over big and make Mary a bigger star. Yet what was less thrilling was her billing. While the script's cast list headlined Annabel above Flo, and in the drama that followed she had more to say and do, the publicity pecking order at Warner Bros. meant Ann Sheridan was promoted as the film's leading lady while Mary was its 'juvenile' star.

———

Mary's movies had enjoyed varying box-office fates. Despite Miles's high hopes and big talk, *The Flying Doctor* failed to make back its budget because it didn't see release in America and barely limped into UK release when Gaumont-British withdrew from the exhibition business. *That Man's Here Again*, budgeted at a mere $98 000, grossed $280 000, the sort of pleasing profit that kept Warner Bros. ticking over. *Confession*, which cost $513 000, managed only $644 000.

But Jack Warner had been right about *Alcatraz Island*. Opening in October at the prestigious 3300-seat Strand Theater in New York, the prison drama played to sellout crowds, and its success continued across the country to a final gross of $721 000 – more than five times its cost. Most critics liked the film and Mary's performance. 'I found she justified all the promises held out for her,' reported *Hollywood Spectator*. 'Possessed of good looks, charming personality and acting ability, she soon should earn wide popularity.' The *Hollywood Reporter* called her 'appealing', and *Motion Picture Herald* said she was an 'outstanding juvenile'. 'The film has a compact plot, smooth performances . . . and a good bit of interesting material on the present residence of Al Capone,' wrote Frank S. Nugent in the *New York Times*. 'Whether the Alcatraz scenes are accurate or not is beside the point; they do make good watching. And so, for all its Class B-ishness, does the picture.'

Mary's star was on the rise. At a preview of Errol Flynn's *The Perfect Specimen*, girls accosted her with an ink pad so they could get her fingerprints along with her autograph. On 8 October she tested for *Jezebel*, a lavish period Southern melodrama that Warners hoped would tap into the anticipation for *Gone with the Wind*, still yet to cast its Scarlett let alone shoot a frame of film. *Jezebel* was to star Bette Davis in a quality role – that of Julie Marsden – meant to placate her after she had walked out on her contract and been sued back to Hollywood from London by Jack Warner. Mary tested for the part of the woman who marries Julie's lover, played by Henry Fonda. It wasn't to be, with the role going to Margaret Lindsay, though director William Wyler liked Mary enough to later date her briefly, Louella Parsons reporting that he zipped around Warner Bros. on his motorbike with her tucked into his sidecar. In the fall of 1937 she also briefly stepped out with the boss's son, Jack Warner, Jr, and with Greg Bautzer, a young attorney then using starlets as stepping stones on his way to amassing considerable Hollywood power. Such titbits kept her name in front of film fans, but Mary's biggest publicity break at this time was a ready-made profile from Warners, widely published to accompany *Alcatraz Island*'s release. It began:

A young woman was running down the hall, her black curls flying in her wake, her tiny shoes almost invisible under the wide cuffs of her dark slacks. At the publicity door she paused for one breathless moment, gasped out a 'Hello' and dove into a big, leather-covered chair where she tucked her feet under her knees and her knees under her chin and turned a pair of guileless black eyes toward her tormentor.

'I'm not late,' she said. 'I'm never late. I set the clocks back sometimes but I'm never late. Don't you dare say that I'm late!'

'Very well,' we agreed, 'you're not late. But you are out of breath. Want a cigarette – or a stick of gum while you catch it?'

She put them both in her mouth, almost if not quite simultaneously. 'I drove out here myself,' she said, 'and didn't have an accident. I've had several, you know. I'm not used to the right side of the roads and streets. But today I got here without any trouble – except maybe one fender is scraped a little.'

'Perhaps we should have an introduction,' suggested the mutual friend, who had arranged the interview. 'This is the Mary Maguire who stole that name from her younger sister. She was a misplaced sprig of Shamrock in Australia before she came to Hollywood . . .'

'I wasn't misplaced,' snapped Mary. 'I was born there.'

'I wish you luck with your story,' continued the friend, unabashed. 'She's a brat of the first water.'

'Nice people, these Hollywood folks,' said Mary. 'Someday I'll tell you what I think of you. I suppose you're going to ask me about kangaroos and duckbilled platypuses,' said Mary. 'Nearly everyone does.'

A comically combative exchange followed. Mary rejected the Mary Pickford comparison. Rattled off the story of her career in Australia. Offered some trivia about loathing gardenias and still liking dolls. Claimed to have never worn slacks before coming to America.

'Why do they call you a brat?'

'I suppose because I am one. I've had my own way most of the time, ever since I can remember. But you don't think I'm spoiled, do you?'

She opened her big black eyes a little and gave one of those angelic looks that can't be described.

Mary claimed she had a special credential from the Australian government that entitled her to transport home if she was ever stranded anywhere.

'I'm told that only five people not actually connected with the government have them.

'And,' she added, evidently embarrassed over this apparent conceit, 'I never chewed gum until I got to America. Now I like it. Want to hear it pop?'

We said we did not.

'I can do imitations. Good ones. I can imitate Hepburn and Garbo and Bette Davis. Shall I do one for you?'

'Now you are being a brat. People have been killed for doing imitations. What else?'

Mary said she was still studying music and dance and was making an effort to unlearn Australian slang. 'That's right,' she said, demonstrating. 'Two months ago I would have said "Righto". But I'm learning to speak real American.'

With that, the interview was over – almost. 'I guess that's all there is,' she said. 'Except that I'm in love and won't tell you about it. Maybe that would make a lead for your interview.'

This was a puzzling puff piece. It contained enough authentic detail – right down to her habit of tucking her feet beneath her as she curled up in a chair – to suggest the Warner Bros. pressman based it on a real conversation. Though Mary's quote about being in love was meant to be read as a bratty tease, it actually did coincide with the beginning of her most public Hollywood relationship – one Warner Bros. *wouldn't* want to exploit for publicity purposes.

25.

Mary set tongues wagging in mid–October 1937 when she was spotted with 20th Century Fox chairman Joe Schenck at the Dunes Club. Built in the desert outside Palm Springs by Mob-adjacent Al Wertheimer, this quasi–legal casino was where stars went to drink quality liquor at a mahogany bar half the length of a football field, chow down on prime beef in the circular dining room and gamble away their enormous salaries at the gaming tables. Joe and Wertheimer were close; a few years earlier, the mogul had let him run a casino out of his Hollywood mansion. Now Joe was renting Wertheimer's Palm Springs mansion and was treated like royalty at the Dunes. Everyone took note of Mary on his arm. 'He seemed very devoted to her,' reported the *Los Angeles Times*. Louella approved: 'Joe has very good taste.' His taste wasn't in doubt. Hers might have been. The gossips were polite but the pairing had to raise eyebrows. Joe was forty-two years older than Mary – old enough to be her grandfather. He was also far from handsome. Even those close to him said so. 'He had charm, the sort that often goes with an ugly face,' remembered Mary Ellin Barrett, his goddaughter and daughter of his lifelong best friend, Irving Berlin. Darryl F. Zanuck's attorney Arnold Grant said, 'He was one of the ugliest men that ever lived, but after you met him

if anybody asked you to describe him you would say he was one
of the most attractive, charming people.' Part of Joe's charm was
that he was a true Hollywood pioneer who loved the movies with
the affection a father has for a child. Which made sense because
he had helped birth the motion picture industry.

Born on Christmas Day in 1876 into a Russian Jewish family,
Joe, his parents and his younger brother, Nicholas, came to
New York in November 1892. The boys were enterprising,
running errands for shopkeepers. Joe also worked in a factory
before becoming a druggist. Showing entrepreneurial flair, he
bought the pharmacy for $600 – and sold it six months later
for $3500. By 1908 the Schencks ran amusement parks, dealing
with local standover mobs and leasing cinema concessions from
Marcus Loew. A few years later they partnered with Loew in
what became the parent company to MGM. While Nicholas
was a cold, hard businessman, Joe was gregarious and loved
the fun and glamour of the new industry. In 1916 he married
silent film superstar Norma Talmadge and before long was producing her movies, along with those of her sisters, Constance
and Natalie, his brother-in-law Buster Keaton, Roscoe 'Fatty'
Arbuckle and Rudolph Valentino. In 1924 Joe became chairman
of United Artists, the company founded by Charlie Chaplin,
Mary Pickford, Douglas Fairbanks and D. W. Griffith, and was
soon after its president. When Darryl F. Zanuck quit Warner
Bros. in 1933 after a falling-out with Jack Warner, Joe proposed they set up a new independent studio called 20th Century
Pictures. Two years later, their upstart company swallowed the
larger Fox Film Corporation to become 20th Century Fox.
A power player, Joe nevertheless had a reputation for being a
loyal and generous friend who could guide a career. He was also
a womaniser. Having finally divorced Norma in 1934, though
they remained on good terms, he loved nothing better than

dancing with starlets all night. And Joe spent big – maybe bigger than anyone else in Hollywood. In 1937 alone he blew $400 000 entertaining himself, his lovers and friends.

Joe also had a dark secret. Mobster William 'Willie' Bioff, backed by Al Capone's former bagman Frank 'The Enforcer' Nitti, had engineered the takeover of the International Alliance of Theatrical Stage Employees. In April 1936 Bioff told Hollywood's movie moguls – including Joe's brother Nicholas, now running MGM – that he could now order the union's 125 000 members to strike, instantly bringing film production, distribution and exhibition to a standstill. The price of protection was $50 000 a year from each of the big studios and $25 000 annually from the smaller ones. Resistance wouldn't just see crippling strikes but might lead to a few of the big studio-owned theatres burning down in mysterious circumstances. The moguls agreed to extortion, which was still cheaper than paying striking employees to return to work and rebuilding ruined theatres. When Bioff wanted to spend his ill-gotten gains without attracting IRS attention, he leant on Joe Schenck for laundering services and had him write a $100 000 cheque in exchange for cash.

———

At the Dunes, surrounded by the famous stars and wise guys who frequented the joint, Mary wouldn't have had an inkling of the dangerous game her date was playing. What she knew was that Joe Schenck – one of the movie industry's most fun, fascinating and powerful players – liked her an awful lot. Sure, there was a big age difference. But she only had to look at Marion Davies for an example of a happy personal and professional relationship between a young star and a fabulously wealthy and powerful older man. Marion had been twenty-one when she met then 54-year-old W. R. He hadn't just made Marion a star but had also taken care of her three sisters, just as Joe had done with Norma Talmadge and her siblings.

A few weeks after their first weekend away, Mary and Joe headed to Palm Springs again to party at the Dunes. Mary had the attention of 20th Century Fox's boss. But Warners wasn't doing her film career any favours. Mary's next assignment was a supporting role in a B-thriller, *Mystery House*. Wasn't this a little beneath her? Hadn't she just topped the 'lucky thirteen' list of future stars? Mary got the script on Friday, 29 October. Her role was the daughter of a man murdered at a remote lodge filled with potential killers and victims. It was a rote character in a perfunctory production, and she was ordered to a full dress rehearsal the next morning before the cameras rolled on Monday. Mary did her rehearsal, but leading lady June Travis developed a sore throat and swollen glands during the day. On Sunday she got sicker and the studio substituted the actress they had on stand-by: Ann Sheridan.

Mary quit the film. She wanted dramatic work, not another ingénue role that would have her again billed beneath Ann Sheridan. Warner Bros. took her refusal in stride, suspending her without pay for the two weeks it would take Ann Nagel to finish the film. Newspapers reported Mary had mutinied against the studio. It wasn't quite as dramatic as that, though refusing roles was usually a move made by more powerful stars like Bette Davis or Jimmy Cagney. Mary digging in her little feet let Warners know they had to give her more respect. Jack Warner read the columns of Louella Parsons and Sheilah Graham like everyone else, so he knew that Mary was stepping out with Joe Schenck – and would have guessed the Fox mogul was giving her career guidance.

Mary and Joe remained close. When he was due to arrive back from New York, she went to the train station to meet him. He gave her a huge $1500 diamond bracelet. They went back to the Dunes and partied with the likes of Cary Grant and Myrna Loy.

Though he was a fixture in her life, Joe wasn't her only powerful admirer. In mid-November Charlie Chaplin and wife Paulette Goddard had their monthly spat, this one triggered because the Little Tramp invited Mary over 'for a spot of tennis'.

Carmel and Lupe got a neat break when Mary's agent popped in to the Hillside house. 'My word, I just happened to remember – they need about twenty young girls for the new Deanna Durbin picture,' he said. 'Why don't you let me take you out to the studio to try for it?' Carmel didn't think they'd have much chance, but Lupe was hopeful it would at least get them out of school for a few days. The girls arrived at Universal and were hired instantly by *Mad About Music*'s director Norman Taurog. 'Hurry up, we can use you right away!' he told them. Just like that, the younger Maguires were playing opposite fifteen-year-old Deanna, Hollywood's hottest young star. For the film, Carmel and Lupe had to learn to ride bikes, something the horse-loving girls had never done. Mick bought them bicycles to practise on, but with so many hills around their house, the girls kept crashing into fences and bushes. 'By the time we mastered it we were just covered with bruises,' Carmel laughed. 'I'd rather a horse any day!' Slower, steadier and more serious Joan was taking acting instruction from the world-famous theatre director Max Reinhardt and auditioning for stage roles at the Pasadena Playhouse. Even Mick was reported to be breaking into the movie business, shopping his pugilistic skills around as a fight coordinator. Only Patricia was letting the side down. 'She is lazy,' straight-talking Bina told Eve Gye of *The Australian Women's Weekly*. 'She is having a marvellous time and refuses to diet or settle down to the grind of the film world.'

Patricia had one of those marvellous times when Mary threw her and Bina a combined birthday at the Trocadero. Joe Schenck paid for Rudy Vallée to take over the band, and the Maguire family were surrounded by many of Mary's famous friends, including W. R. and Marion, Charlie Chaplin, Spencer Tracy, Tyrone Power, Sonja Henie and Joan Crawford. To ensure Patricia's twenty-first was just that little more memorable, Mary gave her a beautiful original gown designed by her pal Orry-Kelly. Later that week, Mary and co-star John Litel acted scenes from *Alcatraz Island* on *Let's Go Hollywood*, the half-hour Warners show broadcast from the Hollywood studios of the California Radio System.

At the beginning of December, Louella Parsons, echoing the 'lucky thirteen' survey, predicted Mary would reach stardom in 1938, alongside Joan Fontaine and Hedy Lamarr. But even as the column appeared, Mary was struck with food poisoning and shed five kilograms in a weekend. 'Which is one way of losing weight,' quipped Sheilah Graham of what was the rising star's seventh Hollywood illness or injury.

Mary was soon back on her feet and at the studio awaiting her next assignment. Hanging around her workplace was fun in itself, as Sheilah Graham observed when she popped into the Green Room for lunch in mid-December. Mary, petite in white slacks, was with Aussie Marcia Ralston. Fellow antipodean Errol Flynn, resplendent in his green Robin Hood tights, paid the girls no mind – and similarly ignored Olivia de Havilland, gussied up in her Maid Marian outfit – to chat with his buddy David Niven. Henry Fonda, bewhiskered with big sideburns and dressed as a Civil War–era gent, focused his attention on some tasty baked halibut, while Bette Davis in cute curls and wearing a dressing gown, pow-wowed with director William Wyler. Just another day at the office. Soon after Mary enjoyed Christmas celebrations with her movie mates. *Tarzan* and *The Thin Man* director W. S. Van Dyke put on a huge house party, where two energetic bartenders whipped up gin slings, old-fashioneds and all other conceivable cocktails. Out the back, a crackling fire warmed cockles as surely as the alcoholic nectar being poured at yet another bar. Mary was in the thick of it, belting out carols with her mates Rosalind Russell, Jimmy Stewart, Harold Lloyd, Myrna Loy, Spencer Tracy, William Powell and the Marx Bros. A visiting Australian reporter's head spun at the heady cocktail of glamour and booze. 'Bar to bar, toast after toast,' he marvelled.

Another journalist from Australia, Guy Austin of the *Sunday Sun*, visited Mary at home and saw how in demand she was and just how much she had learnt from Bina about cultivating the right people. While they chatted over tea, the phone rang every ten minutes, with six calls from Warners Bros. alone. Among the news flashes: she was no longer needed for a promotion in New Orleans but the Hollywood Chamber of Commerce wanted her to ride in the Santa Claus sleigh down Hollywood Boulevard that night. The reporter was amazed by her contacts. 'She bandies the names of William Randolph Hearst, Paul Block, the next biggest newspaper publisher, Joseph Schenck and other studio heads as her social friends, as you and I would speak of the people next door,' he wrote. Mary was frank about the role these powerbrokers were playing in her success. 'It's really due to Hearst,' she said, 'that I'm getting publicity in all his papers.' But Block was doing his bit, too, not surprising given he was a Hearst crony. The postman arrived with a bundle of mail for Mary, with one envelope containing a half-page clipping about her from a Detroit newspaper. 'There's a note here that it's in 28 Block newspapers,' she explained. Guy Austin was impressed: 'It's not what you know but who you know, though in Mary's case add personal attributes of youthful beauty, a little experience, and a lot of horse sense, as well as a bit of British snobbishness

that has intrigued the "biggies" here.' That night Mary's biggest
biggie, Joe Schenck, dressed as Santa, joined his young girlfriend
on the sleigh to wave and bow to the cheering civilians enjoying
Tinseltown's Christmas festivities.

26.

Another biggie had his eyes on Mary. Alfred Vanderbilt, Jr, who had already received $5 million of the inheritance his father had left him, was Hollywood's most eligible bachelor after Howard Hughes. Alfred and Mary shared a love of racehorses – he owned thirty and had one of California's biggest stables – and they double dated with Cary Grant and Phyllis Brooks at a football game. A few days before Christmas, he took her to the world premiere of *Snow White and the Seven Dwarfs* at the Cathay Circle Theater, with the blue carpet walked by everyone who was anyone in Hollywood as thirty thousand fans cheered and millions more listened in on radio across America. Afterwards they went to the clubs, including Cafe Lamaze, and a photo of Mary looking like the cat that got the cream as Alfred lit a cigarette at their table for two appeared in newspapers all over the world. Louella Parsons reported he was so smitten that Hollywood's other beauties were jealous. 'The other evening a couple of them made a few catty remarks when she walked into the Troc on Vanderbilt's arm,' she wrote. 'But never let it be said that Mary isn't a true daughter of Mickey Maguire and that she doesn't know how to defend herself. She came back with as good as they sent and at the end of the third round it was called a draw. No hair pulling, mind you, just

a verbal battle.' Rival columnist Sheilah Graham claimed it was
the other way around: it was *Mary* the fellas were tussling over.
'She is so pretty, with such large, brown eyes that all the males
here – including Charlie Chaplin, Joe Schenck and Alfred (millionaire) Vanderbilt – fight to be her escort.'

James Cagney also wanted her – on screen at least. The tough-
guy superstar had defected from Warner Bros. to upstart studio
Grand National, where he was next to make *Angels with Dirty
Faces*. Just before Christmas it was announced that Mary was in
line to play his leading lady – provided, of course, that Jack Warner
would loan her out. Columnists reckoned he would, the mogul
willing to do anything to make peace with Cagney in the hope
of eventually luring him back to the studio. Meanwhile, *Sergeant
Murphy*, which might have initially teamed Mary with Jimmy,
opened to solid business and would go on to double its budget
with a gross of $279 000. American reviewers focused mostly on
its general merits as unpretentious matinee fare. 'The story is told
with humor, excitement, romance and a hokum ending that brings
cheers from the audience,' said *Boxoffice* magazine. '*Sergeant Murphy*
is an appealing story that any audience will be pleased with,' agreed
Film Daily. *Hollywood Spectator* thought Mary 'very comely and thoroughly capable, albeit I did think her diction was a bit broad for
an American girl'. When it was released back in Australia, Mary
got more scrutiny – and typically mixed reviews. *The Age* thought
her still 'immature', suggested her voice hadn't been properly
recorded and said her close-ups weren't of good enough quality, but
praised her major scene with Donald Crisp for showing 'considerable promise in natural acting and Puckish humour'. The *Sydney
Morning Herald* really couldn't make up its mind:

> Miss Maguire photographs much better than she has in her
> previous American films. Also, her enunciation has improved

. . . although she still fails to put sufficient expression into her acting. This, nevertheless, possesses a certain charm, for all its obvious deficiencies . . . Miss Maguire makes a petite and fascinating portrait as a colonel's daughter.

Mary celebrated Christmas with her whole family for the first time in two years. Then Joe Schenck sent his limousine to whisk her to him in Palm Springs. Though the mogul was Jewish, Christmas marked his birthday. Back in Hollywood just before New Year's Eve, Mary dropped in to the Universal lot to watch Carmel and Lupe working on *Mad About Music*'s elaborate Swiss boarding-school sets. Her little sisters had quickly realised how much standing around and waiting was involved in acting – even worse, because they were under sixteen they had to do hours of tutorial time each day in a curtained-off area of the studio stage. Producer Joe Pasternak was surprised to see Mary on his set. 'I've been suspended,' she joked.

The year closed with good and bad luck for the Maguires. Joan, Carmel and Lupe were selected to be part of Pasadena's annual Rose Parade, with the *Los Angeles Times* running a big photo of the smiling beauties giving a radio interview about how their float was the only international entry and how it would celebrate Australia's sesquicentenary.

Mary had less to be happy about. On a night out at the Famous Door nightclub, she had lost that huge diamond bracelet Joe had given her.

Nineteen thirty-eight started spectacularly for Joan, Carmel and Lupe. In dazzling white dresses, they stood on a Rose Parade float whose centrepiece was a bright red lyrebird made of thirty thousand flowers and framed by green ferns representing Australia's wilderness. The girls waved regally to the million people lining the parade's five-mile route – and were even more ecstatic when their float won one of the day's major prizes.

That night millions more Americans listened to the nationally syndicated CBS radio special 'Forecasting 1938'. Experts in politics, finance and sports made their predictions about the coming year. Syndicated columnist Harrison Carroll listed stars he thought would make it big, before welcoming Mary to talk about her prospects. Tellingly, she focused on the biggest obstacle she had faced: her health.

> Mary: The studio tells me I'm to play one of the leads in *Three Girls On Broadway*. That sounds very exciting.
> Harrison: I should think so: a similar story, *Three On A Match*, served to launch Bette Davis, Joan Blondell and Ann Dvorak to stardom. Now, Mary, what do you say is the most important thing to concentrate on when becoming a star?
> Mary: Undoubtedly, your health, everything depends on that. You have to look well and feel well to keep pace with Hollywood's shooting schedule.
> Harrison: That's a very sensible observation, Mary, and I do hope your big success comes in 1938.
> Mary: I hope so, too, Mr Carroll. I'd like to feel like I'd accomplished my goal in Hollywood. And I'd like to become a star for another reason.
> Harrison: What's that?
> Mary: Well, after your kind predictions on this, the first day of the New Year, I'd hate to make you out a false prophet.

Louella's special New Year's column comprised a jocular list of resolutions she thought best suited Hollywood notables, including, 'Pretty Mary Maguire agrees not to vamp too many eligibles.'

Mary agreed no such thing. A year earlier, the Hollywood scene had frightened her. Now she embraced its nightlife. In addition to regular rhumba dance dates with Joe Schenck, she went out with Edgar Bergen, ventriloquist superstar creator of Charlie McCarthy, and again hit the town with Alfred Vanderbilt, Jr. Then Hollywood's truly most eligible – to say nothing of eccentric – bachelor came calling in the form of Howard Hughes. The producer of *Hell's Angels* and *Scarface*, he was also the fastest aviator in the skies and one of the world's richest men with a $US145 million ($2.6 billion) fortune. On a break from Katharine Hepburn, he now courted Mary. Much to the amusement of her sisters, the handsome Howard would turn up for dates in wrinkled clothes, wearing tennis shoes with white socks, his hair a tad too long. Sometimes he and Mary hit a nightclub but other times he drove them around in her car before stopping to eat at a sandwich stand on Sunset Boulevard. At the end of the night, Howard would hail a taxi, have its driver follow, drop off Mary and then depart in the cab. On another occasion they went out with his friend Pasquale 'Pat' DiCicco, an agent–producer–mobster with links to Charles 'Lucky' Luciano. At this time, DiCicco was suspected not only in the mysterious 'suicide' of his movie-star ex-wife Thelma Todd but also in the beating of actor Ted Healy outside the Trocadero, said to cause his death the next day.

When Mary wasn't out by night with famous, rich, odd and/ or bad boys, Warners kept her busy with other publicity-friendly activities. Reporters might one day find her immaculately dressed at the Santa Anita track, giving advice she had gleaned from her racing-mad dad to her studio gal pals Jane Bryan, Ann Sheridan and Lana Turner. The next day the press boys might find Mary firing the starting gun for a 'bellboy derby' along Hollywood Boulevard, which devolved into chaos as competitors carrying fully laden trays dodged through pedestrians and automobiles, the scene scored with the sounds of shattering glassware and stalled traffic horns.

Away from the publicity spotlight, tragedy struck her circle when Miles Mander suffered a cerebral haemorrhage while filming *Kidnapped*. Mary's mentor was rushed to hospital with vision problems and partial paralysis of his arms, where he was diagnosed with heart disease and high blood pressure. To her relief, Miles pulled through and made a good if slow recovery. Had he died, her life would have been entirely different.

———

Warners announced Mary in a slew of films – *The Dude Rancher, The Defense Rests, Student Nurse, Cowboy from Brooklyn* – half of them with Ronald Reagan, the studio seemingly toying with the idea of making them a screen couple. But production didn't commence on any of these with her, nor on *Three Girls on Broadway*. Even more frustratingly, *Angels with Dirty Faces* was cancelled because James Cagney's previous film for Grand National was such a flop it financially sank the upstart studio. In a few months he would make peace with Warners – and, too late for Mary, the future classic would be made there co-starring Pat O'Brien, Humphrey Bogart and . . . Ann Sheridan.

Mary was without a picture in production but more celebrated than ever, appearing in yet more numerous newspaper and magazine lists of the stars set to make it big in 1938. A survey of directors that included Cecil B. DeMille and Ernst Lubitsch singled her out for her photographic beauty. Max Factor picked her as a future star, while visiting Hungarian cosmetics guru Erno Laszlo nominated her as one of Hollywood's ten most beautiful and interesting women – putting her alongside Greta Garbo, Ginger Rogers, Carole Lombard, Ann Sheridan, Kay Francis, Bette Davis, Olivia de Havilland, Deanna Durbin and Dorothy Lamour. *Motion*

Picture summed up the buzz: 'Endowed with plenty of ummph
. . . [she] has asserted her personality and talent so well that she
is practically the talk of the town.' And, with Carmel and Lupe
in *Mad About Music*, Joan testing for MGM and Patricia exercising 'to get rid of extra pounds before she crashes the field',
the magazine reckoned the movies might soon be overtaken by
'flocks of Maguires': 'If they all click, it will be the biggest bunch
of sisters that has made good in Hollywood.' The Maguire lasses
were also popular with other young Hollywood players, their
Hillside house a hangout for the likes of Lana Turner, Deanna
Durbin and Judy Garland.

Visiting the home, *The Australian Women's Weekly*'s Barbara
Bourchier thought Mary was kept grounded by her siblings,
who mockingly referred to her as 'Maguire'. Fair enough that
she should have a nickname. Patricia's sobriquet Patsy sometimes
became 'Snake Pit'. Carmel was nicknamed 'The Duchess'. 'Lupe'
was a nickname. Sensible Joan, was, well, just Joan.

'She doesn't pretend to be glamorous for a moment,' the
reporter observed of Mary, 'and if she were to try it out her
crowd of very frank sisters would soon kid her out of it.'

Mary wondered aloud whether she should risk stepping out
publicly with Howard Hughes. Her sisters pounced.

'Well, Barbara, what do you think of her running around with
the filthy rich?' asked Patricia.

Carmel chimed in: 'Yes, Maguire's in high society now!'

Mary laughed along and admitted she had indeed 'gone social'
before offering the journalist some fancy Austrian chocolates that
William Wyler had given her.

'Everyone's always giving her things,' wailed Patricia. 'Would
you believe it . . . one chap wants to give her an aeroplane for
her birthday!'

Barbara sought out Mary's direct boss Bryan Foy at Warners.
He echoed what Miles Mander had said after casting her in *The
Flying Doctor*. 'She has a good chance of hitting the top – given,
of course, the right direction, and the right vehicles,' he said. 'She
needs a lot more acting experience, but that will come easily,
because she's very good on the set and takes direction willingly
and intelligently . . . You know, a lot of these young people get
into awful difficulties when they start reading – and believing
– what you people and the publicity departments write about
them. I don't have that trouble with Mary, though. Perhaps it's
that grand family of hers.'

That grand family of hers frequently welcomed Joe Schenck,
who often stopped by the Hillside house before he and Mary
hit the town. Joe got on well with Mick and saw star potential
in Joan. He also shared Bina's ambition for Mary – and the Fox
mogul had a plan that found a receptive audience.

On 4 February Mick sailed back to Australia to wrap up business affairs. The *Los Angeles Times* carried a big photograph of all
six Maguire women waving dockside under the headline 'When
Daddy Goes Sailing Away to Far Australia'. The next day Mary
flew north to attend the premiere of Warners' Technicolor epic
Gold Is Where You Find It in Weaverville, a tiny mining outpost
in the Californian mountain wilderness. Landing in Sacramento,
she continued her journey by train with Olivia de Havilland,
George Brent and Margaret Lindsay, who were actually in the
film, along with Jane Bryan, Wayne Morris and Beverly Roberts,
who were, like her, along for added star wattage. The group finished their trip with buses taking them on a hundred-mile journey
to Weaverville through rain and snow along a sharply curving icy
mountain road. Police escort sirens wailing, the town's brass band
playing and dynamite explosions rumbling from the surrounding
hills, the movie-celebrity convoy arrived in town after dark to find

the main street lit by bonfires and lined by thousands of cheering hillbillies. In freezing conditions, the stars mounted an outside dais for a live national radio broadcast, only to be upstaged by octogenarian and nonagenarian Weavervillans describing their actual experiences of the gold rush in these here parts. Then it was time for the movie, shown in the town hall, with five hundred locals hollering like hell whenever they spotted their own as extras. One old timer's blood ran so hot that he whipped out his pistol and fired three bullets at a baddie on the screen. Show over, the hall was cleared of seats, and the townsfolk served doughnuts, cider and coffee. As a band played, Mary and her fellow Warners beauties, who had accessorised their frocks with coats, mittens and galoshes, whirled around the dance floor with starstruck local gents as the town's maidens watched on jealously. 'It was Hollywood's strangest premiere,' remarked one reporter. Festivities finished not long before dawn. Mary was up soon after to ride in a dog sled and frolic in the snow with Jane Bryan for publicity photos. Exhausted, she slept on the bus all the way back to Sacramento, and then for most of the flight back to Los Angeles. She woke on the plane to have lunch. And to smile groggily for another picture. This would appear to be the last publicity photograph ever taken of her by Warners.

27.

Mary left Warners three days later. When the news was made public, it was simultaneously announced that she had a *new* seven-year contract – with 20th Century Fox. While it's unclear whether Jack Warner intended to renew her contract, it was reported that Joe Schenck had negotiated her release and paid $5000 to seal the deal. Mary's new Fox contract paid $500 a week for the first year – $250 less than what she would have received if Warners exercised their option – but as sweeteners it included only twelve layoff weeks annually. Her salary would also hit $2500 a week in the seventh year – making up for the pay freeze in the first. In the long term the Fox deal would pay more – and it was more likely to pay off in terms of fame given that she had the boss's favour. Though Mary's first studio contract had been pored over, this time there was an element of trust. 'You know,' she said, 'there are still parts of that contract I haven't read.' Had she, Mary would have seen that the Fox shackles were as restrictive as those at Warners, with the studio, among other things, able to order to have dental work done at her own expense and terminate her services if she was sick for more than twenty-one days or disfigured in an accident. On the upside, the studio had to pay all her expenses if she worked more than fifteen miles from Hollywood. As Mary was still a minor – and would remain so until she turned twenty-one – the agreement again had to be confirmed by the court. Industry observers thought her move a shrewd one. 'Watch Miss Maguire go places, now that she is working for Joe Schenck, who is very much enamored of her,' wrote Sheilah Graham.

Joe was powerful and sympathetic to her desire for better roles. But he also wouldn't shoehorn Mary into A-list pictures. Back in 1933, when they set up 20th Century Pictures, he had promised Darryl F. Zanuck autonomy over production. The two men would have to agree Mary was right for any movie. As proof this agreement held, a week after she signed with Fox she tested for *Alexander's Ragtime Band*, an A-picture biography of Joe's best friend, Irving Berlin. Mary didn't get the role. But Joe could guarantee she was seen – with him. For her nineteenth birthday he took her to the Santa Anita derby to hang out with a crowd that included Marlene Dietrich, Fred Astaire, Rudy Vallée, William Powell, Clark Gable and Carole Lombard. A week later, they looked very cosy at the Turf Club Ball, Mary in a white fur wrap, he in a white tux. The next day at Santa Anita's $100 000 Handicap, Sheilah Graham saw the couple 'smiling to the right and left, swinging along, holding hands'. Mary's place in Hollywood high society was truly confirmed on 10 March when Joe took her to the tenth Academy Awards. Held at the Biltmore Hotel, the Oscars that year came with added excitement because it was the first time the winners hadn't been announced in advance. Looking sophisticated in a black frock, Mary sat beside Joe on the 20th Century Fox table at the front of the room, along with Darryl F. Zanuck, Don Ameche, Douglas Fairbanks Jr and Sr, who all brought their *wives*. The ceremony started at 10.30 p.m. – and was immediately brought to a standstill when Cecil B. DeMille delivered a 35-minute speech that seemed as long as one of his epics. Over the next three hours, Mary saw her heroine Luise

Rainer win her second consecutive Best Actress Award, her recent escort Eddie Bergen get a special Oscar for comedy and her previous boss Jack Warner accept his studio's first Best Picture award for *The Life of Emile Zola*. But the night climaxed with Darryl F. Zanuck receiving the inaugural Irving G. Thalberg Award, with Mary and her table clapping and cheering him as he accepted Hollywood's ultimate accolade.

Although Marion Davies had recently retired from making movies, she remained Hollywood's hostess with the mostest, and Mary was always welcome to casually drop by the Beach House – as she did the Sunday after the Oscars to hang with mutual pals like Anita Loos and Cary Grant. Being in Hearst's continued favour also paid off when Mary was chosen to grace the cover of his *Cosmopolitan* magazine. The portrait – of her in a floral hat, green dress and matching gloves, gazing at herself in a hand mirror – was done by 'artist of the stars' Bradshaw Crandell, who also used the likes of Bette Davis, Carole Lombard and Olivia de Havilland as his models. Joan, too, was going places, having landed the lead role in a comedy at Pasadena Playhouse.

Joe stepping out so often and so publicly with Mary led gossip columnist Ed Sullivan to report in his 21 March nationally syndicated column: 'They insist that Mary Maguire is readying a trousseau for her wedding to Joe Schenck.' Other gossip columnists didn't weigh in and neither did the rumoured lovers. Mary's first Fox assignment, *Mysterious Mr. Moto*, began shooting around this time. The film had Peter Lorre as the eponymous Japanese detective, master of jujitsu, subterfuge, feigned obsequiousness and caricatured Oriental speech. Mary was to play Ann Richman, secretary to Henry Wilcoxson's peace-loving industrialist Anton Darvak, who's the target of a convoluted assassination plot orchestrated by the League of Assassins. This was the top-billed female part in a picture whose success was guaranteed because the previous four Moto flicks had all been hits. Popular or not, there was no escaping the fact that this was another B-picture.

Meeting Mary at her new studio on a day when she was doing make-up, hair and clothing tests for *Mr. Moto*, a Brisbane *Courier-Mail* reporter heard how disciplined she had become in pursuit of stardom. Mary said she barely went out at all – she couldn't. Not when she was getting up before six, expected on set at nine and finishing at seven. When she got home she only had the energy for dinner and an hour or so of script study before she collapsed into sleep. She also took acting, singing and French lessons several times a week. 'I don't expect to sing in pictures – or to talk French in them,' she explained. 'But singing and French help my voice production.' And, like any starlet, Mary had to keep the weight off. 'I don't diet,' she said, 'but I try to do without fattening foods – no pastries, no chocolates. I have plenty of exercise – riding, and sometimes golf and tennis, and massages.' The reporter dutifully jotted it all down, but also couldn't help but note that the newspapers reported his interviewee was out and about week after week with seemingly hundreds of her Hollywood friends. As had been the case at Warners, making a movie meant making time for a lot of publicity photos. Mary posed with her *Mr. Moto* co-stars, looking dreamy in Henry Wilcoxson's arms and intrigued as she stood with Peter Lorre. She and Henry were snapped getting some good healthy 'exercise' on their daily walk around the studio – she dressed to the nines and in pumps, him in a three-piece suit and smoking a cigarette. Even more ridiculous was Mary perched on a chair, thoughtfully 'reading' magazines in Polish and Spanish, so the photos could be used to accompany publicity about her in those publications.

Mysterious Mr. Moto's press hype was typically upbeat. Trivia included that Mary had taken up sketching her co-stars and that she'd gotten her wardrobe woman's daughter a job as her stand-in. But it was another troubled production. While the columnists were fed a story about Peter Lorre having to go to hospital with an infected tooth for three weeks, the truth was far, far darker. The star was addicted to morphine, which had first been pre-scribed to him in Germany in the 1920s after surgery. When Lorre made it back to set, he was still injecting himself twice a day, barely able to run upstairs or perform the simplest of stunts. On high days he'd be upbeat, joking and flirting with Mary; on down days he'd retreat to his dressing-room, anxious and in agony. Listening to radio broadcasts of Hitler spewing hate for the Jews only increased his distress. 'The whole world is falling apart,' he screamed at director Norman Foster one day, 'and you want me to make a picture!'

Though Mary's health concerns paled beside those of Peter Lorre, she also was far from being at the top of her game. When a reporter visited the *Mr. Moto* set, he observed she didn't touch her lunch and then promptly fell asleep. Mary also confessed to fainting recently on set, but professed not to know what was wrong with her. Although she claimed to not go out or stay up late while making a movie, her social life at this time appeared hectic. In the second half of April, she was twice spotted dancing and dining with Joe Schenck, as well as hitting the town with playboy Billy Seymour and *All Quiet on the Western Front* star Lew Ayres. Mary also managed to fit in an Easter party at La Conga nightclub, where she was one of the most enthusiastic rhumba dancers. But the biggest party during production of *Mr. Moto* was Hearst's seventy-fifth birthday. In keeping with the party's early colonial theme, Marion's Beach House was decor-ated with hundreds of silk American flags and golden eagles, and

Hollywood's elite sat at eighty supper tables draped in red, white and blue. What Mary wore wasn't recorded, but Norma Shearer was breathtaking as Marie Antoinette; Henry Fonda and James Stewart were Minutemen; and Harold Lloyd came as a Russian ambassador. There was Betty Grable as a Southern belle, Jackie Coogan as John Wilkes Booth, and Gary Cooper as a plainsman. The birthday boy was dressed as President James Madison, while Marion wore one of the period costumes from her 1923 classic *Little Old New York*. Coincidentally, Louella Parsons had just publicly urged Fox to remake that very movie, with Mary updating the role that had made Marion a star. It's easy to imagine Mary, her date Joe Schenck, Louella, Marion and W. R. tossing this idea around while the orchestra played waltzes. That night she was surrounded by many other friends who'd helped her make her way in Hollywood: Maureen O'Sullivan, John Farrow, Jack Warner, Cary Grant, David Niven, Basil Rathbone, W. S. Van Dyke, Orry-Kelly, Anita Loos, Tom Brown and his wife, Natalie Draper, Jane Bryan and her future husband, Walgreens drugstore heir Justin Dart. At the stroke of midnight, a huge cake – a replica of the Independence Hall in Philadelphia – was wheeled out and everyone sang to W. R. as the orchestra played 'Happy Birthday to You'.

Mary didn't know it, but this was her Hollywood swansong.

———

That same day Lon Jones of Brisbane's *Telegraph* echoed Ed Sullivan's earlier wedding report, writing 'it is strongly rumoured that Mary Maguire is getting together her trousseau for her marriage to Joseph Schenck'. Noting that she and the 20th Century Fox boss had been seeing a lot of each other, Lon still reckoned Howard Hughes was the 'No. 1 man with her'. Within days Walter Winchell ran the Joe Schenck claim in his column. Mary had been married off by the gossips before; this time there seemed more substance to the story. She and Joe had been close for six months.

Fox's plans for Mary fuelled wedding speculation. After finishing *Mysterious Mr. Moto*, Mary's long-held wish to visit New York and London was granted when she was cast in *Piccadilly Circus*, which would be shot in England as a vehicle for British superstar Gracie Fields. How much influence Joe Schenck exerted isn't known, but as per Mary's contract this assignment provided her with a lot of perks. As she would be working more than fifteen miles from Hollywood, all of her travel, accommodation and other expenses would be taken care of by the studio, meaning she wouldn't need to touch her salary for the three months she was away. She was to take the train to New York and then sail on the *Queen Mary* on 11 May. It was a sweetheart deal. But when Mary was photographed on Joe's arm and with Irving Berlin after stepping off a plane in early May, her glum expression made her look like she was having second thoughts about everything. Still, she left as planned, with Joe buying her and Patricia tickets on the *Super Chief*, 'train of the stars', putting them up at the Waldorf Astoria in New York and arranging for a chauffeured Rolls Royce to whisk them to Broadway shows and fashion boutiques.

What *really* set tongues wagging was news that Joe was to follow Mary to London on the *Queen Mary*'s next voyage less than two weeks later.

The New York press had a lot of questions for Mary. Rumour now had it she and Joe were going to marry soon after he arrived in London. 'I was bombarded with questions about it and gave a flat denial,' Mary said. 'It appears that for the American press the denial was too flat and in some mysterious way they took it to mean "yes" – don't ask me how but they did.' Bina arrived in New York to chaperone Mary in England, the studio paying her fare on the *Queen Mary*, while Patricia returned to Hollywood. Before the Maguires sailed, Mary found time to catch up with friends, including Margaret Vyner, then also about to head to London with her married lover, the actor and writer Hugh Williams. 'As soon as I marry Joe Schenck, you won't have to worry about a job,' Mary was reported by Sheilah Graham to have said to an unnamed friend at one of these farewells. As for Joe, he refused to confirm or deny that he was to marry Mary. 'We are old friends,' was all he said.

PART THREE

England

28.

Mary had come a long way in less than two years. Last time she'd farewelled a port it had been on the *Mariposa* with Mick, sailing under the Sydney Harbour Bridge on the way to Los Angeles. Now she and Bina were on the *Queen Mary* passing the Statue of Liberty bound for London, a city they had always dreamt of visiting. The Atlantic crossing would take five days. Fox shelled out £160 ($US10 200 today) so the Maguires could enjoy the Art Deco luxury of one of the ship's biggest deluxe suites and facilities that made even the *Mariposa* and *Monterey* seem a little modest. Built at a cost of £3.5m ($US300m) and launched in 1936, the *Queen Mary* had a dining room over three storeys that could accommodate eight hundred passengers at each sitting; two indoor swimming pools; a theatre, dedicated cinema and ballroom with parquetry floor; libraries, shops and beauty salons; six acres of decks.

Faded silent-screen legend Gloria Swanson was also a first-class passenger. Her and Mary's paths had crossed socially in Hollywood, and it's likely they renewed their acquaintance during the voyage. Though twenty years apart in age, they had more in common than having held the title of 'Hollywood's smallest feet'. In 1927, Gloria had turned down a $1 million contract with Paramount when Joe Schenck wooed her to United Artists, promising her the chance to make artistic dramas, which he would soon rail against for their lack of commercial appeal. Reflecting on their stormy professional relationship, Gloria called Joe her 'worthy adversary and masterly teacher'. In 1931, after a scandal over her fourth marriage, the pregnant Gloria fled to France with her new husband. Only then did she write to Joe, appealing to his 'sentimental streak' and saying she needed a break from making movies. Instead, he cancelled her United Artists contract – and her career nosedived into nothingness. If Gloria and Mary did talk during their time on the *Queen Mary*, it may have given the young Australian a different and not entirely positive perspective on Joe.

Truth interviewed Mary about Joe halfway across the Atlantic. It's not clear if it was an on-board correspondent or an expensive shore-to-ship call. Either way, her answer was short: 'He's only the boss – a great friend.' Yet everything else in the resulting front-page article pointed – not unreasonably – to a more intimate relationship. 'It was Schenck who arranged for Mary to be present at social functions, to which not even the greater stars could get an invitation,' it explained. 'He escorted her to the races and big executive dinners, and some of the most exclusive parties in the film colony, and he was a constant visitor to the Maguires' home.' The mogul, it said, was nicknamed 'Daddy Schenck' by the Maguires, and he next intended to make a film star out of Joan.

The *Queen Mary* docked at Southampton on May 16. Gloria Swanson was photographed, looking a little matronly in her thick furs, while radiantly smiling Mary looked fresh and cute in her white blouse. She got a rousing welcome at Waterloo Station, where a crowd gathered, cameras clicked, reporters shouted questions and Fox representatives hustled. Perched on a steamer trunk, Mary waved to fans and even had to be rescued by police from a few overenthusiastic admirers. She found it all simply thrilling.

A portrait of Bina and her five daughters. From left to right: Lupe, Bina, Joan, Patricia, Carmel and Mary, who was then known as Peggy. (Used with the kind permission of Norm Archibald)

From 1933, the Maguires ran Brisbane's Belle Vue Hotel, where they hosted elite members of Australian society and visiting international VIPs. (Trove/SLQ)

Still known as Peggy, she appeared in this advertisement for Charles Chauvel's film *Heritage*. (SLQ)

In the Belle Vue's ballroom, the young star had private dance lessons with world-famous Russian ballerina Olga Spessivtseva.

The Maguires chartered a plane to fly Peggy, Patricia and Bina to Sydney for the preview screening of *Heritage* on 20 January 1935. Pioneering aviator George 'Scotty' Allan was their pilot. (National Film and Sound Archive of Australia)

A poster advertising Charles Chauvel's *Heritage*, noting its prize-winning status. (National Film and Sound Archive of Australia)

Now known as Mary, the star was draped in celluloid by her adoring crew – a candid shot taken during the production of *The Flying Doctor*, 1936. (National Film and Sound Archive of Australia)

The cast and crew of *The Flying Doctor* at a function in Sydney. Beside writer Jock Orton, Mary sits at the feet of Charles Farrell, with Margaret Vyner leaning in over the American star.

Mary and Peter Lorre: a publicity still from *Mysterious Mr. Moto*, 1938. (Alamy)

Above: Both Warner Bros. and 20th Century Fox promoted Mary's sultry image.

Right: Mary had star billing along with Ronald Reagan in 1938's *Sergeant Murphy*. (Alamy)

Hollywood talent: Mary, director Miles Mander and Janet Johnson, early 1937.

Mary at Hollywood's Café Lamaze with millionaire scion Alfred Vanderbilt, Jr – one of the many eligible bachelors she dated.

An ad for Lux soap, featuring Mary Maguire, from *The Australian Women's Weekly*, August 1938. Mary's picture regularly appeared in newspaper and magazine ads like this.

(Trove/NLA)

Mary Maguire, Jane Bryan and Jane Wyman (who would become Ronald Reagan's first wife) – 'three film beauties in bright sun suits' as captured by a press photographer at Palm Springs in 1937. (Los Angeles Public Library)

May, 1938. Mary, looking rather glum, with film mogul Joe Schenck and his best friend Irving Berlin. (Los Angeles Public Library)

Mary and Robert Gordon–
Canning on their wedding day.
(Trove/SLV)

Mary and baby Michael at
his christening in June 1941.

MARY MAGUIRE FINDS U.S. LOVER AND <small>BEAUTIFUL DIVORCEE</small>
IS DIVORCED BY HUSBAND
Brisbane Star's Story
(Special—Exclusive—From "Truth's" London Office.)

BEAUTIFUL, brown-eyed Brisbane actress, Mary Maguire, was divorced last Monday in London by Captain Robert Cecil Gordon-Canning, M.C., wealthy British coal-owner, Fascist sympathiser, ex-internee, poet and playwright. She was divorced—at her own insistence, the gallant captain told the court—on the ground of her misconduct with an American officer. Hers is a story of youth and propinquity ousting comparative age in absentia. Because, though Mary didn't tell "Truth" in so many words, she is nevertheless obviously in love with the young American, Philip Legarra, an aeroplane expert.

Article from *Truth*, 26 November 1944 reporting on Mary's divorce and new love.

Philip Legarra was on an important WWII mission when he met Mary. Studio portrait, c. 1943.

(Courtesy Betty Legarra)

Phil and Mary with niece Betty Legarra at a family gathering, late 1960s.

(Courtesy Betty Legarra)

Mary and Bina checked into the Dorchester Hotel, which, since opening in 1931, had become one of London's most elite destinations. Their suite overlooked Hyde Park and was already filled with flowers from well-wishers. Mary hosted a stream of Australian correspondents, who found her looking absurdly young in her fashionable slacks and so excited about being in the city every Australian dreamed of visiting that she could hardly sit still. While she had arrived in Hollywood anxious and anonymous, Mary had landed in London as an established celebrity bound for even greater stardom. During the three months she was to be on this side of the Atlantic, she hoped to see Don Bradman bat and visit her ancestral home in Ireland. She told reporters she was delighted at the prospect of working with Gracie Fields, having seen all her films, and with their canine co-star Skippy, the wire-haired terrier her Hollywood pal W. S. Van Dyke had made world famous as Asta in the *Thin Man* films. There was much to do before cameras rolled on *Piccadilly Circus*. Frocks had to be fitted. She had to learn her script, practise the songs she'd have to sing and brush up on her footwork, because the role also required her to dance – which she confessed scared her a little.

Meeting reporter Vena Yates, whom she would come to favour, Mary remembered the booster role that Yates's newspaper had supposedly played in winning her the role in *Heritage*.

'You did say *The Telegraph*, Brisbane, didn't you?'
'I did.'
'That's great – do come in. You see it was due to *The Telegraph* that I got my first chance in films.'

The *Sydney Morning Herald*'s Betty Wilson was impressed by Mary's collection of colourful hats, which had apparently already caused Londoners to stare, and her seven-stone stature, purportedly the result of her naturally 'bird-like appetite' that saw her get by on a cup of tea for breakfast, a green salad for lunch and a grilled chop for dinner.

Speaking with *The Australian Women's Weekly*'s correspondent Mary St. Claire, Mary said she was determined to get roles that allowed her to express her individuality:

> 'However, you can always get what you want in Hollywood if you know how to fight for it,' said Mary. Asked if she found the fighting difficult, Mary smiled. 'Well, I am an Australian of Irish ancestors, so I guess I can fight if necessary.'

Queried about going to Australia for a visit, her answer might have been influenced by recent contact with washed-up Gloria Swanson.

> 'I hope to return home at the completion of present contracts, but I can't stay away from films for long.' Miss Maguire said that the star who makes a successful comeback in films even after a year's absence is rare.

Editorialising, Mary St. Claire made good points about Mary's career so far:

> She is coming to be known here as 'the star who has not made a big picture'. Most interest seems to be centred not on what she has already done, but her possibilities in the future . . . Although Mary's Hollywood pictures have not been of the super box office class, she has done well in the parts given her. 'But is that enough to justify stardom?' the film world is asking. Mary needs films, not fame, at the moment to establish herself.

Ever helpful, Bina chimed in when the *Maitland Mercury*'s correspondent said that Mary had been good in *Alcatraz Island*.

Mrs Maguire wrinkled up her nose and gave me to understand that in her opinion Mary was not so hot. 'She's much
better in *Sergeant Murphy*, the racing film which she did next,'
she informed me: 'and we hope she'll be better still in *The
Mysterious Mr Moto*, which we haven't seen yet.'

The Australian scribes didn't ask about Joe Schenck – or at least
didn't print anything. In any event, his trip to England had been
postponed due to business in Hollywood. But Joe made sure Mary
didn't forget him, bombarding her with flowers, phone calls and
half a dozen or more cables a day. He provided a Daimler and
uniformed chauffeur to take her and Bina around London. Indeed,
documents held at 20th Century Fox's archive show that Mary's
expenses – for hotels, transportation, meals, maids, manservants
and miscellaneous items – then averaged £70 ($A8000) a week,
which was on top of her £110 ($A12 640) weekly salary. Joe
also arranged for Mary to meet his friend the press baron Lord
Beaverbrook, with whom he'd chased starlets back in the 1920s.
Beaverbrook invited her to his mansion 'Cherkley', and, following
his lead, British lords, ladies and millionaires then lined up to
throw dinner parties for Mary and offer to sponsor her in society.
One of these aristocrats was pro-Hitler, pro-appeasement Lord
Rothermere, owner of Associated Newspapers, who had written
the notorious 'Hurrah for the Blackshirts' editorial praising Sir
Oswald Mosley's fascists in his *Daily Mail* newspaper.

Out at Pinewood Studios, Mary, Gracie and the rest of the cast
did a script read-through. That the screenplay made any sense at
all was something of a minor miracle, having tortuous origins
that showed just how controlling Darryl F. Zanuck could be with
Fox films. *Picadilly Circus* was based on a treatment called *The
Boy, the Girl and the Dog*, set in Budapest and meant as a vehicle

for Sonja Henie. Zanuck had ordered a complete rewrite and the inclusion of three ice-skating scenes. When this new version was delivered he objected to almost everything. 'Mr. Zanuck does not want to use any of the main characters you have,' read a Fox memo now held at the University of Southern California's archive, 'with the exception of the boy – although there are several aspects of his character that must be eliminated.' The production chief suggested that this male character shouldn't be a stock-market expert but a 'truck-driver – with ambitions to write the Great American Novel'. This development hell continued for months, with the story location shifted to New York and Zanuck's attentions turning to the canine character. 'The way the dog is now written is great, only take out the tricks,' he ordered. Rewrites continued until somehow the yarn was set in England and became a vehicle for Gracie Fields.

Gracie would play Gracie Grey, the leader of a musical-comedy troupe on the skids after falling out with their crooked manager, Sneed. Gracie's niece Avis – Mary's character – and her shifty boyfriend Denis find a lost dog and discover that the mutt is Mr Skip, pet of the world-famous pianist Rene Sigani, who has offered a £100 reward. Denis wants to take the money and run, but Avis insists they tell Gracie so the reward can go towards putting the troupe back on its feet. Meanwhile, Rene is so taken with Avis that he joins this merry band. Jealous Denis conspires with Sneed to undermine the troupe, first sinking the riverboat they've rented as a venue and then sabotaging their big theatre show by trapping Avis and Rene in a theme park castle. Mr Skip saves the day by alerting Gracie and co. to their predicament. The baddies get their comeuppance, the show goes on, and the young lovers marry as Gracie watches on tearfully.

Directed by Monty Banks – Gracie Fields' frequent collaborator and soon-to-be husband – *Piccadilly Circus* was renamed *Keep*

Smiling midway through production (and would be released in the US as *Smiling Along*). Slight but charming, the film gave Mary a chance to demonstrate her comic timing. Her biggest laugh came when, during the sinking sequence, she thinks a squirt of water from floorboards up her skirt is the work of a gent with a soda syphon – and slaps him indignantly. The film showed she could sing a little, dance nicely and even punch out a villain to protect her piano player's precious fingers. Behind the scenes, the production offered other pleasures. Leading lady Gracie was warm-hearted, good-humoured and always ready with a funny story. 'Ah, that reminds me,' she'd say before launching into another amusing anecdote in her broad Lancashire accent. Equally adorable was Skippy, the cast's canine star. Mary, who loved terriers and would soon buy a sweet little Sealyham, was smitten. So was Gracie, who had a paw-print stamp made up so Skippy could give 'autographs' to his fans. Visiting the studio, *The Telegraph*'s Vena Yates reported that the young Australian was held in high regard, not least because she treated everyone as an equal regardless of their status in the cast-and-crew pecking order. Mary certainly won the heart of her stand-in with a personalised photo whose inscription read: 'To Stella – Hoping I will never have a stand-in outside of you. With thanks – Mary.'

London was more sedate than Hollywood – though Mary, now renting a Mayfair Mews house for Bina while she continued to live at the Dorchester on the studio dime, enjoyed a healthy social life. Australian cricketers escorted her to a reception, and she caught up with Douglas Jardine. She went to the Savoy Hotel for dinner with a group that included David Niven, and attended a charity garden party in Regent's Park, where she, Raymond Massey, Adolphe Menjou and Margaret Vyner mingled with fans and charged a few shillings for autographs or kisses. According to one observer, Mary was barely visible behind the admirers crowding her stall.

Yet her number one fan, Joe Schenck, was still stuck in the United States. His trip had been delayed again, this time because he and other studio bosses were summoned to a secret White House powwow with President Roosevelt to discuss proposed laws meant to curb the movie industry's monopolistic practices.

In Melbourne, Mary's maternal aunt Marguerite and paternal grandfather, Michael, gave an interview to the *Sun-Pictorial* to describe reports about any marriage to Joe Schenck as 'absurd gossip'. In modern parlance, this seemed an attempt to 'get ahead of the story'. The newspaper reported on 2 July: 'Both have had letters from the Maguire family abroad telling them that there has never been a suggestion of such a romance.' Even so, Marguerite still seemed to have her doubts: 'After all that's been published about her it's hard to tell the true story.' The very next day, Mary and Joe were news again when Brisbane's *Truth* ran an exclusive front-page story about their imminent marriage. The article was packed with specifics about Joe's flowers and cables and chauffeured car. Mary Pickford was rumoured to be a guest at the wedding, which would be attended by many other film stars – and all of the Maguire family. The source for the story could hardly be impeached: all these glittering details had been in a letter from Bina dated 20 June. Given the paper had been handed such a scoop, the article's mocking tone was perhaps payback for Mary recently buttering up Vena Yates of rival Brisbane newspaper *The Telegraph*. The article said she had until recently been a 'beautiful, rather dumb, little schoolgirl' before continuing: 'No matter whether one likes Mary as a screen actress or thinks she just isn't one, it must be admitted that nothing more fantastic has ever befallen an Australian girl in search of fame.' The unattributed piece went on to depict her as a gold-digger willing to overlook the fact that Joe was 'no oil painting': 'If a girl is ambitious and has not that incurable romanticism of the young dreamers, very possibly she would like to be wife of a man whose millions excite the world, and who could dictate to her own film companies like Mary Pickford if she wished to.'

The ink still drying on the *Truth* story, Mary issued her strongest denial yet. 'When will these rumours end?' she said in an exclusive given to Vena Yates. 'Mr Schenck is a great friend of my father and family and often visits us. I am definitely not contemplating marriage with him or anyone else at the moment.' Then 20th Century Fox – in effect Joe himself – took the unusual step of releasing an official rebuttal: 'The report would be equally feasible or equally ridiculous if Mary's name were coupled with that of any of several young men who escort her. The Schenck rumours began in America early this year and have recurred from time to time with no foundation whatever.'

Mary met with Vena again a few days later at Pinewood Studios. 'I'll probably lose my job if these rumours continue,' she worried. 'But his visit to England has nothing whatever to do with me, and what on earth Mr Schenck thinks of all these stories I don't know. As I told you the other day, Mr Schenck is a great friend of my father's and he is frequently at our house. Once or twice he has taken me out just as he has often taken out other members of his company.' Even sympathetic Vena was aware of the inconsistencies in such denials. Everyone was. Mary and Joe hadn't been out once or twice but had repeatedly hit Hollywood's hottest spots, enjoyed weekends away at Palm Springs, and been cosy at many of the film colony's swankiest events and parties, including seating her among wives at the Fox table at the Oscars. While the mogul had discreetly seen other women, he hadn't publicly bestowed a diamond bracelet on another girl or signed her to his studio in such public fashion. Joe was chummy with Mick, but he hadn't been visiting him at the Hillside house during the nearly two months the old bruiser had spent getting to and from Australia earlier in the year. Vena's facial expression saw Mary's temper flare. 'Please don't sit there looking as though you don't know whether to believe me or not,' she snapped. In the end, after quizzing her co-workers, who all said there was nothing to the rumours – as they could be expected to do, as Fox employees – Vena wrote that she believed Mary.

A few days later, Joe finally sailed from New York aboard the *Normandie*. With this the liner's 100th Atlantic crossing, the *Brooklyn Daily Eagle* sent a reporter to get quotes from notables heading up the gangway, including Benny Goodman, who dissed English swing bands, and Alfred Hitchcock, who praised American roast beef. Usually gregarious Joe was taciturn. 'I am a disappointment,' he said. 'I have no news.'

Given how much attention Joe had showered upon Mary, it is likely he wanted to marry her – and that Bina believed her daughter was in favour of the wedding when she penned her *Truth* letter. Around this time, Mick also told the *Los Angeles Times* he thought his daughter was about to become Mrs Joe Schenck.

Being a girlfriend to a mogul was one thing and a wife another. While marrying Joe might not have guaranteed stardom, it would have given Mary a powerful position in Hollywood. Yet she appears to have refused. To understand why it's instructive to look at what a marriage proposal from this movie mogul may have entailed. The only way to do this is to skip ten years ahead to the third woman to whom Joe was seriously linked: Marilyn Monroe. In 1948, according to several biographers, Joe hired the aspiring actress to be a party girl who would hang out at his mansion and have sex with him and his friends. But he became so fond of Marilyn that he proposed. Well aware of his age and physical limitations, Joe said he wouldn't mind if she had other lovers – just so long as she didn't sleep with the same man twice in a row. He also told her it wouldn't be too long before she would inherit his fabulous wealth. Marilyn thought it over and refused.

Mary may have been made a similar offer. Joe was already in his sixties when they met, and newspaper reports of her other high-profile escorts in late 1937 and early 1938 suggest he hadn't insisted on an exclusive relationship. In the end, Mary's romantic nature may have won out over her career ambitions. However it happened, they were done personally – but Joe was still her boss and she was still locked into an ironclad contract.

29.

Joe doesn't seem to have seen Mary when he arrived in England, and he spent most of the next six weeks on the Continent. Nor did he stay long enough to attend the London premiere of *Alexander's Ragtime Band*, where Mary hit the red carpet and was interviewed for the newsreels, along with the film's subject, Irving Berlin, and rising star George Sanders. Joe set sail from England on 31 August and arrived in New York on 5 September to find his life about to be turned upside down.

It was now public knowledge that Joe had given Willie Bioff a cheque for $100 000, with the payment appearing awfully like a pay-off for union peace. Joe called the allegations 'ridiculous', but he had to know he was in deep trouble. The federal government was gunning for him – and if he told the truth, the Chicago Mob might literally do just that.

Mary had dodged a bullet with Joe and was happy the next time she spoke with Vena Yates. 'She appeared heart-whole,' wrote the *Telegraph* reporter. 'Or should I say perhaps that her heart and her enthusiasms are divided among so many things – the chief of them being her work – that there is simply no room in them for any serious thought of romance or marriage at the moment.'

Mary was heart-whole, but Bina was again suffering from the cardiac complaint that had troubled her in Brisbane. Mick sailed to be by her side, arriving in September, followed shortly after by Joan. With Bina recovering well, she and Mick made plans to return to Hollywood to look after Carmel and Lupe. But Joan was intent on staying in London to make her mark in the theatre. Determined to do so on her own merit, she stuck a pin into a random page of the phone book and came up with her new stage surname: Joan Shannon.

Mysterious Mr. Moto opened in America to mostly good reviews. *Hollywood Spectator* thought it the best of the series, *Boxoffice* reckoned the character advanced another notch towards 'top flight popularity' and *Film Daily* rated the cast as 'excellent'. *Variety* thought the story hackneyed and the dialogue not brilliant, but conceded that the important element – action – was in abundance. The reviewer criticised Mary's love interest as 'colourless' and thought she seemed more like his boss than his secretary. Australian reviews ran the usual gamut. Sydney's *Daily Telegraph* thought she showed 'new confidence', while *The Sun* opined that 'her work shows considerable improvement on former appearances. Her voice has gained a richer tone and her delivery is steadier and has more polish.' *The Australian Women's Weekly* said 'she does a great job – though the part is not one that calls for subtle acting'. But *Table Talk*'s verdict was vituperative:

> I have seen this Australian actress in several parts now, and they are all modelled along the same, slight lines. It would seem that those responsible for giving her the parts fully appreciated her limitations, and thus made her characters as elementary as possible . . . but if the Hollywood powers-that-be are quite satisfied that Mary will never improve one iota, why give her parts at all? That is a mystery I defy even Mr Moto to unravel.

On the same day Joe Schenck arrived back in New York City, Darryl F. Zanuck did a deal for Mary with Walter C. Mycroft, head of production at Associated British Picture Corporation (ABPC). Fox would now charge £160 a week for her when she was in production on an ABPC film, helping the studio recoup the cost of her salary and most of her expenses. That this happened so soon after Mary and Joe's friendship soured could have been seen as him using his power for payback. But despite his many flaws, he wasn't one to hold a grudge, having remained on good post-relationship terms with Norma Talmadge, as he would later with Marilyn Monroe. If he had a hand in the decision, which seems likely, he was actually giving Mary what she wanted most: a chance at leading roles in the classy dramatic pictures for which ABPC was known. Indeed, Fox documents specifically mention that the deal wasn't intended to make a profit but to find Mary roles that would be beneficial to her career. Of course, from Joe's point of view, it also wouldn't hurt that the deal would keep Mary away a while longer. Her absence from Hollywood would help him keep his pride. It might also stop her being subpoenaed about how he spent his money if the federal government's case came to that.

But staying in London under a Fox contract deprived Mary of another opportunity to be loaned out in Hollywood. Maxwell Arnow, who had remained her admirer even after she defected from Warners, had himself left the studio and was now casting *Gone with the Wind* for David O. Selznick. Mary's former studio mate Olivia de Havilland got a plum role as Melanie Hamilton, while Breezy Eason directed the first scene shot of the epic production when he used his action skills to orchestrate the burn-ing-of-Atlanta sequence.

Mary was announced as the lead in ABPC's period Russian drama *Black Eyes* but before it commenced production she went to Paris for what was meant to be a two-week holiday. On the first day she ran into ABPC production chief Walter Mycroft in the lounge of her hotel, where he was spending the weekend. Though he had met her many times before, seeing Mary in this new context apparently inspired an epiphany. 'You may not know it, but you are going straight back to London to begin work on my picture,' he told her. Mycroft was talking about an A-picture called *The Outsider*. And he meant to really *star* her in the film: Mary would be top-billed over her leading man George Sanders. While she had been a supporting player in *Keep Smiling*, this was the realisation of another of her long-cherished goals. Her name would be up in lights in London before her twenty-first birthday.

London was tense and grim when Mary returned. Trenches were being dug and sandbags stacked in the expectation that England would soon be at war with Germany over Hitler's annexation of the Sudetenland region of Czechoslovakia. Then at the end of September came relief mixed with shame: Prime Minister Neville Chamberlain had appeased the Nazi dictator in order to avert war, then returned to 10 Downing Street waving a scrap of paper he said ensured 'Peace for our time'.

The Outsider was based on the Dorothy Brandon play of the same name that had been filmed in 1926 and again in 1931, with both versions shown in Melbourne when Mary had lived there. She was playing Lalage Sturdee, a talented young pianist made lame as a child by a quack doctor. While her friends enjoy pool parties and tennis afternoons, Lally is relegated to the sidelines, tortured by society's pitying gaze and the fear that her boyfriend will eventually take a more robust specimen of womanhood as his wife. Her only hope is George Sanders' arrogant and eccentric Dr Anton Ragatzy, who has a thriving practice curing cripples with his experimental electrical stretching rack, in defiance of the medical establishment that includes Lally's own surgeon father. After initial resistance, she agrees to a year-long treatment, during which time her boyfriend proves faithless as Ragatzy's bedside manner becomes increasingly irresistible.

Mary worked long hours on *The Outsider* for seven weeks from early September, getting to set before dawn and filming until well after sunset. Each day began with the studio's stylist subjecting her to an intensive hair-care routine, which included egg shampoo, herbal rinse, setting her locks in curls and waves, and then brushing for half an hour. Only then was she ready for rehearsals, which started at nine o'clock. All the effort was worth it, with Mary glowing in the production. Less glamorously, *The Outsider* also required her to spend days on end confined to the rack-bed on the film's nursing-home set. In between takes, she found it easier to remain prone while the cameramen adjusted lighting rather than climb out and have her stand-in take her place. Visitors to the nursing-home set would invariably creep over to her and speak in gentle whispers, as though she really was an invalid.

A little lonely now that Mick and Bina had returned to America, Mary took comfort in the fact that Elaine Hamill, whom she had known in Brisbane, was playing the role of her nurse. She could also get a taste of home at Tony's, the new ultra-smart West End restaurant run by an expat who'd worked at Sydney nightspots Romano's and Ambassadors. Aussies gathered there to enjoy the house specialty, chicken supreme, and a glass or two of fine wine as they talked about what was happening back home. Carlton had beaten Collingwood in the VFL Grand Final; there had been another bloody awful plane crash that saw eighteen people killed when a Douglas DC-2 crashed in the Dandenong Ranges; and Prime Minister Joseph Lyons' government was increasingly in disarray. *Keep Smiling* opened to so-so reviews and even Vena Yates was less than thrilled at how her friend had been utilised: 'Why rush an actress all those thousands of miles for a part such as the one Mary has in *Keep Smiling*?' she later asked. Those who had followed the Schenck saga could guess at the answer. 'She plays her part well and if there is no indication of brilliance it is the fault of the part and not the player.'

The Outsider wrapped in late October. After a two-week break, during which ABPC was only required to pay Fox an £80 retaining fee, Mary started work on *Black Eyes*, top-billed in the script above her co-star Otto Kruger. The film was a remake of the 1935 French movie *Les Yeux Noirs*, which had helped catapult French actress Simone Simon – one of Mary's doppelgangers – to fame and a 20th Century Fox contract. *Black Eyes* was set in Russia before the Great War, with Mary playing Tania – another sickly waif with a talent for the piano – whose darling father deceives her into thinking he's a big businessman when he's merely a head waiter. Director Herbert Brenon knew a little something about Australian actresses, having collaborated on numerous films with Annette Kellerman – the most famous of which was 1916's *A Daughter of the Gods*, controversial as the first feature to show a female star completely nude. There was nothing nearly as racy about *Black Eyes*, which required Mary only to be wooed by a sinister lothario played by Walter Rilla before succumbing to the charms of a more innocent chap played by fellow Australian John Wood.

Around this time, another piece of news from home had to make Mary heartsick: Marjorie Norval, that plucky regular at Belle Vue functions, had got out of a car at Brisbane railway station on 11 November and not been seen since. A £500 reward hadn't produced any useful information. Tragically, an RAAF plane involved in the search hit a high-tension wire, crashed and exploded, killing all four crewmen. A botched abortion and cover-up, just like Bertha Coughlan's fate after leaving the Belle Vue in 1923, eventually emerged as the leading theory, but Marjorie's body was never found and the mystery endures.

A Fox telegram dated 11 November indicated that Mary
expected to be back in Hollywood a month later. She told studio
executives that she'd like their help getting a work permit for her
chauffeur-manservant, 26-year-old Irish-born Drummond Pilson.
It's not known whether Mary was simply again being nice to a
worker who depended on her, or whether she had feelings for
this man. In any event, Fox told her they couldn't help and that
he would have to go through normal immigration channels.

During production of *Black Eyes*, Mary still found time for a
social life. She went to the London premiere of *Marie Antoinette*
with Hal Diamond, part of the American comic trio Diamond
Brothers, and accompanied John Wood and another Australian
actress named Judy Kelly to the annual Film Ball at the Royal
Albert Hall. Mary also cheerfully lent her presence to charitable
fetes and competitions.

Patricia was back in town, having arrived on the *Normandie* with
Miles Mander. Fully recovered, Mary's mentor was in London for
the premiere of his latest film *Suez*, for which he was winning
rave reviews as Benjamin Disraeli. But finding time to catch up
with Patricia and Miles wasn't easy. Mary was annoyed that on
several occasions while she was entertaining guests on her scheduled days off, Walter Mycroft called up asking her to come in
and shoot this or that angle or scene for *Black Eyes*.

As winter approached, Joan's profile was increasing. She had
attended the premiere of *Suez* with Miles, their photo making the
society magazines, and had been cast as the lead in a pantomime
to be staged in Glasgow for two months from early December.
But Patricia remained adrift. Though she had apparently done
some singing and radio drama work in Hollywood, she had listed
her occupation as 'none' with immigration authorities and put on
more weight than thought sensible for a girl with even a vague
hope of being an actress at the time.

Mary's health problems continued. She had fainted on set halfway into making *Black Eyes*. Coming back to consciousness, she insisted on continuing. 'It's nothing,' she told cast and crew. Then, on 27 November, she had piercing abdominal pain. Again, she insisted on carrying on – only to collapse and be sent home. The next day she was rushed to hospital for an appendectomy. As much as was possible, director Herbert Brenon shot around her, and Walter Mycroft kept her co-stars Otto Kruger and Walter Rilla busy by finding them roles in another of his films. Per ABPC's agreement with Fox, they didn't have to pay for her services if she was sick. While the American studio wasn't obliged to pay Mary's salary, they did have to cover her expenses as she was still officially on assignment more than fifteen miles from Hollywood. She was 'convalescing charmingly' according to Brisbane's *Sunday Mail*, which published a photo of her smiling from her hospital bed, cheered up by her Sealyham terrier and a profusion of flowers. Mary stayed in hospital until 9 December – which meant missing out on Joan's European debut in Glasgow – and then departed for Switzerland to convalesce.

Mary returned to *Black Eyes* on 10 January, doing her love scenes with John Wood. She appeared recovered, taking tea with a reporter for *Framlingham Weekly News*:

> She looked fit and strong again, and I asked her how she had made such a complete recovery. 'When I reached my nursing home in Switzerland I told the people I left "black eyes" at home and they became very sympathetic and looked after me well,' she said with a wicked twinkle in her eye which bespoke a born leg-puller.

Vena Yates visited the set and found her friend – nicknamed 'one-take Mary' by her colleagues – at the top of her game, faultlessly learning, rehearsing and performing six script pages per day. 'We are getting through splendidly and will be finished well within the scheduled time,' said her director.

Mary had a lot of wonderful opportunities to consider after she finished *Black Eyes*. Fox wanted her back in Hollywood. ABPC hoped to star her in further films. Gaumont-British was said to want to loan her for a production. And Mary had also been offered the lead role in a West End stage adaptation of the recent hit movie *Prison Without Bars*. She wasn't just in demand because of her beauty: she had proved herself as an actress.

The Outsider launched that week with a lunch at the Dorchester Hotel – including kangaroo soup served in her honour. 'Without exception the critics have expressed their delight in Mary's fine handling of the part,' Vena reported. She wasn't exaggerating. 'The bewitching beauty and talent of Mary Maguire, young Australian actress, is a great asset to British films,' said *The Era*. 'She gives a strong dramatic performance here.' The *Sunday Express* concurred: 'It is good to see the very young and lovely Miss Maguire have a real chance in a good-sized part. She looks angelically appealing, and wins the utmost sympathy.' The *Daily Sketch* also thought her great: 'Mary Maguire, as the crippled girl, yields with a lovely simplicity and a trustfulness that claims our sympathy and creates suspense.' Mary was on a career high and appeared spoilt for choice when it came to her next move.

But her future wasn't hers to determine – not as a Fox contract player. 'I'm saying nothing and am leaving it for the office to decide for me,' she said diplomatically. 'I honestly don't mind which way it goes.'

What Mary could control were her earnings, after she legally emancipated herself from Mick and Bina in the Californian courts on 27 January 1939. There was no suggestion her parents had in any way compromised her career or misappropriated her money – as was so common with other child stars – and it was more likely that, about to turn twenty and living away from them in London, Mary simply desired the freedom over her own finances.

Director Herbert Brenon had tempted fate by saying *Black Eyes* would finish on time. With just a few days of filming left, Mary was laid out by a serious case of influenza. Production shut down again as she tried to recuperate. Being sick put Mary down in the dumps, not helped by the fact that Joan was still touring Scotland and Patricia had returned to Hollywood. True to her reputation as a trouper, she was back on set a week later even though not fully recovered. When Herbert Brenon called cut on Mary's last scene, she forgot herself and announced she was returning to America *and* taking a long-overdue holiday. Now Mary tempted fate when she added, 'And nobody and nothing on earth is going to stop me.'

What Mary didn't know was that more than a month earlier Darryl F. Zanuck had decided not to exercise the option on her contract, which would have seen her signed for another year at $750 a week. Instead there now came a substitute offer. Fox was willing to renew her at $500 per week. She agreed verbally, confirmed the deal in a telegram and signed the new paperwork sent to her by Fox lawyers. Then Fox revealed its true intent: they were selling her contract to ABPC. Mary was reportedly happy with this – though she didn't know Fox was pocketing £1000 ($US80 000) from the deal.

Mick was furious. Arriving in London, he took Fox to task. While Mary was legally emancipated from him and Bina, she was still a minor and unable to legally sign a binding contract under American law. Why, he asked, should Fox set the terms of any agreement with ABPC after the studio had already advised in writing that it wasn't renewing her contract? Mick argued that she was free under British law to make her own deal with ABPC. Further, as Fox's actions had made her believe she had to stay in London through February, she would now happily bill Fox for all her expenses. Remarkably, given how often the studios had the upper hand in such matters, Mick had Fox over a barrel. They had to cancel the deal. Mary didn't bill for the month's expenses, but nor did she repay the nearly £800 in 'personal expenses' she'd billed to the studio in the past nine months. The studio had no choice but to conclude that he was right – and the deal was cancelled.

Mary signed with ABPC in mid-March, though the terms of the contract aren't known. On a cold and foggy morning, she and Maureen O'Hara represented the company at a film industry soccer game for the newsreel cameras. Soon after, Mary was again too sick to work, her influenza having returned with such a vengeance that she was under doctor's orders to take a complete rest. Her mood was lifted when Joan returned from Scotland and by the news that her mother and other sisters were coming to live in England. Despite her ill health, she was reported as racing around Elstree, in Hertfordshire, trying to find a house big enough for them all. She then took a cruise around Madeira, hoping the sun and sea air would speed her recovery.

Bina, Patricia, Carmel and Lupe arrived on 11 April, and Mary was photographed laughing with delight as she took the bottom position in a stack with these sisters. The symbolism was telling: she was supporting her siblings. All except hard-working Joan. But no sooner had the clan set foot in London than it was decided the new arrivals were to live in France, where Carmel and Lupe would finish their educations at a convent school. Mary claimed it as her idea. 'First I thought of giving them a house in London,' she said. 'Then I changed my plans, made it Cannes instead so that I could have a good excuse to go to the South of France between pictures.'

Moving the Maguire family was complicated by a very large piece of furniture they had insisted on taking from Brisbane to

Hollywood and London and on to Cannes. 'One thing they have to carry around the world with them is a large dining-room table – the only one they have been able to find which will house comfortably the whole family,' Brisbane's *Telegraph* reported. Given they were a family of seven rather than seventeen, it seems more likely the table in question was kept not for its size but because it had been made for the former King of England, Edward VIII.

The Maguires and their table moved into Villa Esterel, which Mary rented from an aged countess. The mansion was surrounded by gardens of magnolia and mimosa, and had big sun-drenched balconies that offered sweeping views of the Bay of Cannes and Esterel Massif. It was prettier than anywhere they had lived before, and Mary hired five servants to ensure her family was well looked after. Bina recognised it as a fine place for her daughters to find wealthy husbands, given how many rich and powerful European men flocked to the French Riviera. A *Truth* columnist recalled Carmel and Lupe 'startling the natives along the waterfront at Cannes with their lissome young Australian bodies . . . the two imps really were kids then. Kids who knew where they were heading, even at that supposedly tender age!' 'The season was in full swing,' Mary St. Claire of *The Australian Women's Weekly* wrote. 'The Maguire girls were lovely and charming. To the villa flocked young English aristocrats, Continental millionaires and well-known society people.' *Truth* columnist Ruby Eve caught the 'Blue Train' across France for a reunion with the Maguires, sharing her carriage with Mary Pickford, also a regular guest at Villa Esterel. Other visitors included actresses Mae Murray and Norma Shearer, debonair actor Paul Lukas and his fellow Hungarian the Baroness Orczy, author of *The Scarlet Pimpernel*. It was in Cannes that Patricia first met Lord Beaverbrook's younger son, the racing-car driver Peter Aitken, and Carmel made the acquaintance of Derek Dunnett, sole heir to the Carter's Tested Seeds fortune. Disappointingly, both men were married.

Mary left her family soaking up the sun and entertaining the rich and famous, and returned to London to continue working. But she was unwell and lonely. That was until Miles Mander introduced her to one of his old friends: the aristocratic soldier-poet Robert Gordon-Canning.

30.

Robert Gordon-Canning cut an impressive figure: standing six feet, four inches, he was broad shouldered and carried himself with military bearing. Though not conventionally handsome – his long face attenuated further by a bald pate framed by fair tufts – Robert was a man of charm, intelligence and wealth. Women were drawn to him though he had a reputation for being romantically aloof – harsh, even – and at fifty he was yet to marry.

Robert and Miles had been friends for nearly twenty years, and the two men had much in common. Born six weeks apart with silver spoons in their mouths, they had both served King and Country in the Great War before seeking lives as artists, activists and adventurers. Robert was born on 24 June 1888 and claimed ancestry from the poet Lord Byron and British Prime Minister George Canning. After graduating Eton and despite the asthma that would trouble him all his life, he joined the 10th Royal Hussars cavalry regiment and found himself on the Western Front soon after the start of the Great War. Robert was there for the impromptu truce in No Man's Land in 1914 at Christmas when British and German soldiers stopped fighting to sing carols and exchange gifts. The experience left him with the lasting feeling that the two nations should be allied – and that the slaughter that began again the next day was even more senseless. Nevertheless, Robert did his duty for the next four years. He distinguished himself in fierce battles at Ypres and Arras, was promoted from lieutenant to captain, and received the Military Cross for his bravery. As a leader of one of the last-ever cavalry units to see modern warfare, he hated the endless sacrifice of horses and, beloved by his men, he was called 'Lucky Bobby' after a bullet ripped through his helmet but caused only a tiny wound atop his head.

With the war over, Robert remained a Hussar reservist but turned his attention to wandering in the Middle East and North Africa. Like Lord Byron, he pursued literature. His 1920 book *Flashlights from Afar* is a collection of war poetry, many of the grim blank verses penned on the front lines. In 'The Somme Battle-Field', he observed: 'The spirits of the dead and living that have passed this way have photographed their agony on the air/The air is full of the terror of the living, the curses of the wounded, the moaning of the mutilated.' His 'No Man's Land' depicts the hellscape he called home for four years: 'Shell-holes, grenades that have failed to explode and dud shell; rifles, haversacks, gas helmets, derelict, in all stages of rottenness; and human bodies twisted and distorted, the delight of rats.' Robert's postwar travels were more romantic. 'From Alexandria to the Italian Alps', contained in his 1922 collection *A Pagan Shrine*, heralded a belief in the spirituality and superiority of the ancient and natural over the modern and artificial: 'I have left the parasite fountains/ Of gold, and disease, and show/For the old and the silent mountains/And the pure pale airs of the snow.' He was also moved by youthful beauty, with 'To a Young Girl of 16 Years' a feverishly overwrought ode to the sun-kissed body of a virgin: 'Someone, someday will take thy full-blown flower/Then why not I, thy young bright bud of May/Open with my lips all in one warm passionate hour/Thy quivering petals for a summer's day.' The aphorisms that filled this volume's final pages depicted a soul still wearied by the war and Western society. 'Duty is a banquet hall for the elders, but a burial ground for youth,' claimed one. 'The cruelty of tiger and savage is infinitesimal when compared to that of civilisation,' said another. Then there were Robert's suspicions about the opposite sex: 'The divinity of a woman is her Satanic soul'. Robert later expanded on this theme in an unproduced play, *Saviours of England*, about husband-hunting American girls. These women, he wrote, were like American cocktails: 'Direct, unsentimental, never subtle. They give one a hearty slap on the back.' Neither could they be trusted. 'I am an American girl,' said one vamp, 'like a rock under the mid-day sun – a warm exterior but a cold interior.'

In the early 1820s, before he became prime minister, George Canning as foreign secretary advocated a Britain-first policy and argued for the independence of Spanish colonies. At this time, Lord Byron went to Greece to help fight for their liberation from the Ottoman Empire, spending his fortune on the cause and dying of illness while preparing an attack on the Turks. One century later Robert, influenced by his claimed forebears, found his cause visiting Morocco, where the country's Berber-speaking Rif tribes were at war with their Spanish colonial oppressors – who were getting military support from the French. By 1924 Robert was secretary of the Rifs Association in London, where he had a fellow activist in Miles Mander, who had been to Morocco with a theatrical troupe. While Miles limited himself to writing pro-Rif articles, Robert applied to the War Office for permission to take a Red Cross hospital to the rebels. MI5 suspected him of running guns to the Rif and lobbying to prevent the export of British warplanes to the Spanish. The security service began monitoring Robert, with the first letter they intercepted from him to a Rif colleague opening with: 'How are you? Still working against the French? So am I.' Nevertheless, returning to Morocco in late 1925, Robert got permission from the French, who had encircled the Rif mountain base, to cross the lines to meet with rebel chief Abd el-Krim and secure terms of a truce. When Robert returned in January 1926 these terms were rejected, and France and Spain launched the vicious final assault that would defeat the Rif.

Three years later Robert played peacemaker again, this time in Palestine, working as a mediator between the British government and Arab leaders enraged that, in their opinion, the Balfour Declaration was robbing them to enrich Jewish immigrants. When riots broke out soon after, leaving more than two hundred and fifty Arabs and Jews dead, Robert was suspected of having incited the violence and having worked against British interests. It was a claim he hotly denied, for he saw himself first and foremost as a patriot. Speaking at the 1933 dinner of the Old Comrades Association of the 10th Royal Hussars, he summed up his beliefs:

> England is today, in the words of Winston Churchill, still the best country to live in for either Duke or Dustman. The glory of England does not reside in our politicians, in our financiers or in our journalists with the vulgarity of the popular press, but in the Royal Family, in the landed aristocracy, in the constable and in the rank and file of such Regiments as the 10th Hussars. People who, in a position of responsibility, in the words of Shakespeare, 'Hold their honour higher than their life.'

Robert eschewed political party membership until he read Sir Oswald Mosley's *The Greater Britain* in early 1934 and concluded that The Leader of the British Union of Fascists (BUF) had a convincing program for the development of the country. His and Mosley's mutual friend William Allen — another former Rif

ally – introduced the two men. They clicked personally and polit-
ically, with Robert joining the BUF and donning the Blackshirt
uniform. He was convinced the party could save England from
war, injustice, economic collapse and communist overthrow.
He quickly became one of The Leader's most trusted advisers
and friends, and even devised the party slogan 'Mind Britain's
Business'. By the mid-1930s, his pro-Arabism had dovetailed with
his growing anti-Semitism.

Robert's pamphlet *The Holy Land: Arab or Jew?* argued for Arab
rights in Palestine while saying Jews already there should be guaranteed protection and legal rights. He also claimed to support the
establishment of a Jewish homeland – just not in Palestine. But
his anti-Semitism was never hard to find: 'The British Union
pities the Jew for the universal dislike he inspires throughout his
history, but the cry of "persecution" comes too glibly from the
mouths of those who by their money power have long persecuted
Christendom.' Fascism appealed to Robert's conception of himself
as a leader and soldier in a war against Jewish influence. His
bombastic booklet *The Inward Strength of a National Socialist* celebrated the 'barbaric splendour' of the movement as a mystical and
militant force that could destroy the 'world of Judaic capitalists'.
Celebrating himself and his comrades, he wrote: 'The National
Socialist is a crusader – a warrior in the very best sense; he does
not fear DEATH. If necessary he runs to meet it.' In reality the
BUF's two major physical confrontations – 1934's Olympia Rally,
where their biff boys attacked anti-fascists, and 1936's Battle of
Cable Street, which saw a planned Blackshirt march cancelled
when a hundred thousand people turned out to protest – didn't
lead to anything like glorious martyrdom.

Anyway, as he approached fifty, Robert wasn't one for street
fighting, and he wielded a pen rather than a knuckleduster.
As the BUF's foreign policy director, he wrote and edited the

international pages of the *Blackshirt* newspaper, and was chairman
and reported financial backer of *Action*, the party's other publication. Robert also undertook a lot of overseas fact-finding trips.
At the end of 1934 he visited the United States to meet with
President Roosevelt and study the New Deal. On that visit he
caught up with Miles Mander in Hollywood, with the two men
enjoying their familiar 'friendly international arguments'. They
likely also debated the merits of the movies. Robert had recently
attacked Hollywood films that celebrated 'criminal heroics' and
appealed to the 'cruder sex emotion of the audience and whose
narrative content contained barely concealed ideas bordering
on the pornographic'. He was hard on British pictures, too,
slamming *The Private Life of Henry VIII*, which had actually
co-starred Miles, for not showing 'the greatness of monarchy'.
Filmmaking, generally, he believed was 'debased' under 'financial democracy' – an unsubtle reference to the industry's Jewish
moguls on both sides of the Atlantic – with 'ideas of service,
responsibility, duty . . . buried out of sight'.

But Robert's main international interest was fascism in action,
and in the mid-1930s he travelled to Spain, Portugal and Italy
to study their regimes. Unsurprisingly, his greatest enthusiasm
was for Germany, which he visited frequently, with MI5 suspecting Mosley was using him as a go-between to deliver secret
information to Germany. Robert did have access to the Nazi
Party's inner sanctum, furnished by Hitler's foreign policy adviser
Joachim von Ribbentrop, whom he met in London during one of
the German's frequent visits to Britain. Via these connections in
September 1935, Robert attended the Nuremberg Rally, where
he watched Hitler reveal himself as never before when he read
out the race laws that laid the legal foundation for the system-
atic persecution of the Jews. In his report for *Blackshirt*, headlined
'The New Germany Rejoices', Robert lovingly described fifty

thousand parading members of the Hitler Youth and a crowd ten times that size erupting in a chorus of '*Heil*, Hitler!'.

Yet all paled in comparison with the public debut of the huge new army called the Wehrmacht. Germany's illegal rearmament was demonstrated in a furious mock battle using hundreds of infantry troops, artillery units, tank groups, and fighter and bomber squadrons. The spectacle, filmed by Leni Riefenstahl for her propaganda movie *Day of Freedom: Our Armed Forces*, ended with planes flying in an aerial swastika formation – celebrating that the Nazi symbol had just been made Germany's sole national flag. The demonstration was said to show how the Nazis could defend the Fatherland from aggression. In reality Robert had just seen what blitzkrieg would look like in four years' time. His article fawned over Hitler's intensity, integrity and willpower, and his ability to stand for hours on end to take the salute of his SA and SS soldiers. 'As an Englishman proud of the heritage and tradition of my country,' he wrote, 'I can say without any hesitation as he passes by, and from the depth of my heart, "Heil Hitler."'

In July 1936, Robert was reportedly part of a group comprising Catholic Mosley supporters, Spanish fascists and MI6 operatives who arranged the secret transport of generalissimo Francisco Franco from the Canary Islands to Spanish-controlled Morocco so he could lead the military rebellion against the new Republican government. Within a week the Spanish Civil War was being fought on the mainland.

Four months later in Berlin, Robert had the chance to offer his personal *Sieg Heil* to the Führer when he and William Allen were best man and witness respectively at Sir Oswald Mosley's secret marriage to aristocratic British beauty Diana Mitford. The wedding had been organised by Diana's good friend Magda Goebbels, wife of Nazi propaganda minister Joseph Goebbels, and was held at the Goebbels' ministerial house opposite Hitler's

Chancellery. In an upstairs room Diana, looking radiant in a pale gold silk tunic dress and attended by her fervently Nazi sister Unity, watched in awe as Adolf Hitler, dressed in uniform, approached across the Chancellery's park-like grounds. After the guest of honour arrived, the small party moved to the drawing room, where the short ceremony was carried out by a registrar. Rings exchanged, Hitler gave the newlyweds his present – a photograph of himself in a silver frame – and joined the wedding party at a lunch put on by Magda at the Goebbels' lakeside home. Diana kept everyone entertained by spilling the details of a then-secret scandal: King Edward VIII was head-over-heels in love with an American divorcee named Wallis Simpson. With Goebbels in control of Germany's newspapers, secrecy about the marriage was maintained. For the next two years Robert was one of the few who knew that Mosley and Mitford had wed – let alone where it had happened and in whose presence.

Robert had at least two personal audiences with Hitler – who on one occasion sought his views on the tribal resistance to Mussolini's occupying fascist army in Abyssinia – and came away from these encounters sure that the Führer wanted only peace with England. 'There always seemed to be such an apparent desire the whole time to come to terms, to be friends, so to speak, with Great Britain and the British Empire,' Robert would later recall. 'Several times in the course of the conversation Hitler told me, like he told Mr Chamberlain and Mr Lloyd George, of his admiration for the British Empire – and still in my own heart I had a feeling that he meant that.' Robert might have admired Hitler, but the feeling apparently wasn't mutual, with MI5 claiming the Nazi leader later responded to a report furnished by Robert: 'To be a true National Socialist one must have both an intellect and a heart; this man has neither.'

But Hitler would have approved of Robert's intensifying anti-Semitism. 'Locusts of Humanity' ran the headline of his March 1937 *Blackshirt* article about Jews in British society:

> Jews–Jews–Jews – all pervading . . . They are only 350,000, so we are told, and yet by their universal presence they might be well over a million . . . The horde of locusts sweeping over the deserts, over the mountains; descending upon the fertile fields of civilisation, eating clean all the wealth, passing, leaving a desolation behind them, appeared at this moment an apt simile to me. They know no country, no frontier; excluding desolation, persistent, inhuman, rapacious . . . The British Union stands by prepared to give battle to these locust hordes.

Writing about the prospect of war for *Action* a few months later, he appeared even more unhinged:

> The lure of Satan is the cause of this dangerous situation and the madness is apparent. For how could any individual in his or her right senses be a follower of Jewish Bolshevism, having seen its handiwork in Russia, France and Spain? . . . Yet this madness has attacked such diverse people as dandy [Foreign Secretary Anthony] Eden, tithe-stuffed Bishops, weedy intellectuals, and honest British workmen. All these have been in turn led into the church of this monster, blinded with lies or with specious promises.

When Jewish refugees from Germany were settled at the Kitchener Camp near his mansion in Sandwich Bay, Kent, on the English Channel, Robert and other fascists, including Lady Grace Pearson, tried to stir up hatred against them with a letter-writing campaign to the local press. He penned his own poisonous missive, claiming Sandwich citizens had been disrupted by this 'Central European mass' and that the place's beauty was 'endangered by the presence of this foreign excrescence'. Linking Jews to disease was but a warm-up for playing to even baser fears. 'Only recently a young girl assaulted by two of these aliens was put on probation for two years, while the culprits were exonerated,' he wrote. 'Sex-starved they may be, but it is not for British womanhood to appease their appetites.' Refused publication in a local newspaper, Robert went ahead and printed his letter in *Action*. A subsequent investigation found there had been no such crime, meaning he either reported a dangerous rumour or concocted a hateful lie.

Despite continuous MI5 surveillance – he was suspected of soliciting Nazi funds for the BUF on his visits to Germany – the security service took little interest in his anti-Semitism. That was because Robert was only an extreme example of a prejudice then depressingly pervasive in Britain, with Mass-Observation, the social research organisation started in 1937, finding that many people believed Jews brought on their own persecution. 'A nasty side of our nation's character has been scratched up,' E. M. Forster wrote of this blind prejudice in his 1939 essay *Jew Consciousness*. 'People who would not ill-treat Jews themselves, or even be rude to them, enjoy tittering over their misfortunes . . . The grand Nordic argument, "He's a bloody capitalist so he must be a Jew, and as he's a Jew he must be a Red," has already taken root in our filling-stations and farms.' George Orwell soon after observed anti-Semitism that was 'not violent but pronounced enough to be disquieting' from people who claimed not to be prejudiced but who nevertheless were sure Jews were cheating on the black market and dodging war service, among other evils. 'I have heard this kind of talk even from country people who had probably never seen a Jew in their lives,' he wrote. Far-right propaganda of the type produced by Robert, the BUF and other anti-Semitic fascist organisations tried to fan these flames by promoting the idea that, in retaliation for their poor treatment in Germany, Jews with political, financial and media power were hellbent on drawing the world into a war of revenge. Admiration for Hitler, too, was commonplace in England, the United States and other Western democracies, with the Führer's many admirers including such disparate figures as the Duke and Duchess of Windsor, Lady Astor, Gertrude Stein, Charles Lindbergh and the United States ambassador to the United Kingdom Joseph Kennedy.

———

Robert fell out with Mosley from mid-1938. He had come to think The Leader was too self-absorbed and had been wrong in firing true believers like firebrand William Joyce and former Labour MP and *Action* editor John Beckett while hiring feckless opportunists. Robert said the BUF had lost its way. Rather than cause a scene, he gradually withdrew from the party, though he contributed a few more articles to its newspapers. There were later suspicions that this break was staged in order to allow Robert more latitude to engage with other fascist entities without creating an official link to the BUF.

By early 1939 the enmity between the men was very real. Robert had previously promised to cover some of Mosley's expenses, but reneged when presented with a demand for £9000. The Leader launched legal action against his former friend. Now Robert washed his hands of the BUF. But he was far from done with fascism, having joined The Link – ostensibly an Anglo-German friendship society, though suspected to be a Nazi front – and the British People's Party, a pro-peace, far-right and anti-Semitic organisation.

Despite his proclaimed fascist politics, Robert still considered himself a patriot. In April 1939 he applied to work for the British government in Cairo, saying his knowledge of and contacts in the

Arab world would be valuable if war was to come. His expertise was acknowledged but his application was rejected following a damning MI5 assessment: 'He is regarded as an unscrupulous adventurer and from a security point of view a most undesirable candidate.'

31.

'It was a case of love at first sight,' Mary said of meeting Robert Gordon-Canning. 'Bobby conforms to my idea of the ideal man. I always wanted to marry a man who looked like Clive Brook, the film star. He was my childhood hero, and Robert is a very "Clive Brookish" person. When I met Bobby nothing else mattered.' The comparison to Clive Brook was in the eye of the beholder, though both he and Robert were lean, tall, possessed of a piercing grey stare – and thirty or more years older than Mary.

Robert's first invitation was for Mary and Patricia to visit his ancestral estate in Hartpury, Gloucestershire. There he owned two magnificent properties. The Hill House was a Tudor house dating to the early fifteenth century and near to Limbury Hill, whose ancient woodlands Robert adored. Then there was Tween Hills, a beautiful red-brick country house erected in the 1720s. Both properties had stables, gardens and views of the six hundred acres of rolling pasturelands and forests that he owned. As The Hill and Tween Hills were leased to tenant farmers, Robert and his young guests instead stayed at Hartpury House, his child-hood home, now owned by his aunt. Built in the early 1800s and set amid vast gardens of topiary, statuary and ancient oaks, this elegant country home had some twenty bedrooms over three wings, high-ceilinged dining, lounge and billiards rooms and a well-stocked library. Its brick stable complex alone was bigger and grander than most Australian mansions.

Robert's aunt made the Maguires welcome. She had a fondness for Australians ever since she had given over the lower floor of this house for use as a military hospital for wounded Diggers during the Great War. The estate also included a chapel and church, where generations of Robert's esteemed family had been laid to rest. The Gordon-Cannings were revered by the good folk of Hartpury, having gifted land on which were built the village's town hall and school.

On another day Robert showed his new inamorata his red-brick Georgian mansion 'Sandilands' at Sandwich Bay, Kent. Mary had to be astounded by its three-storey grandeur on absolute English Channel beachfront. What a location: not only could you see the French coastline but Robert's smattering of neighbours were some of England's most well-to-do people, including Lady Astor, the country's richest woman after the queen consort. A few miles inland from Sandilands, Robert had a 130-acre farm, where he ran a herd of prized dairy cattle. Then there was his luxury London flat in Chesterfield Hill, Mayfair, and his commercial buildings in London, one of which had until recently been leased to Anna Wolkoff, a prominent dress designer whose work had appeared in *Vogue* and whose clients included Wallis Simpson. There would have been a good chance fashion-plate Mary knew Anna and her work. On top of all that, Robert's already considerable wealth was soon to be bolstered with an £85 000 (£5.2 million) inheritance from his mother, who had died at the end of 1938. A war hero, a poet, an aristocrat and a millionaire: this was the sort of man Mary had been groomed to marry.

Robert liked that Mary was unlike other actresses. 'He first fell in love with me because I was the first film star he had met who did not talk shop,' she said. He was glad Mary no longer played bridge or golf, activities he didn't think becoming of women, and that she was happy for him to school her in the aristocratic pastimes of fishing, shooting and hunting. Robert also liked that Mary was the most beautiful and famous of the five Maguire sisters, just as Mosley's wife, Diana, was the most radiant of the six Mitford girls.

Robert was persuasive when he said he was a patriot and a pacifist, whose only political interest now was preventing another war with Germany. In such discussions he was skilled at sublimating his anti-Semitism into rational-sounding pro-Arab arguments, sparing all but fellow travellers his most poisonous opinions. Mary didn't take an interest in politics, and it is unlikely that Robert risked their romantic relationship by forcing his more extreme positions on her. Mary did know he was a fascist and that he didn't care for Jews, but neither of these positions were then particularly unusual in upper-class British society. It seems clear that she didn't share his views, but she also didn't rule him out as a lover because of them.

———

Mary had been seduced by a secret Nazi spy. At least that was the plot of her next film, *An Englishman's Home*, adapted from the play of the same name by Guy du Maurier. First staged in 1909, it had then been part of the literary trend exploiting national paranoia about an invading enemy – which in turn led to the creation of the forerunner to MI5 that now had Mary's real-life boyfriend under surveillance. The new relevance of *An Englishman's Home* – which would see release in the United States as *Mad Men of Europe* – had occurred to producer Neville E. Neville when he watched Neville Chamberlain return to *his* home at 10 Downing Street after appeasing Hitler. A movie version, updated for the age of radios, parachutists, bombers and poison gas, was initially a tough sell to investors because the Nazi regime was so sensitive to actual or implied criticism that even Hollywood hadn't dared put out a film about the German threat. But that changed after Warner Bros. released *Confessions of a Nazi Spy* in April 1939, and Neville now found a commercial magnate willing to fund his film to the tune of £100000. Seeing an opportunity to encourage military enlistment, Britain's Air Ministry placed squadrons of its latest planes at the producer's disposal.

Filming started at the end of May at Denham Film Studios in Buckinghamshire. Neville cast Mary, now on loan from ABPC, as Betty, pretty oldest daughter in an ordinary English family infilt- rated by a suave European spy, played by Austrian-born matinee idol Paul Henreid (an actor who was in reality such a fervent anti-Nazi that he had been designated an 'official enemy of the Third Reich'). When the story begins, this handsome villain has already got Betty wrapped around his little finger as he finalises the installation of a radio transmitter in the attic of her fam- ily's home. Despite the threat of war, her dad believes peace will prevail and tut-tuts at preparation measures such as trenches, gas- masks and air-raid wardens. He's proven disastrously wrong when enemy parachutists land all over the countryside. Guided by the spy's radio, the invaders smash their way into the family house and make it their stronghold. Next they use the transmitter to guide bombers to their targets in London. Poor old dad is executed for standing up for family, home, King and Country. Betty and the rest of her family get clear of the house just as it is blown to pieces by the Air Ministry. Radio beam lost, the enemy bombers turn back, and soldiers arrive to mop up the bad guys – with the most handsome of them sweeping Betty off her feet.

Even before *An Englishman's Home* was finished, the German regime was livid. 'Without any attempt at disguise, it proclaims

Germany as the enemy invaders who slaughter English citizens,' seethed a Nazi newspaper. Neville E. Neville rejected the claims. 'The picture preaches hate against no nation,' he said. 'Nor can the invaders be identified with any particular nationality. The uniforms they wear are wholly imaginary and specially designed. And none of the foreign characters have anything to do with Germany. Our reply to Nazi accusations is simply this: if the cap should fit any national head, let that nation wear it.' Given the film's publicised anti-Nazi genesis, and the fact that its invaders wore uniforms and helmets very much like those of the Wehrmacht, Neville may have hoped for exactly this sort of free publicity from Goebbels and his goons.

Robert Gordon-Canning probably wasn't thrilled with his new girlfriend's involvement in the movie. But he stayed out of her career, and she stayed out of his politics.

According to a letter sent home to Australia by one of Bina's guests at Villa Esterel, there had been much excitement at Denham when Queen Mary visited, and Mary was chosen to show the young princesses Elizabeth and Margaret around the studio.

With *An Englishman's Home* to be distributed by United Artists, the company's co-founder and Maguire family friend Mary Pickford visited the set and declared herself pleased with how the production was progressing. Despite her approval, the film was troubled from start to finish. Eight writers worked on competing versions of the script, all pretty much ignored by the director, Albert de Courville, who daily bemused his cast – which again included Mary's Australian friend John Wood – with hastily improvised dialogue. Screaming matches broke out between writers and inexperienced executives put on the payroll by the film's financial backer. An unnamed actress hurled an inkwell at one of these neophytes. The monstrous main set appeared to have been designed by someone with no idea of what a middle-class home's lounge room looked like. It was huge, measuring forty by thirty feet, with half a dozen couches and window seats, books in three languages, pricey art and some very attractive antiques. There was also a parquet floor decorated with nine rugs.

Mary tripped on one of those many rugs while filming a dancing scene on 22 June. She fell heavily and was unable to stand without a lot of pain. Taken to hospital, doctors confirmed her ankle was broken and would need to be set in plaster. She would be unable to work for at least ten days and might be out of action for as long as a month. 'The accident to Miss Maguire is most serious for her and for us,' said Neville. 'She seems more concerned about the film than herself.' The producer was racing the clock as war clouds darkened. '*An Englishman's Home* has a topical theme and we had hoped to get it out as quickly as possible,' he said. 'It is urgently wanted both in Britain and the United States.'

Mary hobbled into Denham three days after the accident and insisted on working. Two minutes after going on set, she fainted from the pain and was carried off by the producer. Having recovered, she winced through one take before finally accepting she wasn't up to working and returning to hospital. 'It was the gamest thing I ever saw,' Neville said. Mary didn't stay away long; a relieved Neville said, 'Now, by altering the script, we have been able to carry on production which at one time we feared would have to be held up indefinitely. We have arranged that Miss Maguire acts in positions that do not impose any strain on her injured leg – leaning against doors, tables, chairs.' Mary risked aggravating her injury by having her cast removed and wearing shoes with special supportive heels. Less than two weeks after her accident, she was running through scenes if required. 'Tough work,' observed the *Daily Mail*, 'tough girl.'

Filming finished in mid-July; Mary was photographed beaming and wearing ordinary heels as she judged a bathing beauty competition. Her rapid recovery wasn't the only reason for her smile: Robert had just proposed and she had accepted. Mary was about to fulfil the last of her life's goals by getting married.

Ever the traditionalist, Robert wrote to her parents seeking permission. Straight after the beauty pageant, Mary flew to Cannes to seek their blessing in person. Upon her return, Mary threw herself an engagement dinner party and invited Mary St. Claire of *The Australian Women's Weekly*. 'Woman's place is in the home,' said the bride-to-be, flashing an enormous solitaire diamond ring. Even so, she said she would continue making films occasionally. Mary tried to set the record straight about her politics. 'I have no fascist sympathies,' she said, 'and do not intend to take part in my fiancé's political life. I hope to remain wise enough after my marriage to stay outside the ambit of Robert's political activities. I was given my big chance in Hollywood, where there are many Jews.' This wasn't simply a platitude – both of Mary's bosses, Jack Warner and Joe Schenck, were Jewish. 'It would be both ungrateful and unkind of me to ally myself because of marriage with the fascist party,' Mary said.

Mary St. Claire, fond of editorialising, continued:

> Although she is taking no part in politics, Mary will probably go to Nuremberg for the Nazi Party rally in September, which her fiancé usually attends. She is also bound to be thrown much in the company of the Freeman-Mitford sisters, who are friends of Hitler. Captain Gordon-Canning is a close friend of Sir Oswald Mosley, who married Diana Freeman-Mitford.

If Mary made that comment about Nuremberg, she was breathtakingly naïve to think she could claim not to be anti-Semitic and still go to the Nazi rally where race laws had been announced. And if she made the comment about Mosley and the Freeman-Mitford sisters, she didn't know very much about her fiancé's relationships. What is possible is that the *Australian Woman's Weekly* reporter made assumptions based on old information: Robert was only recorded as having attended the 1935 Nuremberg Rally, and by the time of his engagement he was bitterly opposed to Mosley.

Mary and Robert were to marry in just a month's time in the private chapel on his Hartpury estate. Joan would be Mary's bridesmaid. Carmel wouldn't be able to attend, busy with modelling assignments in Cannes, and nor could Patricia and Lupe, working as entertainers at a casino in Turin. Bina and Mick weren't sure if they would attend. From their hotels to Hollywood, her parents had always loved hosting and attending parties – that they might miss Mary's big day and her entrée to British society was puzzling, explained perhaps by reservations if not about the groom then about how fast their daughter was rushing into marriage.

Then, almost as soon as it had been announced, the wedding was postponed because Mary got some very bad news.

32.

Mary had pulmonary tuberculosis in both lungs, and her condition was worsening. She had been diagnosed around the time Robert proposed, after he insisted she see a specialist about her persistent chest trouble. The doctor wouldn't have been able to say when she had contracted the disease, which has a long incubation period. Mary may have been infected by the ballerina Spessiva back in 1934, though at the Belle Vue she would have come into close contact with many other secret sufferers. Mary probably already had TB by the time she got to Hollywood. Early symptoms – fatigue, weariness, weight loss, chest pain and a mucusy cough – were easily misdiagnosed as influenza, bronchitis or simply the malaise of a young woman who smoked and had a busy work and social life. The diagnosis was devastating but also may not have been a complete surprise to her. After all, Mary had gone to Arosa in Switzerland at Christmas and Madeira in Portugal a few months later; both were popular destinations for respiratory ailment and TB sufferers who had been told to seek cold mountain or warm seaside air to aid recovery. These trips were both reported as Mary's attempts to shake off the 'bad chill' she had caught making *That Man's Here Again* two and a half years earlier. Neither had worked, and she was now very sick.

With tuberculosis widely considered a shameful condition of the lower classes, Mary had to be relieved the newspapers didn't push too hard for information or speculate about what really ailed her. 'Too much hard work caused my illness,' she told Sydney's *Sun*. Brisbane's *Truth* had the good graces to refer to 'chest trouble'. In sickness as in health, Mary would be with the 'right people' as a 'guest' of Lady Carnarvon's Nursing Home. This genteel facility had been founded by and continued to be run by Almina, Countess of Carnarvon, best remembered for inspiring the Lady Cora character in *Downton Abbey*, whose exteriors were filmed at her magnificent Highclere Castle. In 1939 her nursing home was so discreet, elite and richly appointed that wits reckoned it the best private club in London.

Though Mary's surroundings were plush, her confinement was far from comfortable. She underwent artificial pneumothorax, in which a big needle was used to force nitrogen into the chest cavity on one side of her body to collapse the lung so it could be 'rested'. After a few days the lung was reinflated and the procedure repeated on the other lung. Side effects included knife-like chest pains and spitting up more blood than usual. The biggest risk of the procedure was heart failure caused by fatal embolism.

Doctors told Mary that she would need up to a year to recover. *If* she recovered – there was no cure for tuberculosis, reckoned to have killed one in seven people who had ever lived. In the previous year alone, it had claimed more than twenty-five thousand victims in the United Kingdom. Facing such a fate was the less romantic side to Mary agreeing so quickly to marry Robert. She later said that when he proposed she had been getting sicker by the day and feeling very alone with all her family except Joan far off in Cannes. Making films was out of the question in the immediate future; her income would dry up and diminish her ability to provide for her family. Marrying a man of means was a hedge against such hardship. Besides, Robert seemed to genuinely care for her; he visited the nursing home often when many lesser men might have made themselves scarce or withdrawn the proposal. He may even have thought Mary more alluring than ever, given he belonged to a class of people who believed that consumptives were strangely beautiful: British romantic poets. His claimed forebear Lord Byron had once said he should like to sicken and die with tuberculosis for how intriguing it would make him to women. Robert now said he no longer wanted to wait to marry Mary even if she was carried to the altar on a stretcher.

Mary's illness led to her reaffirming her Catholic faith and perhaps reflecting on the redemptive journey of the consumptive. Like her fiancé, she and her people – as followers of French Carmelite nun Sister Thérèse Martin, whose statue stood in her aunt Marie's convent in Melbourne – also saw a strange beauty in tuberculosis. Sister Thérèse's posthumous autobiography *The Story of a Soul* recounted the agonies and ecstasies leading to her death from the disease aged twenty-four. Mary knew the story of the 'Little Flower of Jesus' and may have drawn strength from her example.

Robert had himself to worry about in early August when Geoffrey Mander – Miles's older brother and a progressive member of parliament – raised suspicions about The Link with Home Secretary Sir Samuel Hoare. A day later in the House of Commons, Sir Samuel sensationally confirmed that the organisation was a German propaganda instrument partly funded by the Nazi regime. Geoffrey Mander now wanted to know if its members were under surveillance; Sir Samuel said they were but added he was powerless to ban the group unless it operated illegally. 'Nazi Gold Paid to Agent of "Link"' screamed the *Daily Mirror*'s front-page headline. As a prominent member, Robert knew his position was precarious.

Robert and Mary brought their wedding forward: they would be married by Father Lowry at St James's Church in London on 10 August. 'A chest complaint has tied me here for the last few weeks,' Mary told the *Daily Herald* from the nursing home. 'But we both felt we did not want to postpone the ceremony.' Mick and Bina were now coming. If they had harboured any reservations, they set them aside to make their sick daughter happy. There could be no honeymoon – Mary would leave Lady Carnarvon's in the morning, be married, and then return to her suite. 'The nurses will put me to bed again,' she explained, 'and I am afraid I shall not be able to leave before the end of the month.' Following another six weeks of bed rest at Robert's mansion in Sandwich Bay, Mary optimistically reckoned she would be 'quite fit again'.

On the morning of the wedding, Mary took communion from Father Lowry in the nursing home. She posed cheerfully for newspaper photographers in her sickbed as nurses did her hair and make-up. Her lung treatment made it impossible for her to wear a wedding dress, so she instead slipped into a specially designed blue satin robe with a hood that had been modelled on a Carmelite nun's habit. White orchids were fastened to the front with a spectacular diamond brooch Robert had given her; on her wrist she wore a matching bracelet. Flanked by nurses, Mary was carried from Lady Carnarvon's in an invalid chair by two male attendants as news camera flashbulbs popped and staff watched from a nursing-home window. After a short car journey, Mary was startled to see a cheering crowd outside the church. 'I never thought there would be such interest in our wedding,' she said. 'It was almost impossible to get through the crowd . . . I think all the world loves a lover and ours was a true lovers' romance.'

Mary was embraced by Bina, regal in a purple dress and sable cape, and Mick, beaming in his suit. For her parents, it was a moment of mixed emotions. This was what they had always wanted for their daughter, but she looked so fragile. She was transferred into a wheelchair and her father took her into St James's. The majestic Gothic church — with its soaring arches, stone columns, stained glass and marble statuary — had been decorated with huge standards of lilies and delphiniums. Alongside Joan, pretty in an ensemble of blue romaine, Mick wheeled Mary up the aisle. As she passed by, her actress friends Janet Johnson, Margot Grahame and June Clyde burst into tears. Robert stood proudly at the altar wearing a double-breasted suit and a carnation in his lapel, attended by his brother Frank, along with his friend and fellow fascist William Allen.

Robert knelt beside Mary and held her hand as Father Lowry conducted the short service. Under the circumstances, the Catholic vow to be true to each other 'in good times and in bad, in sickness and in health' was particularly poignant. The groom slipped a wedding ring of French design with interlaced diamonds onto his bride's finger. Father Lowry pronounced them man and wife. The last of Mary's life goals had been achieved. 'He held my hand as I was wheeled into the registry to sign, and he stooped and kissed me,' she said. 'That was the greatest moment of a hectic week of planning and preparation.' As they signed the register in the vestry, Australian soprano Marie Nyman sang 'Ave Maria'.

Outside, the Gordon-Cannings, Robert standing beside Mary's invalid chair, smiled for news photographers, whose pictures of what *Truth* called 'the most unusual wedding London had seen in years' were published around the world. Family and friends went to the nursing home, where Mary's suite was gaily decorated with pink lilies, blue delphiniums and deep red roses. The couple took time to talk to reporters. Asked about her acting plans, Mary affirmed she would make two movies a year when she had recovered. 'I think it is advisable to retain some interest in films,' she said. 'But I will not start work for a year. During that time I am going to receive medical treatment. Robert is a dear. He looks after me so well and comes to see me lots. Now I'm married I feel I shall get better much quicker.' Robert didn't want to talk about his wife returning to work. 'Her health is the most important consideration at present,' he said.

The bride and groom cut their three-tiered wedding cake, topped with a model movie camera and bearing the badge and colours of the 10th Royal Hussars. A Champagne toast was raised. Six years younger than Robert, Mick would have got good comic mileage out of calling him 'son'. Mary's gifts from her new husband were revealed as far more lavish than just diamond jewellery: he had bought her a mink coat and a Rolls-Royce, and declared she would have a yearly dress allowance of £2000 ($125 000). Robert had also arranged for her to be presented at Court the following year and would have her portrait painted in regal fashion by society artist Vasco Lazzolo. Congratulatory cables poured in from her film friends, including Mary Pickford, Gracie Fields and Franchot Tone.

But all the excitement threatened to overwhelm the bride. 'As Mary had to be kept quiet, the hundreds of telegrams and gifts were not all opened,' *Truth* reported. When evening came, her friends left. Bina and Mick said their goodbyes, heading back to Cannes. Robert also bade his bride farewell, departing for Scotland to shoot grouse.

That night the girl born Hélène Teresa Maguire, who had been known as Peggy and then Mary Maguire, before that day becoming Mrs Robert Gordon-Canning, had to feel a mixture of emotions. Her life was imitating scenes from her films. Robert romancing her in her hospital suite echoed *That Man's Here Again*. Friends surrounding her invalid bed that afternoon was just like *The Outsider*. As in *The Flying Doctor* she was alone on her wedding night. And that very evening was becoming something out of *An*

Englishman's Home. Outside Mary's window, much of England was – for the first time – subject to a blackout as hundreds of British bombers droned overhead and an equal number of RAF fighters flew to intercept them, testing readiness for the war that now seemed inevitable. She was not yet twenty-one and had achieved all of the things she had dreamt of back in Melbourne. Yet Mary might not enjoy any of it for long. If tuberculosis didn't kill her, an apocalyptic war might.

––––––

'I'm not a tragic bride because I had a wheelchair wedding,' she told Mary St. Claire of *The Australian Women's Weekly.* 'I'm the happiest girl in the world. I do not feel the frail, tragic figure I seem to present to the world because my new-found happiness is already banishing the shadow of the long period of recuperation lying ahead of me.' Mary professed not to be disturbed that her new husband was presently hundreds of miles away. 'People have asked me how I felt about going back to hospital while Bobby went to Scotland to shoot grouse,' she said. 'We discussed all that. It is the ideal arrangement until I get well. I don't want Bobby to brood or worry.' Besides, her family had been perfectly supportive, her many friends ensured her room was filled daily with fresh flowers, and she had received lovely gifts from all over the world. 'But Bobby's presents I shall never forget,' she said. 'I've got to think hard or I shall imagine he's a fairy-tale prince and I am still in the movies.'

Mary was also in a reflective mood. She recalled that not so long ago, Victoria's Department of Education had tried to stop her from appearing in *Diggers in Blighty* and that but for Loreto's mother superior she might now be a nun. 'Events have moved swiftly in my life,' she said. 'When I look back over my career I am amazed at the experiences I have undergone in a few short years.' She was also looking to the future. 'I do not intend to take part in any of my husband's political activities,' she stressed again. 'With an occasional film I shall find plenty to do.' Mary said her next movie, to be shot in the New Year, would be *Society Hostel*, and that she would play the wife of a popular social figure. But she was far more excited about playing this part in real life as the chatelaine of Sandilands. 'I learned cooking and dressmaking and did a domestic science course at Queensland University,' she said. 'This will stand me in good stead, because, though a staff of eight servants is installed at Sandwich, Kent, I shall be able to take over control of my house without any fears about my new role, which is more thrilling than any I've ever had in films.' Mary was also excited by the prospect of visiting Australia at the end of 1940 to show 'my Bobby' the place of her birth. 'I would like him to love the sea, the sun, and the open spaces for which I often pine,' she said.

Once settled back in England, she hoped to start a family. 'Both Robert and myself are very fond of children, and hope we will be blessed with a son and a daughter.' Confessing that she was still deeply religious, Mary hoped that the adulation and glamour of film stardom had not spoiled her. 'Now I am married I hope to live a quiet peaceful life,' she said. 'I am determined that our marriage, which I believe was made in heaven, will be a success. I do not believe in divorce and hope that our lives will be devoted to each other. Career or ambition will not come between us.'

Once upon a time, everything Mary wished for came true. Now, almost nothing she hoped for would eventuate.

33.

A week after her wedding, Mary's condition worsened. Returning from Scotland, Robert took her to Sandilands, where the sun and sea air of late summer might help her breathe easier. He hired nurses to care for her night and day. 'It is considered that complete rest in the quiet in the country for at least two months is now the only thing,' Vena Yates reported in *The Telegraph*.

There was another compelling reason for Mary to leave London: the city was being evacuated in preparation for war. On 24 August, Robert's pal Joachim von Ribbentrop, now Germany's foreign minister, surprised the world by signing the Nazi–Soviet non-aggression pact with his Russian counterpart Vyacheslav Molotov, removing one of the last major obstacles to Hitler's territorial ambitions in Western Europe. Sandbags and gasmasks returned to London's streets ahead of the German bombing expected upon war breaking out.

Tended by her nurses and staff of eight servants, Mary recuperated comfortably in her own room, which Robert had ordered redecorated in soothing blues and whites, beneath a bedhead that featured a carved lotus flower, which he said was the Muslim emblem of fidelity. But for a young woman used to the excitement of high society in Hollywood and London, the sprawling

Sandilands had to be isolating, not least because she was eighty miles from Joan and her friends in London. Adding to her loneliness, Robert often had business and political affairs to tend to in the city. Confined to her bed, Mary would have passed much time listening to the radio, waiting for the news that everyone was dreading.

It came at 11.15 a.m. on Sunday, 3 September 1939. The BBC broadcast Prime Minister Neville Chamberlain telling the nation: 'This country is at war with Germany.'

Robert was beside himself with frustration and anger. England, he believed, should not be drawn into a ruinous war to defend Poland – which would quickly be overrun by German forces; this was a view he set down in a letter to Miles Mander in Hollywood.

Mary was more concerned about the safety of her father, mother and sisters. Within days, the French military requisitioned Villa Esterel and the Maguires evacuated to Paris, forced to leave behind their car, most of their clothes and their beloved table. For a few days, Mary didn't know where they were. Then a cable arrived from Paris: they were safe. By the end of the week, they were back in London, where they took up a maisonette in Devonshire Place.

Although Britain was officially at war, the feared bombing of London didn't come. Life went on pretty much as usual. For Robert and many others across the British political and social spectrum, this breathing space meant that a negotiated peace was still possible.

With its pro-Nazism exposed, The Link disbanded four days after the war began. But less than two weeks later, its leader, Admiral Sir Barry Domvile, formed the British Council for Christian Settlement in Europe (BCCSE), with John Beckett, Ben Greene, Lord Tavistock and Robert as its founding members. The council held its first meeting in Robert's Mayfair flat, and he took the role of treasurer. With the BCCSE's stated goal a negotiated peace with Germany, membership was soon swollen by left-wing pacifists, and its cause received some support from a handful of independent Labour politicians and from Lord Beaverbrook. Beneath the pacifist façade, the BCCSE was firmly fascist, working to become an umbrella organisation of far-right groups, and it was also anti-Semitic, hence the emphasis on Christian settlement. The British government saw it as The Link by another name, and police closely watched its leaders.

The *Daily Mirror* hated The Link and so running its stand-by sultry publicity photo of Mary with the headline 'She Fell For a Spy' was an unsubtle dig at Robert. The subhead – 'On the films, of course!' – clarified that the article was actually a review of *An Englishman's Home*. The movie reached cinemas at the end of September and had the distinction of being the first to depict the new war. As producer Neville E. Neville had intended, the enemy troops on screen were perceived as 'Teutonic terrorists' to be driven 'back to the Fatherland'. The release was contentious, though this time the British government raised concerns. The Air Ministry demanded minor cuts to ensure the RAF's secrets weren't compromised, and the Ministry of Information insisted on a title card reassuring audiences that the events depicted were impossible because England stood ready to meet all threats. A puzzled *Daily Record* reviewer noted: 'After seeing the horrific air raid on London, which is the climax, anyone might wonder, if it is impossible, what all this black out and gas mask stuff is about.' The film got mixed reviews, though most critics were chilled by what it envisaged. 'Air-raid scenes are well done, and if you can enjoy, under present conditions, the spectacle of hostile planes dishing out death and destruction, here is your chance for a topical thrill,' said the *Daily Mirror*. 'A bang up-to-date, if not altogether convincing drama, but it's not for the nervous!' Writing in *Tatler*, James Agee admired Mary's bosom and concluded 'the film is bosh and very exciting bosh'.

Mary was confined to her bed at Sandilands but more visible than ever because *Black Eyes* was soon also on release. 'A scholarly and attractive British period piece,' reckoned the *Daily Express*. The *Daily Mail* wrote, 'Mary Maguire is a charming heroine', and thought the film pleasant if hampered by its creaky story. *Variety* wasn't so sure: 'Mary Maguire, as the daughter, is charming in the earlier scenes, but sags a bit when emoting.' The *Daily Herald*'s critic spoke for many: 'Dialogue and acting have all the subtlety of two slices of bread and butter. Yet there is something soothing about the whole thing's artless, artificial development. I was left in a rather pleasant state of apathy.'

ABPC's Walter Mycroft optimistically hoped to star Mary in comedy *The Middle Watch*. Crushingly, she had to turn the movie down. 'I am not feeling fit enough to return to films yet, but I hope to later,' Mary said.

The 'Phoney War' continued. In October, George Bernard Shaw urged peace in a letter to the *New Statesman*. Actors John Gielgud and Sybil Thorndike were among members of the National Peace Council who wrote to Neville Chamberlain asking him to consider a peace proposal put together by neutral powers. Former Prime Minister Lloyd George argued in the House of Commons that Britain should negotiate with Germany. To this chorus, the BCCSE added its voice with a leaflet, paid for by Robert, titled 'A Statement on the European Situation', which said the war wasn't solely Germany's fault and could also be blamed on the British and French governments' insistence on upholding the unfair Treaty of Versailles.

Robert sent the pamphlet to John Moore-Brabazon, a friend, Sandwich Bay neighbour and government minister, along with a rambling letter in which, among other claims, he said Germany had only rearmed to meet threats from its neighbours. Moore-Brabazon's reply was withering, calling the claims 'pure buffoonery' and 'very nearly subversive'. 'What I think you fail entirely to understand is that we happen to be fighting in order that you may be able to send such a pamphlet out,' he wrote. 'In any of the countries we are fighting you would be given very short shrift.' The BCCSE made more enemies with its first public meeting on 14 October in London. 'They praised Hitler,' the *Sunday Express* reported of the 150 attendees. 'They reviled the British Government. They ended by sending a resolution to Mr Chamberlain calling on him to start peace negotiations.'

Mary would have been angry with Robert for attracting this sort of attention. 'My wife is always irritated with me,' he later said of her attitude to his agitation. She actively disliked John Beckett, as mentioned in a November 1939 note in his MI5 file. 'Gordon-Canning has been personally acquainted with Beckett for some time and apparently liked him. This feeling was certainly not shared by Mrs Gordon-Canning. He had been persuaded by Beckett to join the British Council for Christian Settlement in Europe as Treasurer, though he had no intention of speaking on public platforms.' Through the last months of 1939, Robert juggled his BCCSE activities, running his estates and taking care of Mary, which included driving her to London for unpleasant treatments every two weeks.

Mary wasn't well enough to accompany Robert to a Christmas Eve eggnog party hosted by a wealthy Sandwich Bay neighbour. 'What would you do if 100 parachute troops landed here?' a friend of Robert's asked him during the soiree. 'Well, I should ask them in to have some beer and then somebody would come along and round them up,' Robert replied in his version of events. But that's not how the party's hostess heard the conversation. 'He said he felt he would not be doing right to mankind if he did not do all he could to help the Nazis,' she later recalled. 'He praised up the Nazi regime and said that if a submarine came and needed refuelling and revictualling they would know where to find a friend.'

———

As the New Year got under way, Mary's health was improving. Now Walter Mycroft wished to star her in comedy *Spring Meeting*. Mary wanted to do it, but her doctors said she wouldn't be able to work until the middle of the year. She had also put on weight and would need to diet before she went back in front of the cameras.

In late January, Mary was well enough to accompany Robert to St Peter's Church, where glamorous tennis champion Kay Stammers married a member of the Welsh Guards before a congregation of lords, ladies, earls and countesses. But a plan for Mary and Robert to go to the south of France for her further recuperation was abandoned when they were refused permission to leave the country. A reason beyond wartime restrictions wasn't given – the denial was because MI5 had intercepted letters Robert had been exchanging with American fascist writer James Barnes, in which they discussed a meeting in Italy. The security service suspected Robert of using Mary's convalescence as a cover for some sort of subversive activity. After the British Navy's attack on the German tanker *Altmark* in Norwegian waters on 16 February, a letter Robert penned to Miles Mander in Hollywood raised yet more MI5 concerns. 'When history comes to be written by non-partisans the blame can be properly assigned,' he wrote. 'And who broke Norwegian neutrality first? War and chaos are only necessary to the international financier, and are harmful to every good Briton and German. May 1940 wash your mind of pure humbug.' Miles was dismayed at such seeming disloyalty and said so, leading Robert to later believe his friend had betrayed him. He should have been looking closer to home. The BCCSE had been penetrated by agents who reported that John Beckett openly talked of fifth column activities. In late January he was said to have made 'intensive efforts' to make contacts in the military so they might 'turn their rifles in the right direction' when the time was ripe. MI5 said he admitted to being pro-Nazi and 'working night and day for Germany'. The loose-lipped Beckett was also said to have claimed Robert was ready to help any Germans on the run in England.

At the start of February, Beckett arranged for Lord Tavistock to meet with the German legation in Dublin to receive peace terms supposedly approved by Hitler. The plan would see the Nazis grant quasi-independence to Czechoslovakia, Poland and Austria; then Germany – in tandem with allied nations – would disarm and join a new League of Nations. Robert arranged for Lord Tavistock to meet Lord Halifax, British Foreign Secretary and the architect of previous appeasement. If rejected the BCCSE planned to try to force the government's hand by distributing millions of copies of a leaflet, 'Germany's Peace Terms – Official', to ensure every Briton knew there was a way to end the war. Robert and Tavistock were to pay for the campaign that MI5 warned might be 'devastating' as propaganda.

Halifax consulted with Prime Minister Neville Chamberlain, and the Tavistock plan was rebuffed. The *Daily Mirror*'s front page denounced the BCCSE pamphlet as 'German propaganda fostered by Hitler's admirers in this country'. The *Daily Telegraph* agreed, shaming the leadership with their fascist pasts: Lord Tavistock had blamed Britain for the war; John Beckett was bosom buddy of William Joyce, now spewing hatred from Berlin as 'Lord Haw-Haw'; Ben Greene was a Nazi propagandist; Robert Gordon-Canning had been prominent in The Link and BUF. The BCCSE was left looking not just treasonous but also moronic when the Nazis disavowed the peace terms as 'invention from beginning to end' and denied Lord Tavistock had met anyone of significance at the Dublin legation. A Nazi spokesman in Berlin pointed out that Germany had only one goal: victory. Robert was given the thankless task of explaining the BCCSE's embarrassment. 'We were warned unofficially that if the British Government reacted unfavourably to the terms some such step would be taken,' he backpedalled to the newspapers. 'The German Government obviously must not give the impression to their own people that they are suing for peace.' In his attempt to save face, Robert had called German integrity into question. It was an insult not likely to be forgotten in Berlin.

Robert was burned by the experience. He had again tried to play patriotic peacemaker only for his loyalty to be called into question in Britain. He wrote to Tavistock to resign from the BCCSE, saying he would take no further part in peace efforts. 'The British people have accepted the war and are going to fight to the end,' he concluded. Brisbane's *Truth* interviewed him in London. 'I have always been a man who tried to make arrangements, not only between Germany and this country, but between others opposed to each other to prevent war,' he said. Mary, he told them, was untroubled by the controversy and resting at Sandilands. 'My wife takes no interest in political or party activities like this,' he said. 'She is progressing excellently and hopes to be completely cured of her illness in two months' time.'

Robert had hoped to make peace with Germany, but Mick was spoiling for a fight with Hitler. In the months after the family evacuated from Cannes, he got bored sitting around. So, in February 1940, aged forty-five, he signed up for the British Army, with a small *Truth* article about his enlistment saying he had been rejected for service during the Great War. In April 1940 Mick found himself on the forward lines in France as an officer's batman in the British Expeditionary Force (BEF). An *Exchange Telegraph* correspondent found him holding court in a village café. 'Dandy being back,' he said, blue eyes twinkling. 'Enjoying every minute.' He told the reporter he had joined up because he 'just felt he had to have another slap at the Jerries . . . I got the feeling of wanting once more to be a soldier. I came over last time and was wounded in 1916.' No evidence can be found in official Australian military records of Mick serving in the Great War, and his service wasn't referred to in any other newspaper article about him. But he was doing his bit now and had no doubt that Germany was facing a KO. 'Lick Hitler?' Mick said. 'Why, that's only a question of how long it will take. The boys all feel the same about it. They are just hugging to get going.' Mick and his mates wouldn't have to wait long.

The Maguire women were shocked that Mick was in harm's way. 'He just came in one day and told us he was off to France,' Bina told the *Daily Mail*. 'We simply didn't believe it. Now we're all longing for his first leave.' They were, she said, getting used to 'living pinch', having gone from a Cannes mansion to their London maisonette, and from an annual income in Brisbane of £2000 ($A180 000) to Mick's annual military allowance of £70 ($A6300). 'We haven't been able to get any of our money from Australia,' Bina said. 'When the little bit we have here has gone I really don't know what we should do.' To help the household budget Patricia, Joan, Carmel and Lupe were sewing their own clothes and talking about forming a sister troupe to make extra money. A photo of the sisters showed Lupe and Joan admiring Patricia in a sheer dress while Carmel stood by sketching the outfit.

Bina vowed that no matter what, they would stick together. 'One thing is certain,' she said. 'We shan't leave London; we'll manage to keep going somehow.' That resolve would soon be tested beyond their imagination.

34.

Robert was no longer officially involved with fascist groups but continued to associate with some of the movement's key players. During the spring, he hosted a dinner party at Sandilands attended by Aubrey Lees, member of The Link, Nordic League and fascist secret society the Right Club, and Major-General John Fuller, fascist and anti-Semite, godfather of mechanised warfare, friend to Hitler and one-time acolyte of occultist Aleister Crowley. The discussion was purportedly about reconstruction and demobilisation after the war. Unsurprisingly, MI5 was increasingly suspicious of such gatherings. Charles Maxwell Knight, head of the B5(b) unit to counter political subversion – and later the inspiration for Ian Fleming's character 'M' – urged a round-up of all British fascists for fear they constituted a fifth column. He wasn't alone in his belief that if the Germans invaded England, Mosley and his fellow travellers might attempt to seize power. One only had to look at Norway, where, as Hitler's forces attacked in early April, pro-Nazi politician Vidkun Quisling had attempted a coup d'état, his surname immediately becoming a synonym for 'traitor'. Britain was in the grip of fifth column mania, with citizens reporting their neighbours for looking shifty or using lights to signal the enemy. Yet despite MI5's urging and popular paranoia, the home secretary for the moment refused to arrest Britons on the basis of what they *might* do.

Robert knew this could change. On 25 April, though he had already resigned from BCCSE in the letter to Lord Tavistock, he did so again in writing to John Beckett, though his real reader may have been MI5; he had to suspect it was intercepting such correspondence.

> My reasons for resignation at this moment are not because I am frightened of being incarcerated by the Government, which they would probably do in any case, if they decide to take drastic action . . . but because I consider that the activities for peace at the moment should not be carried on, but await a more favourable moment and secondly because I have so little time to attend to this business being at the time rather pressed by an urgency of private affairs.

Robert was, in effect, saying that Mary came before politics.

On 10 May, Germany invaded France, along with Belgium, Luxembourg and the Netherlands. In London, Neville Chamberlain resigned and Winston Churchill became prime minister.

With the BEF in the firing line, the Phoney War was now real – and going disastrously. Inside a week, France looked lost. As the Germans advanced, the BEF and French Army were forced back to the Channel, with some 400 000 soldiers trapped at Boulogne, Calais and Dunkirk. If they were killed or captured, Britain's war was as good as lost.

Mary had to have been terrified. Her father was in France. While later family lore said Mick was at Dunkirk, dates strongly indicate he was at Boulogne, which from 22 May came under fierce attack by Nazi planes and tanks. But Mary also had her husband to worry about. Robert's friend and former tenant, fashion designer Anna Wolkoff, was covertly the secretary of fascist secret society the Right Club and involved in espionage that might have changed the outcome of the war as surely as the BEF's destruction in France. Tyler Kent, a cypher clerk at the US embassy in London, had copied secret cables between Winston Churchill and Franklin D. Roosevelt that revealed the American president was disposed to help the British war effort even though such action would violate the US's Neutrality Acts. Wolkoff had brought Kent and his stolen cables to another of Robert's friends, Right Club founder and Scottish MP Archibald Ramsay, who it was feared might make them public to embarrass Roosevelt and force him to abandon Britain to the Nazis. Maxwell Knight's agents had penetrated the Right Club's inner circle and already concocted a sting that proved Wolkoff had contacted William Joyce in Berlin and provided information for his 'Lord Haw-Haw' broadcasts. Now Maxwell Knight, his agents and Special Branch swooped and arrested Wolkoff and Kent – and, in doing so, discovered, along with a cache of stolen cables, the Right Club's secret ledger of influential British members (though the roster didn't include Robert). The sting was the justification MI5 needed to convince Churchill that wartime Regulation 18B should be used against British fascists who were a potential fifth column.

Burly plainclothes detectives from Special Branch carried out surprise raids on 23 May. Mosley was the first to be arrested, followed by Archibald Ramsay, John Beckett and more than two dozen others. The detentions were announced in the House of Commons, and the men were soon behind bars in Brixton Prison. No charges were laid and no periods of detention were specified. While appeals were to be permitted, the detainees and their lawyers would have no access to the evidence used against them.

When the BCCSE's office was raided, a letter from Beckett to Lord Tavistock was found and provided strong evidence of pro-Nazi planning. In the correspondence Beckett detailed who he reckoned should run the British government once the country had been conquered by the Germans. The 'Coalition Government of National Security', he said, should be led by Tavistock as prime minister, with Mosley as leader of the House, Beckett himself as home secretary and minister for 'National Security', with Major-General Fuller as Defence minister. Under Beckett's plan, Robert would be in charge of Britain's Dominions – including Australia. Incredibly, MI5 misfiled the letter and it didn't become part of the interrogation of the interned fascists.

Robert wasn't arrested that day, but he and Mary feared that Special Branch would come through their front door at any moment. One hundred miles away in Boulogne, Mick and his BEF mates were fighting for their lives under fierce German attack. Dunkirk would soon become more famous, but this battle saw Britain's first desperate attempt to mount the mass evacuation of soldiers. Supported by RAF Spitfires, Royal Navy warships blasted their way into the harbour. Navy gunners engaged Panzer tanks on shore as German planes strafed and bombed mercilessly. Thousands of BEF troops were embarked in bloody scenes that saw several Royal Navy ships destroyed or disabled and two captains killed by shrapnel on their bridges. When the surviving ships got away it was with decks crammed with the wounded and awash with blood.

Mary spent nailbiting days worrying about the two most important men in her life. Miraculous news about both arrived on 24 May – her father was safe from the Nazis and her husband was safe from prison. Mick had been evacuated unhurt from Boulogne and the next day was granted a few hours of leave to see his family. The old bruiser swore bitterly as he described the ruthless machine-gunning of French women and children, and the terrifying experience of facing Nazi air raids and tanks. 'Those Germans can't win,' he told Ruby Eve, at the Maguire maisonette for this brief reunion. 'I'll be glad to get back to France to help carry on the big fight.' Mary, meanwhile, told the *Truth* scribe that Robert would not be subject to detention because of the letter he had written to Lord Tavistock renouncing pacifist action and resigning from the BCCSE. 'It is believed the authorities now possess this letter,' the newspaper reported, 'and that they are now not likely to interfere with Gordon-Canning.'

Remarkably, back in California, Joe Schenck was looking at life behind bars. That $100 000 cheque to Willie Bioff had triggered an IRS investigation, and he was before a federal grand jury. Joe would soon be indicted for perjury, having claimed under oath that the money was a loan, and for defrauding the government of more than $400 000 in income taxes. If convicted on all charges, he faced up to 107 years in prison.

The court would soon hear that Joe had failed to report big gambling wins to the IRS and claimed gambling losses as business expenses. He had also deducted, as one paper put it, 'free-handed expenditures on women and pleasure parties in Hollywood, New York and Europe'. The prosecution called on a 'parade of be-furred young women' to testify that in the past decade the mogul had lavished gifts on them ranging from $50-a-week jobs to expensive automobiles. One early 1930s starlet, Grace Poggi, said that back then Joe had given her the use of his yacht, an apartment and furnishings worth $7000.

Had Mary stayed in Hollywood, she would likely have been called on to testify as the most recent recipient of Joe's generosity. Unless, of course, she had married him and thus couldn't be compelled to speak against him in court.

Mary and Robert returned to Sandilands, where the German threat was visible from their upstairs windows. Across the Channel, huge columns of smoke rose over Dunkirk as hundreds of naval vessels and little ships desperately sailed for the city to rescue the 330 000 Allied soldiers trapped there. But the war might soon be on the Gordon-Cannings' doorstep. Throughout British history Sandwich Bay's proximity to the Continent and its flat, wide beach had made it a landing area for invading Roman, Viking and French enemies. It was feared the Germans would be next and Robert's old fascist comrade Lord Haw-Haw had even mentioned it as such a site in his taunting 'Germany Calling' broadcasts from Berlin. Thus Sandwich had become an officially designated defence area of army patrols, searchlights and gun emplacements. Soldiers erected anti-invasion scaffolding on beaches and mined the roads and bridges leading inland. Understandably scared, many of their wealthy neighbours had fled. But the Gordon-Cannings remained – and did their bit for the war effort by billeting ten soldiers in their bathing hut and providing milk from their dairy.

MI5 sought more evidence against Robert. Sandwich Bay fascist Lady Pearson, arrested and briefly detained until her Conservative MP brother kicked up a stink and had her released, claimed that Robert had recently hosted Oswald Mosley and Diana Mitford at Sandilands. The security agency should have realised this wasn't true – the two men were in a bitter political and legal feud. Besides, Sandilands and Sandwich Bay were swarming with British soldiers, making it difficult to believe England's most infamous couple had gone unnoticed by all but one aristocratic neighbour looking to save her own skin. But MI5 took the allegation on face value. Maxwell Knight's agents soon had a more credible witness in Mrs Moore-Brabazon, who provided them with the 'very foolish' letter Robert had written her husband. When the interviewing MI5 lawyer asked 'to be put in touch with any person who had heard with their own ears any disloyal observations', he was instantly rewarded with the name of the Sandwich Bay neighbour who had hosted last Christmas's eggnog party. He went to see her that evening, describing her as a 'pleasant, very talkative' and 'well-moulded, middle-aged ＿＿ lady, who is married to an Englishman'. On condition of anonymity, supposedly to protect an unnamed prominent man, she related her story about Robert saying he supported the Nazis and would aid a German submarine crew should one land at Sandwich Bay. To this day the woman's and man's identities remain redacted from MI5's declassified files. Other Sandwich Bay women were also found to relay suspicions about Robert. Patricia Wentworth, the popular mystery novelist, 'laid information against' him, as did Blanche 'Baffy' Dugdale, one of Britain's leading Zionists, who had every righteous reason to detest him. Several other women, whose names remain redacted, also spoke against Robert. Records of these allegations were destroyed, but surviving files indicate none of the information was of any consequence.

At the start of June, driving back to Sandwich Bay from one of Mary's medical appointments in London, Robert was annoyed to see that a bridge near Sandilands was being mined and that a trench had been dug across the road. 'Nobody could tell me anything about that bridge . . . I kept trying to ring the police in order to find out, if I could, what was happening, but I could get no information at all,' he later said. 'If at any moment we had to evacuate our place down there I wanted to know how to get away.' A short time later he discovered that a bridge on his farm had been blown up. This time he called the local military authorities. 'We are living here,' he said angrily to an officer. 'I have got a sick wife and I have a tremendous amount of stuff to get out, please inform me in future.' Realising how he was coming off, Robert cooled down and invited the officer and his men to come for dinner at Sandilands as a break from the monotony of army life. The offer was rejected.

On 4 June, after the miracle evacuation of Dunkirk, Winston Churchill made history with his speech about fighting the Germans on the beaches. But his powerful address identified another enemy to be defeated. 'Parliament has given us the powers to put down Fifth Column activities with a strong hand,' he thundered, 'and we shall use those powers subject to the supervision and correction of the House, without the slightest hesitation until we are satisfied, and more than satisfied, that this malignancy in our midst has been effectively stamped out.'

MI5 was determined that Robert was part of this malignancy and should join his fascist friends behind bars in Brixton Prison. Yet Home Secretary John Anderson still refused to grant a detention order against him unless presented with more evidence.

MI5 soon had some. The same day as Churchill's speech it sent the Home Office a report saying, 'military authorities of Kent are very disturbed at Gordon-Canning's attempts to get in touch with members of H.M. Forces and to obtain confidential information from them'. This related to his complaints about bridges being blown up near his house. MI5 had also found an earlier report claiming Robert had been heard telling John Beckett he was 'perfectly ready to harbour enemy aliens'. This information had been furnished years earlier by a BUF member with MI5 links. This was almost certainly William Joyce, who was such a long-time friend of Maxwell Knight that the spymaster had, after the outbreak of war, tipped him off to his imminent arrest, allowing his escape to Berlin where he became the poisonous Lord Haw-Haw.

Nevertheless, the home secretary remained unconvinced of sufficient cause for a detention order, though he did sign a defence regualation order, DR 18A, which restricted Robert's movements.

Special Branch came to Sandilands just before noon on Saturday, 8 June. They ordered Robert and Mary from the house, now requisitioned for military use. This Englishman's home was no longer his castle. Upon arrival in London, Robert had to officially report his Chesterfield Hill, Mayfair, address to the Metropolitan police. Writing to the Home Office, he complained bitterly of his treatment, pointing out that for two months he had helped feed and house soldiers, and that his herd was producing milk for the British public. 'Are such actions considered as being liable to be prejudicial to the public safety?' he asked.

Mary's beloved co-star Gracie Fields was also affected by the paranoia. Having survived cervical cancer in 1939, she had married *Keep Smiling*'s director Monty Banks. But now, with Italy in the war, his Italian citizenship put him at risk of internment as an enemy alien: a fate that had already befallen thousands of Italians and Germans living in England. Gracie and her husband – reportedly at the urging of Churchill – fled to Canada. Her reputation took a battering.

———

MI5 continued to press for Robert's detention. On 10 June, Sir Alexander Maxwell, undersecretary of state for the Home Office, said the matter would be reconsidered if a signed statement about Robert's willingness to help a Nazi submarine crew could be obtained from his unnamed Sandwich Bay neighbour. An MI5 lawyer took the statement, with the informant updating her allegations to say Robert had flouted the blackout and made life difficult for authorities: '[He] leaves his lights on and quarrels with the police,' she said. 'Last week he seems to have changed his attitude towards the searchlight boys. He is now being very nice to them. The boys told me that.' But, in defiance of the Home Office's instruction, she was not asked to sign the statement. 'I told her

I was not proposing to ask her to sign it,' MI5's lawyer blithely explained in his report, 'as I knew her word was as good as her signature.' Yet even with everything MI5 had collected in recent months – not to mention fifteen years' worth of intercepted letters – the agency still didn't have much of a case. 'There was little evidence that Gordon-Canning was of hostile association and less still that he had recently committed any act prejudicial to the public safety,' admitted an officer in a document where he nevertheless argued for Robert's detention due to his BUF connections and willingness to aid German invasion. The problems with these assertions were that Robert had left Mosley's party about a year before the war began and that reports he had pledged to help Nazi invaders were hearsay that flew in the face of his patriotic war service and reputation.

But the noose continued to tighten. On 29 June, Diana Mitford was arrested, and on 7 July Admiral Sir Barry Domvile and his wife were taken into custody. These latest detentions suggested even Mary's freedom was at risk.

Then it hit the pages of the *London Herald*: Robert had been detained under 18B – and released conditionally. Except that hadn't actually happened. Furious at the slander, he consulted his lawyer with a view to libel action.

Tensions escalated further from 10 July, when England started fighting for survival in the Battle of Britain. This was Hitler's bid to destroy the RAF. Once Germany achieved total air superiority, the Nazis would invade England.

Times were dark and getting darker. Yet Mary thought she might have news to brighten their lives. After a year of painful illness, official persecution and escalating war, she believed she was pregnant. On the afternoon of Friday, 12 July, she and Robert welcomed their doctor to their Mayfair flat. Examining Mary, he confirmed she was about six weeks along. That meant she was due to give birth around 22 February – when Mary herself would turn twenty-two.

But the couple's joy was that very moment shattered when Special Branch detectives and Metropolitan police barged into the apartment. Robert was under arrest.

35.

Robert was read his 18B detention order and handed a copy. Two short paragraphs explained the reasons for his arrest: he had been a BUF member, collected money and subscriptions for the party, and written articles for *Action*. 'You are,' it concluded, 'pro-Nazi in sympathy.' Robert wasn't then – nor would he ever be – allowed to see the 'statement of the case' MI5 had used to finally convince the home secretary. The document referenced all the accumulated evidence, along with a new allegation that amounted to anonymous hearsay once removed: 'At the beginning of June 1940, at a dinner party, a statement was made by one of those present that Gordon-Canning gave pro-German parties and boasted how fine it would be when Hitler came here.'

For Robert the arrest was horrific, shameful, infuriating. For Mary the moment was even more awkward because she knew the arresting detective – he had previously been on duty at one of her film studios.

As police searched the apartment and confiscated documents, attention turned to Mary's loyalties. Was she plotting against the British Empire? 'It was altogether fantastic, with allegations that I had flashed signals to submarines lurking off Sandwich,' she later recalled. Her doctor objected; he argued that causing Mary such anxiety might endanger her and the baby. The detectives backed off.

Robert was escorted from the building. Mary was allowed to accompany him as far as the gates of Brixton Prison. They said their goodbyes. He assured her an appeal would surely find the detention unwarranted; she assured him she would do everything she could to secure his freedom. The prison gates swung shut behind Robert.

Mary was now an expectant mother with tuberculosis whose husband had just been jailed as an enemy in the greatest battle the British Empire had ever known. Bereft, angry and confused, she returned to her mother's apartment to try to understand what had happened. How could her husband be in prison? She knew he was a fascist and that he didn't like the Jews. But neither were crimes, and Robert hadn't been in the BUF for up to a year before they met — at least that was what he had said. As for him being pro-Nazi? Robert didn't want war with Germany, and it was true he admired Hitler, but he was also a patriot who would die before being disloyal. Locking her husband up for his political beliefs, Mary may have thought — wasn't that the very thing the Nazis did? Surely the Home Office Advisory Committee would realise the mistake and recommend his release.

Robert began his imprisonment with 'reception', in which he was put into a cell the size of a telephone booth and made to wait . . . and wait . . . and wait. Ordered out, he had to strip, bathe and undergo medical examination. Allowed to dress, though personal possessions were impounded, he was issued coarse beige sheets and led across an inner courtyard to the four-storey F Hall. Robert's bleak cell — one of two hundred — measured a little over two metres wide by three metres deep. There were four brick walls. A bed board and lumpy mattress infested with bed bugs. A small chair and table. A washstand with enamel basin and jug. And a chamber-pot. To see out the high-set window meant standing on stacked furniture – and then the view was of the dismal court-yard. Robert had been born to the manor but now had to accept this squalor as his new home. Unlike even the most common of convicted criminals, he had no idea for how long. He was in the dark in more ways than one. Official lights out was 9.00 p.m. On the night Robert was arrested the sun set twelve minutes later than that. But with the blackout in force and winter approaching, he would have less light with every passing day. If still in prison in a few months, he might spend fifteen hours a day in darkness.

Small articles notifying the public of Robert's arrest made front pages everywhere the next morning. Mary, visibly distressed, told her story, including news of her pregnancy, to Ruby Eve. *Truth* reckoned she had 'found herself the centre of a drama of real-life which most writers of film stories would relish as a plot'. Mary broke down and cried at the thought of giving birth to a baby whose father was behind bars.

Robert was allowed out of his cell around nine that morning. He emptied his chamber-pot and got a little fresh air in the court-yard, where prisoners were allowed to talk and shuffle around in pairs. After an hour, it was back into his cell until lunch, usually a dreary assortment of vegetables. Robert was allowed another hour in the yard in the middle of the afternoon. Prisoners were then able to sit in the open doorways of their cells and talk while they ate their dinner of bread, margarine, a little cheese and a pint of cocoa. Robert was locked in his cell at 4.00 p.m., where he would remain until the following morning. He would be allowed one visitor a week, on Wednesdays, and would be able to send and receive two single-page letters a week.

Mary's comfortable Mayfair flat was no comfort in the days that followed because detectives returned to conduct further searches. No doubt the men enjoyed their work, rummaging through the clothes of the beautiful movie star played a fool by the wealthy Nazi, even if the few documents they confiscated contained nothing incriminating.

Mary met Robert's lawyers to plan his appeal. Then she made jars and jars of jams to cheer up her husband, for he was allowed to receive food and even a little gin. When Wednesday came around, Mary went to the manicurist and hairdresser. Looking her best – and 'glamorising' the staff – she went to see Robert. Unable to embrace, they sat on either side of a screen in a partitioned cubicle, with a warder present the whole time. It was another film déjà vu – she had acted with John Litel in a scene just like this in *Alcatraz Island*.

Mary was offered a lucrative contract for a stage tour with leading comedian Jack Hulbert. She refused, saying she needed to be able to visit Robert each week. Showing a brave face, Mary attended Janet Johnson's wedding to wealthy Charles Birkin, whom she had met during her brief stint in Hollywood. The bride and groom were a picture of wartime romance. Janet's stage career was continuing with a play at St Martin's Theatre, but she was also doing her bit by driving an ambulance. Charles was a successful short-story writer now working for the War Office. When he inherited his father's title, Janet would become Lady Birkin. Mary couldn't do her bit – not with her illness, pregnancy and MI5's suspicions that she was up to no good. Instead, she kept busy handling Robert's business affairs, including the sale of produce from Sandilands. She also wrote to Sir Ernest Bennett, one of her husband's acquaintances, seeking 'help over certain matters connected with her husband's treatment in prison'.

The Home Office's Advisory Committee, already concerned over the quality of evidence used to justify Robert's detention order, heard his appeal on 28 August at the Berystede Hotel. During the interrogation, Hubert Wallington, King's Counsel, and other committee members asked Robert questions about his activities in Morocco and Palestine; when and how he'd made Mosley's acquaintance and joined the BUF; his trips to Germany and meetings with Hitler; and his membership of and resignation from the BCCSE. He had to account for his submarine comment at the Christmas party; the claim he had told John Beckett he would help the Nazis if he had the opportunity; the reason he had planned to meet James Barnes in Rome while Mary convalesced in the South of France; and his queries about the demolition of bridges in Sandwich Bay. The committee wanted a timeline of his break with Mosley and the BUF, and to hear his views on the present war and how he would conduct himself if given his freedom. As a measure of how little it appeared to matter to officialdom, Robert wasn't interrogated about his anti-Semitic writings or activities – and he was canny enough not to volunteer his poisonous views to the committee.

Robert was a convincing witness. The committee accepted that his efforts in Morocco and Palestine had been peaceful; that his overseas trips and meetings with Hitler and other Nazis had been merely fact-finding missions; that his allegedly sinister comments, activities and plans were entirely innocent, misheard or hadn't happened; that his break with Mosley and the BUF was irreparable; and that if released he would engage in no subversion or sabotage. 'Gordon-Canning's interests are now almost entirely limited to the management of his estate, and his personal affairs, and the care of his wife in her illness,' the committee reported, before recommending to the home secretary that Robert be released.

MI5 lodged a strenuous objection. 'Gordon-Canning's history, his position, his wealth, his powers of leadership, his known pro-Nazi views, all combine to render him a very dangerous man,' wrote an MI5 lawyer. 'We should be failing in our duty if we did not oppose, as strongly as we can, a proposal to release a man who at least may possibly be a Fifth Columnist and who we regard as such.'

Robert would remain behind bars while MI5 furthered its case for his continued detention.

———

On Sunday, 7 September, with the RAF close to collapse, Hitler made one of the decisive mistakes of the war. Abruptly changing tactics in retaliation for a minor British air raid on Berlin, he allowed Hermann Göring's air force to begin the terror campaign on London that quickly came to be known as the Blitz. That night, hundreds of German bombers staged a devastating raid, concentrated on the docks and East End, which left 430 people dead and 1500 seriously wounded. With one exception, the Blitz would continue for the next seventy-six nights.

Just over a week later, Spitfires and Hurricanes defended the city against seven daylight waves of German bombers and fighters. But as darkness fell, Londoners knew the RAF would be unable to stop the Luftwaffe's next attack. Thousands fled their homes to sleep in increasingly congested Tube stations. Mary instead sheltered with Bina and Carmel in the deep basement of her Mayfair home. The sirens wailed yet again as 250 German Junkers Ju 88s and Heinkel He 111s rumbled over London, the skies around them lit up by anti-aircraft fire.

Just before midnight, Nazi bombs began raining down on the West End. Then the police were at their basement door. They had to get out. Two timebombs had landed nearby – one two doors away at Number 30 and the other at a vacant lot next to Number 40. Simply stepping onto the street was dangerous, with steel splinters and brick fragments from other explosions flying in all directions, but the trio fled safely to shelter elsewhere. Only now did Lupe, who had been out with a friend, manage to get home. Terrified to find the house deserted, she called out for her mother and sisters. Then the timebombs detonated. The Mayfair apartment shuddered as Number 30 became rubble. Lupe and her friend fled along the street past the fire service fighting the blazing aftermath of the explosions. A tearful reunion followed.

Despite the nightly danger, Mary refused to evacuate. 'I am not going anywhere further than taxi distance from my husband,' she told Ruby Eve, who that week had her own close call when a bomb fell through the roof of her West End flat but failed to detonate.

Inside Brixton Prison, the 18B detainees felt the helpless horror of the Blitz especially keenly. Many of the men had endured years of combat in the Great War and subsequently suffered from shell shock, now known as post-traumatic stress disorder. Plunged into darkness and confined to their cells, they endured long nights listening to bombs whistle from the skies. Unlike most Londoners, they had nowhere to shelter.

MI5 continued its arguments for Robert's detention, claiming that he had been up to no good in Palestine in 1929, that he had later wanted to set up a fascist movement there, and that he would assist the Nazis given half the chance. The Advisory Committee asked why it should believe hearsay from anonymous informers over the word of a man they had interviewed personally and at length. In a long reply, MI5 officer S. H. Noakes referred to a 1929 letter from Palestine's chief of police about Robert and cited his mid-1930s *Action* articles to support the claim he had tried to form a Blackshirt movement. Noakes also vouched for the trustworthiness of MI5's informants and explained the operational need to protect their identities.

In November, Robert was again brought before the Advisory Committee, this time questioned by Sir Norman Birkett, KC, one of England's finest legal minds, most skilled orators and future alternate judge at the Nuremberg trials. No record of the interrogation survives, but on 14 November the committee reversed its recommendation for Robert's release, citing MI5's most recent evidence as swaying the decision. His fate now depended on the decision of the new home secretary, Herbert Morrison. And he was in no hurry to pass judgement.

On the night of Saturday, 23 November, Mary was at the wheel of her car, Bina in the passenger seat, as they drove back to Mayfair after dropping off a friend at home. Conditions were terrible: the streets blacked out, the weather foul, German bombers carrying out a minor raid and London's skies lit up with antiaircraft fire. Mary and Bina had ignored their friend's plea for them not to head back onto the streets.

The car skidded and overturned, coming to rest just a few yards from, of all places, Brixton Prison. There was blood everywhere inside the smashed car. Mary, now six months pregnant, had to fear the worst. But the blood was Bina's, her face severely lacerated. Firemen dragged the women from the wreckage, took them into their nearby station and summoned an ambulance. At the hospital, doctors pronounced that Mary and her unborn child were fine. But Bina required extensive surgery. Granted compassionate leave, Mick was soon at her bedside. Later, in the telling, Bina would leave her grandchildren with the impression that her faint scars had been caused by shrapnel from a Nazi bomb smashing her on Waterloo Bridge.

In mid-December, Robert and his fellow detainees, George Pitt-Rivers and Archibald Ramsay, sent a telegram to their alma mater Eton for its five hundredth anniversary celebrations. The telegram read: 'Etonians fighting for the fatherland, for honour for truth at _____, remembering the playing fields of Eton, salute her. Floreat Etona!' When published in newspapers, their location

('_____') was said to be 'indecipherable' though it was no secret the three men were in Brixton Prison. The phrase 'fighting for the fatherland' seemed especially provocative, given the f-word was most commonly used in reference to Germany, whose bombs had now killed around ten thousand Britons.

———

The Maguires were living with the horrors of war directed against civilians. Even so January 1941 was a hopeful time in their household. Mary was due to give birth in a month. Sure she would have a boy, she had decorated the nursery in blue and had knitted numerous blue clothes. Bina had also made an elaborate blue layette. The christening was to be at St James's Church, where Mary and Robert had been married, with Father Lowry again doing the honours. The baby would wear a beautiful point lace robe that had been in the Gordon-Canning family for more than a century.

With so many suffering so badly, the Maguires were counting their blessings. Mary had come through her pregnancy well despite her illness. Mick was mostly out of harm's way at an army base in Western England, where he had to wash what seemed like five thousand dishes a day and dodge only the occasional German bomb. Patricia would soon find purpose as a Women's Auxiliary Air Force nurse and be busy tending wounded soldiers. Joan's career was taking off, and she had been touring in popular stage farce *Rookery Nook* opposite veteran comic actor Ralph Lynn for six months, with the run to continue into the middle of the year. Carmel, now seventeen, was engaged to seed heir Derek Dunnett, whom she had met in Cannes and who had since divorced his wife. Lupe, now sixteen, was the second-favourite debutante of that year's admittedly surreal social season. Bina had to feel immense pride – her baby was graduating to womanhood just as her favourite daughter was about to become a mother for the first time.

In the third week of January, Ruby Eve came over to the Mayfair flat for tea and to catch up with Mary, Bina and Carmel. She also felt lucky to be alive. In the past week, she had come home from doing a broadcast for the Ministry for Information to find her latest house destroyed by a Nazi bomb. She sought refuge at a friend's place, but then another raid began – a time-bomb landed in front of that house, so Ruby had to flee again. Days later, she was doing war work in a canteen when a bomb hit, killing three of her friends right in front of her. Now, as she talked with the Maguires, bombs again fell on the West End. The women grabbed for Mary's coats – mink, sable, fox – against the freezing weather and rushed into the street just as a house on a nearby corner was blown to smithereens.

'Keep Calm and Carry On' embodied the British spirit. The propaganda newsreel *London Can Take It!* asserted that the city's people could never be broken. While the mental health epidemic that authorities had expected under such bombing didn't materialise, the experiences were still deeply traumatic for many people, and particularly so for those with pre-existing anxious conditions. The pressures of Hollywood had not long ago tipped Mary into a nervous breakdown. Now she spent every night wondering whether a bomb would kill her, her unborn baby, her husband, or her mother, father or sisters. Every morning was to see the death and destruction left by the latest raid, knowing it would probably begin all over again when the sun went down.

Mary reached her breaking point not with a bomb but with bombshell news. On 25 January the Home Office finally announced its decision: Robert was to remain behind bars indefinitely. On hearing this, Mary collapsed and was taken to London Clinic and Nursing Home in Devonshire Place. Robert, through his lawyers, paid £1000 to three of Britain's best doctors to look after her. While Ruby Eve reported that Mary was 'improving', her condition worsened quickly. On 3 February, with her pregnancy in danger, she underwent an emergency caesarean section.

Mary had been right: her baby was a boy. He weighed eight pounds and was delivered safely. But the frail young mother didn't come out of the operating room in anything like good shape. Suffering major surgical complications, Mary hovered close to death.

36.

Robert got the news about Mary – and was afforded some small measure of mercy. David Margesson, Secretary of State for War, intervened on his behalf, urging Home Secretary Herbert Morrison to allow the prisoner to see his wife. Under escort, Robert arrived at the hospital, met by the Maguire clan. They were all relieved that Mary's condition had improved to 'serious', though she was still on the 'danger list'. In the two hours they spent together, the couple decided their child would be named Michael Robert, for the boy's grandfather and father. 'Captain Canning looked exceedingly well,' Bina told a reporter from *The Citizen*. 'Naturally he was tremendously thrilled with his son. The baby is a beautiful boy.'

Mary's condition was upgraded to 'satisfactory' and Robert allowed to visit again the following day. Soon it was reported that the birth and her antenatal care had cost £10 000, which enraged one left-wing newspaper back in Australia. Robert didn't care about the expense, instructing his lawyer to buy his wife a flawless emerald ring as a surprise gift.

Once she was well enough to leave hospital, Mary moved to a cottage in the village of Oxshott in Surrey, where she and baby Michael were safer from German bombs. Their residence was far smaller than Sandilands, but, with hundreds of thousands of homes destroyed or damaged in the Blitz, they were lucky to have a roof over their heads. With the war effort absorbing labour, Mary received regular visits from a nurse rather than having eight servants wait on her. Even so, she made a good recovery, though she remained heartbroken over her husband's internment. By spring she was well enough to make another movie. 'I was so lonely with my husband in Brixton Prison that I decided to return to work again,' she said.

That Mary chose propaganda film *This Was Paris* for her comeback might also help prove her patriotism, particularly as the movie warned against the dangers of fifth columnists. Set in the French capital in the lead-up to the German invasion, it starred Ann Dvorak as a fashion designer and volunteer ambulance driver named Ann Morgan who's investigated by MI5 as a possible Nazi operative and fifth columnist. There were shades of Anna Wolkoff's treachery in the potentially fascist dress designer, though this fashionista is ultimately shown to be an innocent patriot. Ben Lyon played drunken Australian journalist Butch, investigating German spies, with Mary as his brassy girlfriend, Blossom Leroy. Produced by Warner Bros., the film was shot at London's Teddington Studios, which was run by Doc Salomon, Jack Warner's old friend and the company's first-ever employee.

For Mary, Blossom was a new kind of role. 'The surprise of the picture is that Mary Maguire, sweet and simple heroine of such pictures as *The Outsider* and *An Englishman's Home*, goes tough for the first time,' wrote Eric Wigham of the *Manchester Evening News*. Mary wasn't exactly 'tough' in the film, but she was polished and confident, and she had a harder edge than in previous performances.

This Was Paris blurred the real and reel experiences of the war. Like her character Ann, Ann Dvorak was doing her bit driving ambulances. Several bar scenes were set in a famed Parisian watering hole, Harry's New York Bar, with the actual owner, Harry MacElhone, who had fled the German invasion, playing himself. There were reminders everywhere of the war effort, whether at the studio gate with its sign 'Act victory, think victory, or damn well shut up', or in the fact that the production cars and trucks were rolled through scenes to preserve precious petrol. Ann Dvorak wrote to Jack Warner about the esprit de corps on the production. 'It would do your heart good to see how everyone carried on in the face of difficulties that seem positively insurmountable,' she told him. 'One man was working rather late one night and his home was bombed. When he got to the ruins all he could find was his wife's arm. See what I mean? What they don't realise in Hollywood is that it is very important to keep the film business going in England. The money it brings into the country buys all sorts of fighting planes.'

———

In early June, Mary took Michael to be christened. Robert wasn't given clemency to attend. She dressed in black to match her boy's robe and looked positively exhilarated when photographed outside the church. Lord William Montagu Douglas Scott, brother-in-law to the Duke of Gloucester, became the boy's godfather; once a prominent fascist, he had escaped detention. As had Lord Tavistock, now Duke of Bedford, despite his continued agitation for peace and the fact that MI5 thought him likely to lead a puppet government if the Nazis invaded or won the war. There seemed no rhyme or reason to who was imprisoned and who remained free, though the suspicion was that the higher one's social rank the more forgiving the government tended to be of fascist beliefs.

Conditions at Brixton had eased – the food was better and prisoners were allowed more freedom. The *Daily Mirror* portrayed it as an orgiastic country club for coup plotters where inmates cheered every time there was an Allied defeat or disaster. 'Prison officers are overworked taking in food and wine to them,' an article claimed. 'They complained they didn't get morning papers early enough. Now they get them while still in bed.' A prison official told the paper: 'I have to line up at shops to get my cigarettes, but the Fascists get all they want and smoke all day. They are cocky and arrogant. One of them even has a pet budgerigar. Each week married men are allowed to visit their wives, who are kept in Holloway Prison. They are locked in rooms, and prison officials have orders not to disturb them.' But while fascist wives interned at a separate prison were allowed to visit their husbands – and Churchill arranged it so that Oswald Mosley and Diana Mitford were eventually held together – Mary was only allowed to see Robert weekly under the watch of officials. Meanwhile, MI5 was spying on her while trading memos and minutes about her activities.

At least Mary's reputation was still relatively intact in Hollywood – thanks to the recent rise of Louella Parsons' latest gossip columnist rival Hedda Hopper, who wrote:

> She seemed to vanish into thin air and there's been much speculation as to her fate. So Miles Mander would like her friends to know he's just had a letter from Mary's father stating that she's very much alive, has a brand-new son, and is working in an English production, *Banana Ridge*, and turning her salary back to the government. Mary's husband, the wealthy young Robert Gordon-Canning, who joined up at the beginning of the war, is imprisoned somewhere on the Continent.

Mick may have written a letter about his daughter's health and the birth of his grandson, but the rest appears as though Miles was gallantly putting a more acceptable story about Mary into circulation in Hollywood.

On 22 June, Robert's friend Joachim von Ribbentrop's pact with the Soviet Union proved as worthless as Neville Chamberlain's scrap of paper from Munich. Operation Barbarossa saw the Nazis invade Russia. The war was another step closer to engulfing the entire world.

Robert's lawyer, William Rollo of Withers & Co, wrote to Sir Norman Birkett asking for his client's case to be reconsidered with a view to release under restrictive conditions. Birkett agreed to interview Robert again. Prior to the hearing, Robert talked with Rollo at Brixton Prison. 'Canning expressed very strong National Socialist views,' reported the MI5 officer listening to the lawyer–client conversation, 'going so far as to express approval of concentration camps and the Gestapo.' It's unclear why Robert would broach these subjects when he knew that his conversation was being monitored in the lead-up to his appeal. As part of that process, Rollo submitted to the Home Office Advisory Council an unusually frank letter from a doctor to describe Mary's predicament:

> There is no doubt at all that her health is being severely and sadly affected both by the confiscation of her house at Sandwich and more particularly of course by the prolonged separation from her husband. Her nervous stability and mental balance were disturbed by the severity of her confinement six months ago. It involved, as you know, owing to the active lung trouble for which she still has to submit to regular irksome treatments, a hazardous caesarean section followed by major surgical complications, which for a time endangered her life. There is a considerable disparity between their ages, and though she is bound to her husband by the ties of strongest affection, she is an impressionable and impulsive young woman of great

attraction with many acquaintances eager to console her and to lighten her loneliness. I do not hold any brief for Captain Gordon Canning, but if this woman's reason is to be preserved, and at the same time a happy marriage safeguarded, then on ordinary humanitarian grounds I believe it is urgently necessary to rearrange his further detention under conditions whereby husband and wife may enjoy some measure at least of ordinary normal companionship and intercourse.

On 14 August, Robert faced Sir Norman Birkett in his second appeal at a building in Mayfair. He spent the morning answering all the questions he had been asked previously before being allowed to lunch with Mary. Then it was back to being grilled by the committee. During the interrogation Robert said he had always been opposed to the Gestapo and that the number of German concentration camps — at that point widely understood as detention centres for political opponents rather than industrial extermination centres — should be diminished not increased. He said he'd accepted that the war had to be fought and that peace by negotiation was no longer possible. He promised to refrain from socialising anywhere his opinions on the war would be sought. He agreed to live a quiet life with his wife and son wherever he was allowed. He said he would do Red Cross or war work or perhaps farming. He confessed he was frightened at the prospect of being released only to do something that put him back behind bars.

Mary, he claimed, remained his guiding motivation. 'I will tell you this first of all,' he said. 'If I got released my wife would stay in bed all day and do nothing.' She was, he said, the reason he had forsworn much fascist action before the war. 'I had to make a home for her, she was unpolitical and much younger, and I had to sacrifice a good deal of my political activities to make a home for her, and it takes only a reasonable human being to

understand how unlikely I am to be keen to enter politics again.'
Robert reaffirmed that he was nothing but a well-intentioned
patriot. 'My whole life has been spent in trying to foster good
relationships, and I have gone with my own money to try and do
that,' he said. Robert was gambling that his interrogators didn't
know or care about the hatred he'd tried to stir against Jews at
Kitchener Camp or through his articles in *Action* and *Blackshirt*.
'It is terrible to live in this country, and love one's country, and
yet have these charges made,' he told them.

Robert had said everything the Advisory Committee wanted
to hear. Their conclusion was unequivocal:

> The Committee has most anxiously and carefully studied
> Gordon-Canning's character. They are of opinion that he
> is a truthful man, and that his statements, to which they
> have referred, should be accepted. They are indeed satis-
> fied that he is a man of high character and sincere patriotic
> intentions . . .

The report said Robert had been a 'wealthy, freelance, dilettante
dabbler in political affairs both here and abroad' who had 'been
full of cloudy ideas and at times inclined to express them too
freely'. He was, they realised, still a fascist whose heart wasn't in
the war.

> But that a man of his upbringing, his training, his many
> friends, all honourable men, can ever have contemplated trait-
> orous or consciously disloyal action such as assisting the enemy
> is utterly beyond the Committee's belief. They are positive
> that he is not, and never will be, a Fifth Columnist or inten-
> tionally disloyal in any way.

The Committee listed his pledges – to refrain from political
activity, expression of fascist views and even 'opinions likely to

irritate or disconcert his hearers' – and said they believed 'he may now be trusted to keep those promises'. Part of their belief rested on Robert's commitment to Mary:

> Mr Rollo was able to describe to the committee how Gordon-Canning's thoughts and affections and anxieties are now centred on his wife and child; and said that she, though younger than Gordon-Canning, is mature for her age, is opposed to his political interests, and may be trusted to use a good and restraining influence upon him, should such influence ever be required.

The recommendation: 'The order for his detention may now safely be suspended on suitable conditions, the Committee feel satisfied and sure.'

MI5 didn't respond for nearly two months. Case officer S. H. Noakes, who had previously vehemently argued against Robert's freedom, now agreed that his conditional release posed 'no unwarranted danger to security'. But the final decision rested with the home secretary.

Seven weeks dragged by. On 24 November 1941, Herbert Morrison's decision was handed down: Robert would remain in detention.

Robert was outraged. He took his case to the royal family, writing to the Duke of Gloucester, a brother-officer of the 10th Royal Hussars:

> Any suggestive innuendos of treachery etc . . . are spread by discreditable secret agents and are absolutely unwarranted and as shown to and appreciated by Birkett completely unsubstantiated: those reports might be more believable if they were about certain very bellicose politicians with no active service, or even offer of service, to their credit.

Robert went on to say he felt sure the real reason for his detention was not his membership of the BUF but that he had angered
powerful Jews in MI5, seemingly having no idea that the security
service had recommended his release:

> On the Arab question I came into direct conflict with polit-
> ical Zionism whose chief is Dr. Weizmann, a prominent
> supporter, [and Lord] Bearsted, both extremely influential
> in our Security Department. Hence I believe the real reason
> for my imprisonment. David Margesson has taken an interest
> in my case and should be able to exert an honest influence on
> Military Intelligence, in his capacity as War Minister. I beg
> of you therefore to intervene on my behalf in co-operation
> with David and to obtain my immediate release as advised by
> Birkett. [his emphasis]

Perhaps angered by such an allegation, MI5 now told the duke's
private secretary that 'there was good reason for supposing Gordon-
Canning to be disloyal and prepared to assist the enemy', and
advised him to advise His Royal Highness not to intervene on
Robert's behalf. MI5 also noted that Robert's comment about
Weizmann and Bearsted 'to some extent shows how Gordon-
Canning's mind is working'.

On 7 December 1941 the Japanese bombed Pearl Harbor, the
United States declared war on Japan, and Germany declared
war on the United States. The world was now at war. With the
Americans in the fight, Churchill had Roosevelt's full support,
which meant men and materiel would soon arrive in England.

As Robert fumed in Brixton against Jewish people, Mary
shared her first Christmas with her baby son and her doting
family. She had no reason to suspect that MI5 was still worried

about her activities. The Air Ministry had forwarded a report that Mary was in possession of a number of photos taken by the Photographic Reconnaissance Unit. 'You should see letter from Air Ministry,' wrote an MI5 officer on 3 January:

> The results of P.R.U. work . . . are regarded as highly secret, and I understand we should dislike any copies falling into the wrong hands. I have spoken to Wing Commander John, the Provost Marshal's Staff, to ask what action if any they are taking, and you will no doubt consider waiting for his reply so as to avoid overlapping action.

That nothing further came of it suggests a misunderstanding. The pictures may have been from *An Englishman's Home*, which had been made with the cooperation of the Air Ministry.

The start of 1942 brought heartening news for Mary. Although she had made only one movie in the past two and a half years, she made the grade when British theatrical exhibitors released their list of the hundred or so most bankable stars. Granted, she wasn't near the top, but she was still in good company as a 'Group III' player along with Ingrid Bergman, Joan Fontaine, Veronica Lake, Ray Milland, Maureen O'Hara and Basil Rathbone. If Mary could remain healthy, she might still have a movie career.

Mary's health wasn't the concern in the third week of January: baby Michael's was. He had suddenly taken ill, with a barking cough so bad he was having trouble catching breath. Mary rushed him to Westminster Hospital, where doctors diagnosed severe croup. With her son barely able to breathe, they performed an emergency tracheotomy.

The tedium of Robert's life behind bars was broken in the worst way – he would be taken to see his son. Under escort again, he reached the hospital. There, he was met by his distraught young wife and her family, including Mick, who had been granted special leave.

Mary and Robert could only say goodbye as their little boy slipped away. Michael died two weeks before his first birthday.

Mary and Robert's grief was overwhelming. But she would have to rely on her family for comfort because her husband was promptly returned to his cell in Brixton Prison. Robert was allowed to attend his son's funeral at Hartpury House's private chapel.

Nearly eighty years later, Mary Redvers, Robert's niece, remembered sitting on the stairs of the mansion, awaiting the arrival of the tiny coffin bearing the body of her cousin. The child was put to rest beneath a large granite cross that bore the inscription:

MICHAEL
BEAUTIFUL BEYOND COMPARE
SON
OF
ROBERT AND MARY
GORDON-CANNING
BORN 3.2.'41
DIED 21.1.'42
LOVED WITH A VAST AND INEXTINGUISHABLE
LOVE

37.

Mary nearly died from the grief. Apart from her name being attached to films still in cinemas – *This Was Paris* released in April to good reviews – she vanished from the newspapers and security service files for six months.

It's probable that, during this time, Mary lived with her mother and did nothing that would have interested a reporter or an MI5 case officer. It's also reasonable to assume her sorrow came with much guilt and anger. She probably berated herself for not taking Michael to hospital sooner and likely suspected that her tuberculosis had something to do with his croup. Feeling anger at Robert would have been natural. If not for his political beliefs, she wouldn't have been left alone with a baby.

Behind bars in Brixton, Robert had to feel the same sadness and even greater anger. Released in accordance with the Advisory Council and MI5's recommendations, he would have had more time with his son – and maybe been there to help save the boy.

———

Mary had lost her precious child. Her husband remained in prison and bitter at the world. If he had been willing to rail against the Jewish people in a letter to the Duke of Gloucester before

Michael's death, it seems more likely that he wouldn't hold back with his conspiratorial opinions when Mary came to visit. Such ranting couldn't bring Michael back or make anyone feel better.

But Mary might still find some meaning in the career she had always loved. As summer began, she went back to work and won the lead role in *Bedtime Story*. A modern Cinderella comedy, it would mark Mary's British stage debut, with her to play Judy, the poor niece in a household dominated by an aristocratic aunt and her gold-digging daughter. The Fairy Godmother character took the form of an absent-minded but good-hearted uncle, and there was a Prince Charming-style aristocrat, along with a romantic-ally disruptive royal foreigner. A publicity photo showed Mary as a stern-looking adult beauty, hair pulled back, eyes staring down the lens, no trace of smile or smoulder. Starting in late July and running to mid-September, the play would tour the provinces and Wales, meaning that Mary would be unable to visit Robert – which may have been part of the production's appeal.

Though still aching from Michael's loss, and worn down as her husband entered his third year behind bars, Mary did well in *Bedtime Story*. The *Kent & Sussex Courier* noted she had 'delighted Assemby Hall audiences this week with her acting'. The *Yorkshire Post and Leeds Mercury* said of her Bradford performances: 'Last night the holiday audience thoroughly enjoyed the acting of Miss Maguire, who must have been very satisfied with her reception.' The show went on to Brighton and to Hull, whose local news-paper the *Daily Mail* said the 'Gay Little Comedy' was anchored by Mary's performance as Judy. It wasn't the West End she had once dreamt of, but she had to be pleased to have fulfilled her ambition to tread the boards in England – and have a diversion from her grief and an excuse not to see Robert.

By October 1942 there was a renewed push for Robert's release when his old friend Duff Cooper involved himself in the case. This was a magnanimous gesture. In 1938, Robert had publicly criticised Duff when he quit Neville Chamberlain's government over the Munich appeasement. The two men hadn't spoken since. Yet, moved by the evident injustice of Robert's case, Duff visited with Brigadier Sir David Petrie, the new director of MI5, and case officers S. H. Noakes and R. Hollis, telling them he believed Robert could be relied on to fulfil all the previous pledges he had given to stay out of politics. The MI5 men agreed, saying they had recommended his conditional release a year ago. With their approval, Duff drafted a letter to Home Secretary Herbert Morrison, expressing his belief in Robert's loyalty, stressing his bravery in the Great War and emphasising his quarrel with Mosley and his exit from the BUF long before the outbreak of the present war.

> As so far as I am aware, he did nothing after the outbreak of war worse than openly advocate a patched up peace and express the view that Germany was not more to blame than Great Britain. Many people equally guilty, such as the Duke of Bedford and General Fuller, are still at liberty . . . I feel confident that if he gave an undertaking on his word of honour to abstain from politics and from giving interviews to the press during the duration of the war and promised to live on his own estate in the country and to inform the police whenever he left it that he would be as good as his word.

Now there was another obstacle to Robert's release: officialdom worried that cancelling his detention order would set a precedent and lead to other fascists requesting similar leniency. Robert had been detained for more than two years on suspicion of what he might do. He would continue to be kept from freedom and his wife because of how others might react.

———

Even if Robert had walked free then, it would probably have been too late to save his marriage.

MI5 had continued to keep tabs on Mary and, in October, received a report on her from Cardiff police, likely about her coming to the city the previous month with *Bedtime Story*.

Then, on 13 November, an American colonel with the G2 intelligence unit of the United States Air Force contacted an MI5 agent named Ramsbotham. The two men met the following day. After their discussion, Ramsbotham proposed 'no further action'. S. H. Noakes sent a note saying: 'I agree.' The next day MI5 received a police report 're Canning and Mary Maguire'. With the actual documents destroyed, it's not possible to know what this correspondence was about. Yet this was the only time USAF military intelligence was referenced in Robert's MI5 file – and he was sitting in a cell unable to do anything that could affect American Air Force interests.

The chronology suggests that these reports related to Mary because she had started a relationship with an American who was vital to the war effort.

38.

Philip Legarra was everything Robert Gordon-Canning wasn't: young, handsome, working class, an American on the right side of the war. He flew planes like Scotty Allan, Beverley Shepherd, Howard Hughes and so many men Mary had admired. Though not in England as a fighter pilot, his aviation mission might help win the war.

Phil's father, Joaquin Legarra, was born in Tucson, Arizona, in 1875, the son of a Spanish immigrant. His mother, Mary Adams, was from an Irish-American family in New York that claimed ancestry from American president John Quincy Adams. The couple had married in 1898, settled in Arizona and had four children.

Phil was the youngest, born in Nogales on 10 December 1914. A tight-knit family, they moved to California around 1930 and settled in Inglewood, South Los Angeles, where Joaquin worked as the manager of a shoe store. Phil went to Los Angeles' Manual Arts High School, which specialised in training students for practical employment, though work was hard to find as the Depression worsened. By his senior year Phil stood an inch shy of six feet and was darkly handsome, with grey eyes, brown hair and an olive complexion. He was smart, good at maths and English, and popular with his fellow students, who elected him vice-president of the student government. Looking back on his senior year, he may have been inspired by his yearbook, whose foreword exhorted graduates to model themselves on the daring aviators of the day. 'There is about pilots and piloting an adventurous air of unfaltering strength and cool thinking in the face of danger that fires the imagination,' it read. 'The pages of history and the pages of fiction are filled with stirring tales of skill and daring by the few who are destined to guide the footsteps of their fellows.' Meant as metaphor, Phil took it more literally.

At the end of 1935, economically depressed Inglewood received a much-needed shot in the arm when North American Aviation (NAA) relocated its manufacturing plant there from the East Coast. Phil started with the company in March 1937 as a painter's helper on the night shift. It was a lowly position but the company rewarded hard workers, with designers, engineers, mechanics and even pilots as likely to learn on the job as they were to have graduated university. Before long Phil was a service mechanic in the department overseeing final aircraft assembly, and in 1939 took his growing skills to the flight test department.

NAA was booming. Awakened from its torpor by Nazi rearmament and the devastation that German bombers had unleashed in the Spanish Civil War, the American military had realised the urgent need to update and expand its air force. When Phil joined the company, NAA had one thousand employees and orders for 117 aircraft worth $5.2 million. By the end of 1939 NAA had more than 4600 workers and that year delivered nearly eight hundred planes worth $50 million. The plant ran like a precision instrument, with Charles Lindbergh visiting in mid-1939 and calling it 'a very efficient establishment – in many ways the most efficient I have yet seen'. It was a time of much design and testing, with the company's biggest success to date the B-25 Mitchell medium bomber. Another promising project was the plane that became known as the P-51 Mustang. Commissioned by the British RAF just before the fall of France in April 1940, this new fighter plane went from the drawing board of its designer, Edgar Schmued, to its first test flight in just five months.

In this heady environment, Phil's rapid rise through the ranks continued. In 1940 he was made final assembly inspector, and in September 1941 he transferred to field service: the department that looked after airfield assembly, testing, modification and repair. If anyone needed confirmation that NAA was doing important war work, they had it in April 1942 when Colonel James H. Doolittle – another alumnus of Manual Arts High School – commanded the company's B-25s on the retaliatory raid for Pearl Harbor over mainland Japan. And if anyone needed confirmation that NAA considered Phil a rising talent, they had it when the 27-year-old was sent to England to head up the office there, and oversee the assembly and testing of the first major shipment of Mustangs.

With his friend and colleague Wilson Burtis, Phil worked out of the company's offices at St John's House on Smith Square in London. Yet a lot of their time was spent at RAF airfields. 'We were fairly certain, of course, that the Mustang would change the war in the air to a marked degree, because we knew how good it was,' Philip reflected in an article he penned for NAA's in-house magazine, *Skyline*, in 1943. But his confidence was dented after he saw two captured German fighters being flown and heard how highly British airman rated these enemy planes. 'We retired to our hotel room, muttering like old hens, and awaited our Mustangs,' he wrote. 'The first was duly assembled and after a test flight was made ready to go to an experimental field, where we knew we would learn whether or not our aircraft was really a good type.' The verdict from pilots was a thumbs-up. One airman was particularly impressed:

'Oui, Philip,' he called, 'this is a fine kite. It will do a lot of good work over here.' We were all pleased, so we adjourned to the village pub to talk about it. The pilot, Fl. Lt. Clive, whom we all knew as 'India', has since become one of the staunchest of Mustang supporters. He summed up his views in a few words: 'I believe in it.'

Belief wasn't enough. Phil had to learn the science of air fighting in order to understand the testing that would be necessary. He talked to pilots who had fought the Battle of Britain, and ensured Mustangs were flown against every type of British and German fighter and bomber available, the aircraft's attacking and breaking away capabilities recorded, tabulated and sent to operational squadrons to be studied by pilots. As Mustangs began to be delivered, these studies proved their usefulness. 'Many pilots have lived longer as a result of these tests,' he wrote. It was difficult and dangerous work; airfields were subject to raids from German fighters and bombers. 'We have had Mustang squadrons operating from airdromes that were not yet completed,' Phil wrote. 'Personnel members lived in tents. With snow on the ground, it was not pleasant as a steady thing. Because of the constant blackout, work done at night was done with a minimum of light. At times the temperatures were such that gloves had to be worn so that the workman's hands did not freeze to the metal they touched.'

Phil was brutally honest about the stakes. 'Mistakes are non-habit forming,' he wrote.

A mistake made where the plane was born can sometimes cost a pilot and an aircraft. Mistakes in servicing the aircraft take a similar toll. The pilot usually has only one mistake of any magnitude to make; his work must always be every bit of the best that he can muster. A pilot who is not a good worker cannot be carried by the rest of the pilots. The automatic process of elimination relieves him of his job.

The Mustang was well received by the RAF as a low- and medium-altitude attack fighter that was faster than the Spitfire to twenty-five thousand feet. But its true potential was envisaged on 30 April 1942 by a Rolls-Royce liaison pilot named Ron Harker, who suggested fitting the plane with the powerful Merlin engine produced by his company for the Spitfire. Rolls-Royce followed his advice, and by mid-June its director, Ernest W. Hives, believed the conversion was a winner. 'The risk, of course, [is] that if we make the Mustang into a first-class machine, the U.S. will want to collar them,' he wrote. Phil was one of those who saw the hybrid plane's potential and made it his mission to convince his NAA bosses back in the United States of its merit. At the US embassy, he had a very influential ally in American assistant air attaché and pilot Tommy Hitchcock, Jr, a passionate advocate of the Mustang who also had a good relationship with Rolls-Royce. While Phil was a working-class company man, Tommy had the ear of America's political, military and industrial elite. Born into a wealthy New York family, as a teenager he became a heroic Great War pilot. In the 1920s he was an internationally famous polo player, married the daughter of a Gulf Oil founder, became a partner at Lehman Brothers and lived such a big life that he inspired friend F. Scott Fitzgerald's characters Tom Buchanan in *The Great Gatsby* and Tommy Barban in *Tender Is the Night*. When Tommy Hitchcock lobbied, people listened.

On a technical level, Phil ensured that Rolls-Royce shared its conversion information with NAA. In late July 1942, it seemed that keeping up the pressure was paying off when the company received an RAF contract for two Merlin Mustangs. But, frustratingly, work didn't begin until September. Visiting NAA in

Inglewood that month, Philip was dismayed by such slow progress and how little official interest there was in the project. After returning to England, he told Tommy that he felt the Mustang had been given the lowest priority NAA could grant a plane. Tommy cited Phil's frustration in an October 1942 memo, fittingly titled 'Development of a Thoroughbred'. In it, he sought to shame both sides into putting aside petty nationalism:

> Sired by the English out of an American mother, the Mustang has had no parent in the Army Air Corps or at Wright Field to appreciate and push its good points . . . The development of the Mustang as a high altitude fighter will be brought about by cross-breeding it with the Merlin 61 engine . . . it does not fully satisfy important people on both sides of the Atlantic who seem more interested in pointing with pride to the development of a 100% national product than they are concerned with the very difficult problem of rapidly developing a fighter plane that will be superior to anything the Germans have.

Tommy would soon be in Washington, pushing harder for Anglo-American cooperation to make the new Mustang a priority.

Philip hoped he would succeed. The course of the war might depend on it.

39.

Mary met Phil while doing war work as a driver for an American Air Force general. At least, that was the story in an *Australian Women's Weekly* article that appeared much later. This seems a conflation of events. MI5 *did* report that Mary – once suspected to be a spy – was approved for confidential war work with the US Eighth Air Force. This might have seen her behind the wheel of a car for an American general, but that application wasn't made until November 1943, and by then she and Phil had been together at least six months. Given that the initial USAF military intelligence query came in late 1942, it seems probable she and Phil met at this time. It could have been during her *Bedtime Story* tour, when she attended an RAF show in Hull, East Yorkshire, in September to sign autographs for a servicemen's charity, or simply out at a pub or club in London, the post-Blitz nightlife by then serving as cathartic release for the battered city.

'Looking back, I realise that London was hilariously gay then, with only playboys and playgirls left,' Patricia Maguire would later recall. It was in this atmosphere that she again met Peter Aitken, Lord Beaverbrook's younger son, at the Berkeley Hotel. Since they had first met in Cannes in 1938, Peter had divorced his wife, become a captain in the Royal Fusiliers and, while serving on the docks

during the Blitz, fallen down a tank trap and broken both his legs
– one was still in a cast. As a WAAF nurse, Patricia was working
in a dental surgery and, in late October 1942, she burned her leg
and was given a week's 'no duty' certificate but wasn't entitled to
take leave. 'Peter phoned me, however, and we went out,' she said.
'We decided to get married on the dot. Mary was with us, as well
as Peter's sister, but I didn't even have time to tell the family.'

The wedding of these lovers with leg injuries was held at a
small church in Brighton. Bina and Mick got the news by telephone, as did Lord Beaverbrook. 'It was the craziest wedding I've
ever been to, even if it was the loveliest,' Patricia said. 'I still don't
know whether or not I'm AWL [absent without leave]. Maybe the
first policeman I see will pick me up – even if I am only a bride
of a few days.' While Lord Beaverbrook didn't approve of anything his younger son did, he allowed the newlyweds to live in
a cottage on his grand Cherkley estate. Now in the orbit of her
fabulously wealthy and powerful father-in-law, Patricia was soon
meeting the nation's most influential people when they came to
visit, including Winston Churchill. But Peter's leg wound was so
bad that he had to be invalided out of the army. This was even
harder for him to take because his brother, Max, was a heroic
Spitfire pilot who had helped win the Battle of Britain and continued to blow Germans out of the sky.

Five years earlier, Louella Parsons had predicted Mary Maguire was
set for stardom and ribbed her about vamping too many eligibles.
As 1943 got under way, she offered a sobering account of what
had become of the little Australian star she had liked so much:

> The tragic story of Mary Maguire, who was under contract to
> Warners and 20th Century-Fox as an actress for several years, has

come to this desk. Mary went to England and married Captain Robert Gordon-Canning, a titled Englishman. She was married in a wheelchair in 1939 while recovering from tuberculosis, but when the war started her husband was interned because of his strong Fascist views. Then came the death of her 10-month-old baby and Mary collapsed. Report is she was so grief-stricken at her accumulation of sorrows she nearly died. However, more recent word is that she is sufficiently recovered to make a picture.

Louella had her facts pretty much right and was the first to report the truth about her one-time pal's tuberculosis.

Even though Mary might have been well enough to make movies, she wasn't being offered any. Instead, beautiful young Lupe was cast in a minor role in *The Man in Grey*, opposite James Mason, Margaret Lockwood and Stewart Granger.

———

Mary's lack of film work seemed trivial beside Phil's mission to do what he could to help ensure the Mustang was remade into a war-winning weapon. By mid-1943, unbeknownst to Robert, they were 'living in sin' at her Knightsbridge Court apartment, and his work was more crucial than ever.

The Allied invasion of Western Europe would be necessary to defeat Hitler. For that to be possible the Americans and British believed they had to establish air supremacy and destroy Germany's industrial ability to make war. They planned to do this with bombing raids carried out by big American B-17 Flying Fortresses operating out of bases in England and escorted by P-47 Thunderbolt fighters. But the Thunderbolts only had sufficient fuel to protect the Fortresses as far as the German border. Strategists predicted that once the fighters turned back for base, the Fortresses' gunners could defend their planes if they were flown in tight formations.

The theory was devastatingly disproved on 17 August 1943. The Eighth Air Force sent 361 Fortresses to destroy German aircraft factories in a dual daylight raid on Schweinfurt and Regensburg. After the Thunderbolts peeled off, the Luftwaffe inflicted aerial carnage on a scale never before suffered by the Allies. Sixty Fortresses were shot down and eighty-seven were so badly damaged they had to be written off or abandoned at airfields in North Africa. Five hundred and sixty-five men were lost that day, half killed and half taken prisoner or interned in Switzerland. Nearly every plane returned awash with the blood of dead and dreadfully wounded crew. Incredibly, two months later it happened again. Nearly three hundred unprotected Fortresses raided Schweinfurt; sixty planes were lost outright and 650 men – almost one in four – were killed or captured. After that, bombing raids were suspended until suitable fighter escorts were made available.

The P-51D Mustang, as the Merlin Mustang was known, would be that plane. Finally, American and British authorities had listened to what Tommy Hitchcock, Philip Legarra and the plane's other numerous champions were saying. Mass production started at NAA's Inglewood plant in June 1943. Soon after the second disastrous B-17 raid, Mustangs started to arrive for use by the Eighth and Ninth Air Forces, with Philip overseeing delivery, final assembly and field testing. Fitted with supercharged Merlin engines, these P-51Ds could fly at 440 miles an hour to altitudes of forty-two thousand feet. Redesigned with a large additional fuel tank and drop tanks, they would be able to escort bombers right into the heart of Germany and then attack targets at will on their return flights. There was no better fighter plane in the sky.

But tests and design modifications were continually being made to correct issues caused by this very speed and power. Under some conditions, Mustang tails came off. In others, the wings went.

Mary knew what she had to do. It was a terrible feeling – but also a liberating one. She was glad to have laid some groundwork by mentioning her new friend occasionally when she visited her husband.

Around May 1943, Mary went to Brixton to confess. She told Robert she had fallen in love with Philip. He pleaded with her to reconsider. She said she couldn't.

Robert was crushed – and helpless. Detained for his political views and on suspicion of what he might do, he hadn't lost only three years of freedom, but had been robbed of his son's life and his wife's love. While he rotted in his cell, she was out there with another man.

On 8 August 1943, Mary received a phone call telling her Robert might be about to be released from Brixton. After so many false alarms, she didn't believe it and carried on with her morning. But it was true. As abruptly as he had been seized, Robert was set free, albeit on strict conditions. Even though MI5 and Special Branch knew of her adulterous cohabitation with Phil, and Robert's release was dependent on him living at Hartpury House, he was nevertheless allowed to spend a week in London. 'I was unable to believe my eyes when I saw him walk in after his release at noon today,' Mary told *Truth*. This was true – just not for a reason printed in the article. 'Discussing their future plans, Mary said that she had been so taken by surprise that she did not know quite what she was doing.' This was untrue – she was staying with Phil despite Robert's renewed pleas for her to remain his wife.

Robert had no choice but to retreat to Gloucestershire. With his properties Hill House and Tween Hills leased to tenants, he stayed with his old aunt at Hartpury House. Yet it wasn't much of a refuge. In keeping with tradition, from 1940 his aunt had given over the lower floor for use as a military hospital. In its

grand rooms airmen and soldiers were recovering from recon-
structive surgery to repair their battle-shattered faces. To aid their
morale and promote camaraderie, these disfigured warriors all
wore identical blue suits, white shirts and red ties, making them
look like swatches from the Union Jack. Though indebted to
his aunt, they surely took a dim view of Robert. He kept to his
private rooms upstairs. Not that it was easy to find peace there –
his time in prison had caused claustrophobia and for the rest of
his life he would leave doors open.

Three weeks after his release from Brixton, a pair of MI5
officers came to visit. His aunt was thrown into a panic, thinking
her nephew was about to be rearrested. Instead, the men just
wanted to know his opinions of some of his fellow detainees.
During the conversation, Robert told the MI5 officers he was
now certain that his detention had been orchestrated by the Jews.
As one of the officers would report:

> Towards the end of the interview Captain Gordon-Canning
> said that his detention had increased his anti-Jewish feelings
> and he was not sure that he could now say that he was without
> desire for revenge. [We] formed the strong impression that
> Captain Gordon-Canning might well be suffering from some
> form of mild mental derangement . . . We were partly led to
> this conclusion by Captain Gordon-Canning's appearance. I,
> at any rate, thought that he was not completely normal, and
> that when he spoke about the Jews there was a flash of fan-
> aticism in his demeanor. On one or two other occasions he
> had what I can only describe as a rather hang-dog or furtive
> look; but in justice to the man I think that this may be due
> to his long period in prison.

Despite his revolting views and actions, Robert was justified in
feeling himself a victim of unfair treatment. Winston Churchill,

who had spoken of the need for 18B detention in his powerful 1940 post-Dunkirk speech, had in the three years since come to regret suspending *habeas corpus* to put the fascists and other presumed enemies behind bars. In November 1943, after Mosley was released, Churchill sent an approving cable from Cairo where he was meeting with Roosevelt:

> The power of the executive to cast a man into prison without formulating any charge known to the law, and particularly to deny him the judgement of his peers, is in the highest degree odious and is the foundation of all totalitarian government whether Nazi or Communist.

From January 1944 the Eighth Air Force was put under the command of James Doolittle. The following month he launched 'Big Week', an intensive bombing campaign aimed at luring the Luftwaffe into battle where they could be taken on by the Mustangs.

That month the Germans lost one-third of their single-engine fighters and one-sixth of their fighter pilots. By early March the Allies had achieved air superiority, and Doolittle now ordered Mustang squadrons to fly far ahead of the B-17 Flying Fortress and B-24 Liberator formations to engage and destroy Luftwaffe defenders.

German losses worsened. In April more than half their fighters were destroyed and one in five pilots were killed. Replacing men and machines became increasingly difficult, while the USAAF was recruiting from a homeland untouched by war where NAA was now producing the planes in astonishing numbers.

Hermann Göring would later say that he knew the war was lost the moment he saw Mustangs escorting bombers over Berlin.

Philip was immensely proud of his contribution, though sad
that Tommy Hitchcock didn't live to see it. On 18 April 1944,
after problems were identified with the Mustang's ability to pull
out of dives, he jumped into a cockpit to see where the trouble
lay. His plane smashed into the earth.

———

The Maguire family might have been living modestly at the start
of the war but by the time its end was in sight they were living
in a mansion in Marylebone Road in Regent's Park opposite
the Royal Academy of Music. In early 1944, a photographer for
Australian magazine *Pix* visited to capture their lifestyle and show-
case how beautiful each of the girls had become. The photos
show a spacious house, tastefully decorated with art, antique furniture and comfortable lounges. With Mary, Carmel and Joan
watching on in amusement, Mick, now portly and grey though
still a dapper dresser, sparred with Lupe, wearing a blouse and
shorts that showed off the legs Bina reckoned the finest in the
family. Carmel, a ravishing brunette with aquiline features, posed
spread out on the floor, sketching a dress design, with the caption
claiming she had been responsible for many of the outfits her
sisters Mary and Joan had worn on stage. The family was pictured taking tea, Mick and their housekeeper Mrs Bogg serving
Bina and the girls. There were photos of the sisters reading and
knitting in a lovely sitting room, and stepping out on a West End
shopping trip. The Marylebone manse became almost as famous as
their Cannes villa had been, with the family equally embracing of
London's elite and Australian servicemen. In March Carmel, yet
to turn nineteen, finally married Derek Dunnett, now invalided
out of the RAF, at St James's Church, with a huge reception held
at the Dorchester Hotel. Sydney's *Truth* reported the nuptials with

glee under the headline 'Triumphs for the Marrying Maguires'. The article concluded:

> Joan, whose stage career is well under way, and Lupe, the baby, an accomplished dancer, are the only fledglings left in the Maguire nest, but London gossips report millionaire admirers among the callers at the Regent's Park home of Mike Maguire and his clever and charming brown-eyed wife. Once mine-hosts of Brisbane's Bellevue Hotel, this genial pair now dispense their own inimitable hospitality to many a famous personality in London's social and political world.

Shortly after, Bina and Mick were thrilled at the prospect of becoming grandparents again when Patricia announced that she and Peter were expecting their first child.

On 6 June 1944 Mick got a fine present for his fiftieth birthday – D-day and the Allied invasion of Europe. German defeat now looked inevitable but Mary and her family were again at risk in London a week later when vengeance attacks began with V-1 flying bombs. These terror weapons, whose buzzing engines struck fear when they abruptly ceased – indicating they were about to plummet to earth – soon smashed into south-east England at the rate of a hundred a day. On a fine afternoon Phil's friend and colleague Wilson Burtis took a photo from NAA's office window as a couple of these 'buzz bombs' streaked past Big Ben.

Mary didn't have close calls like she had in the Blitz, though she didn't feel safe, especially after 121 people were killed on 18 June when a V-1 hit Wellington Barracks, not far from her Knightsbridge apartment. Though that was the worst single tragedy of the vengeance attacks, Mary felt another one keenly when Doc Salomon and two of his Warner Bros. workers were killed by a V-1 hitting Teddington Studios. The V-1 and the silently terrifying V-2 rockets would claim more than six thousand lives over nine months.

————

In October 1944 Patricia gave birth to a son named Tim. Mary's joy for her sister was tempered by her own haunting loss. Had Michael lived, he would now be three and a half, old enough to understand that he had a cousin.

At Hartpury, Robert traded letters with his released fascist friends, assessing the progress of the war and predicting – though never expressly hoping for – a German pushback in Europe. On the home front, he had accepted defeat in his marriage and filed for divorce, needing to seek written permission from the Metropolitan Police to visit his lawyers in London and to attend court.

Mary's adultery and the name of her lover became public on 20 November 1944 in the Divorce Court when Robert was granted a decree nisi on the grounds of his wife's 'misconduct' with Philip. Mary didn't attend the hearing. Robert recounted how she had mentioned Philip during visits and then a few months before his release confessed to the affair. He said he had begged her to reconsider then and had done so again after being freed from Brixton. Mary and Philip's adultery was confirmed – as was required in such cases – by her housekeeper testifying that the couple had been shacked up for some time.

Mary's star had faded to such an extent in England that her adultery and divorce were reported perfunctorily in only a few newspapers. But Australia's ongoing fascination with the Maguires saw *Truth* send its newly arrived London correspondent L. G. Richards to visit the Knightsbridge love nest the next day. What resulted was a long article headlined 'Mary Maguire Has Found New Love – Captain Husband Wins Freedom'. It began:

The story was the old familiar wartime one of a wife left behind, an engaging Allied officer arriving from over the ocean, friendship, then something more, then a broken marriage. There was a difference in this case, however, for Mary's husband, Captain Gordon-Canning, wasn't away fighting his country's battle when American officer Philip Legarra took over his duties on the home front . . . With Mary not defending the suit, the judge cut the knot, thus putting on record the first check to the steady matrimonial progress of this remarkable Australian family who have come to be known as the Marrying Maguires.

Wearing a black suit and pearls, Mary perched in an easy chair, legs tucked beneath her as always, and told the reporter her side of the story. 'I suppose I was a bit young to be married,' she said. 'I was probably swept off my feet by Robert Canning, who is tall, handsome and distinguished-looking, and was a persistent suitor.' She recounted that they had met through Miles. 'It was something of a whirlwind romance, and I thought I was genuinely in love. Robert treated me like a princess. He couldn't have been kinder, more considerate or generous. But then, I was sickening with tuberculosis all that time. It was a tremendous shock to me when suddenly, while I was very ill, Scotland Yard men walked in and took my husband away . . . I visited my husband while I was physically capable of doing so. Then my son was born and died. I was very ill. Canning was let out of prison temporarily because I was on the verge of dying. But I recovered and resumed my life – such as it was.'

The reporter told her what Robert had told the court about the progression of her infidelity. 'Is that the way it went?' she commented. 'If that's what Canning said, then that's right. That is the English way of putting it.' Her response suggested she had a differing view of events on which she wouldn't elaborate. Mary realised she was now a scandalous woman but professed no regrets. 'Apart from the shock this is going to be to my grandparents in Melbourne and also to many other of my Australian friends, I am unashamed of what I have done.' Philip walked into the room during the interview, described by the reporter as a 'youngish, smart American', though he let Mary do the talking:

> 'I've been married for five years and haven't seen my husband, except intermittently, for the past three years,' Mary said. 'It's distressing, but that's the way it is. I'm sure there are lots of people who won't forgive me for what I've done, but most women would do the same in similar circumstances, I'm sure. There is nothing for me to do here officially during the war because I had tuberculosis. There is no place for me in British war work for that reason. My baby didn't live. I was practically alone in London. Film work was impossible because I had a husband in gaol and I was more or less under suspicion. In any case, I am not apologising for falling in love with someone my own age. That is natural.'

A version of this article appeared in Brisbane's *Truth*, though minus the by-line and padded by more than six hundred words. Much new material comprised a rewrite man's colourful recap of Mary's life:

> Them Maguire gals certainly knew how, reflected the old home town . . . [which] cocked an eye askance at the hairless dome of Mary's bridegroom, when it saw his picture, it nevertheless held its breath ecstatically and ooh'd and ah'd to the limit of its respiratory capacities over the wedding itself. For nothing could have been more filmy than that.

The rewriter reworded Mary's quotes and even put the reporter's description of Phil into her mouth, as though she was commentating on him while he was in the room. This version also contained a new paragraph, wedged between her descriptions of Robert's kindness to her and his sudden arrest:

> *Truth* interposed a question whether Mary hadn't known of the Captain's Fascist leanings at the time of the marriage, to which Mary replied: 'I certainly did not. At that time, I thought Hitler was the only fascist in the world. I didn't understand what it was all about — I was not interested in anything else except setting up a home and becoming — if you like to put it that way — a dutiful wife. It was a tremendous shock to me when suddenly, while I was very ill, Scotland Yard men walked in and took my husband out . . .'

This version added another credulous note from Mary: 'As I told you, I didn't know then, and I don't know now, that Captain Gordon-Canning was associated with fascism in any form.' Did Mary actually expect anyone to believe that? They were ludicrous claims, not least because she had previously been quoted as rejecting Robert's fascism. In the best Maguire tradition, Mary may have been trying to rewrite family history in the newspapers. But if that was the case it was odd those juicy quotes *weren't* in the Sydney *Truth* story, suggesting Brisbane's excitable rewrite man simply made them up. The word 'obvious' doesn't appear once in the original article, and isn't overused in other pieces L. G. Richards filed for the newspaper, but it pops up three times in speculative new sentences about her motivation:

> Though Mary didn't tell *Truth* in so many words, she is nevertheless obviously in love with the young American, Philip Legarra, an aeroplane expert . . . This indicated — without her saying so — that her husband is 21 [sic] years her senior, and that, in gaol, he was not in the race with Legarra, who was

on the spot and not many years older than herself, and obviously dotes on her . . . Mary refused to indicate whether she proposes to marry again, though it does seem obvious. She is very anxious to get back to America, and continue her film career, and hopes one day soon to return to Australia, where she would like to make films, too.

Mary's wedding to Robert had made the papers all around the world. But when she married Philip there wasn't a reporter or photographer in sight. The nuptials – held on 2 March 1945 at the Westminster Register Office, with Carmel acting as witness – weren't glamorous, though if alerted *Truth* surely would have been there for a quote or two. If the couple honeymooned, it went unreported. Any such celebration would have been short because Phil was still busy helping NAA make the P-51 Mustang even lighter and faster.

But that Mustang would never need to fly against the Germans. On Monday, 7 May, London's pubs were packed with people celebrating the wonderful news: the guns in Europe had fallen silent. It wasn't official yet, but the war in Europe was over. The next day, a million people thronged the city to hear Prime Minister Winston Churchill make the announcement. 'Today is victory in Europe Day,' he told them, voice amplified over speakers. 'Advance Britannia. Long live the cause of freedom. God save the King.' The crowd erupted in applause. A two-day party followed.

This was mission accomplished for Phil in England, though the P-51 Mustang would continue to be vital to the war against Japan. After more than three years away, he was ready to go home to California. Mary, too, was finally free – of Robert, of studio contracts, of MI5 suspicion, of the war – and able to return to

America. Just over a week after the German surrender, she had her new passport in her new official name: Helene Teresa Legarra.

Six weeks after that, she and Phil were ready to leave London. There were teary farewells with Bina, Mick and her sisters. But Mary could take pride in what she had done for them. Her mum and dad were living well in the house in Regent's Park. Patricia was mother to Lord Beaverbrook's grandson and pregnant with her second child. Carmel's husband was set to inherit one of the nation's biggest fortunes. Joan's stage career continued to flourish, with her about to star in a production of *No, No, Nanette*. Lupe was so pretty and popular that her future was assured. Mary had once told Stanley Parker of *Table Talk* that one of her goals had been to take care of her family. She couldn't take credit for all of their successes but her stardom had made the lives they enjoyed possible. Mary also had to feel relief at leaving bomb-ruined London, where she had been hollowed out by so much tragedy.

Mary and Phil sailed from Glasgow for New York City on the Cunard liner *Eros* on 2 July 1945. Although she listed her name on the passenger manifest as Helene Legarra and gave her occupation as 'Housewife', the woman who knew herself best as Mary Maguire was hoping to make a comeback as a movie star.

PART FOUR

The Marrying Maguires

40.

Mary and Phil sailed past the Statue of Liberty on 11 July 1945, the same clear summer day the *Queen Mary* led a fleet of eight packed transports into New York Harbor to bring home 35 000 American and Canadian soldiers in the biggest repatriation since V-E Day. While soldiers hugged wives, girlfriends, sisters and mothers, Mary answered questions − not from reporters wanting to know her comeback plans but from immigration officials wanting to know about her health. Placed on a medical hold for her tuberculosis, she was taken to Ellis Island for observation. After further interrogation and X-rays, Mary was allowed to enter the United States. This indignity was nothing more than an immigration protocol, yet it was a world away from how she had once been greeted in Auckland and Honolulu, Los Angeles and London.

Mary and Philip took their time getting back to California, perhaps enjoying some sightseeing on an overdue honeymoon. Mary knew her comeback would be hard work. She had put on weight and was nearly a decade older than when she had first wowed the studios. She had once told a reporter that staying away from films for a year made it almost impossible for an actress to get back into the business. Mary hadn't made a movie in four years − and had left Hollywood almost twice as long ago. None of her British films had benefited from the publicity given to her American productions, and her name no longer meant much to audiences. Then there was the whole matter of Robert, surely off-putting for many in Hollywood, be they Jewish or Gentile.

On her way back to California, Mary wrote to Louella – or someone close to her – to announce her plans. The gossip queen's column soon contained her news:

> Mary McGuire [sic], who left Hollywood six years ago for London and ran into so much personal trouble, is on her way back to Hollywood and a new try at the movies. To be exact, she is in Las Vegas at the moment with her new husband, Philip Legarra, and she has written friends she hopes all the dark clouds have lifted and this will be a new start for her. She was married, previously, in London to an older man who was suspected and tried for his Nazi sympathies. Mary suffered a nervous collapse and her friends feared she might never recover her health. Her new bridegroom is an American who represented an American aircraft company in England.

This was also a world away from the glowing endorsements Louella had once offered. Misspelt surname, nervous collapse, poor health, Nazi ex and a new non-celebrity husband: she might have been Hollywood's least likely comeback prospect.

Mary got a warmer welcome from the Legarra family in Los Angeles. She met Phil's parents Joaquin and Edith, and his brother Rolland and sister-in-law Opal. She made fast friends with their eighteen-year-old daughter Betty, who was thrilled that her uncle, whom she thought a handsome and charming catch, had met and married his match. The Legarras all got together once a week for a family dinner. 'Having a movie star in the family was exciting and interesting,' Betty recalled in 2017, at age ninety. 'She was a blazing personality then. When I first met her she was attractive, friendly and nice to me. She was always happy talking to people and we were happy talking to her.' Betty was struck by Mary's ease and natural beauty. 'She wasn't vain, although she had a right to be. She got on with everyone. She was a very welcoming person.'

Phil was proud of what he had done to beat the Nazis, even if it was not as easily explained as the heroics of returned soldiers who had stormed the beaches of Normandy and fought their way to Berlin. 'The P-51 was our favourite family plane,' Betty said. 'We were all very interested in how the war went and what everyone contributed, and Phil contributed a lot as far as the family was concerned.'

Even across a distance of five thousand miles, Robert intruded on Mary's new life at the end of November when he disgraced the front page of the *Los Angeles Times* – and newspapers all over the world. At an auction of items from the German Embassy in London, he had bought a 250-kilogram granite bust of Hitler for £500. The shameful sale was even filmed by British Pathé's newsreel unit. Another former 18B detainee purchased numerous huge swastika standards meant to have flown over Nazi-conquered London.

Robert and his fellow unrepentant fascist were reported to be loaning their expensive souvenirs to James Battersby, another 18B man, at the auction, so they might be 'venerated' at Kingdom House, the Sussex HQ of newly formed Hitler cult the Legion of Christian Reformers. 'We in the Legion regard Hitler as a divine instrument to break the power of the Mammon system,' said Battersby, who would set forth his beliefs in a book called *The Holy Book and Testament of Adolf Hitler.* 'You cannot serve God and Mammon. Hitler was most definitely sent by God to judge the world.' Robert weighed in. 'Nearly 2000 years ago Jesus was mocked, scorned and crucified,' he said. 'Today He is a living force in the hearts and minds of millions of people in the West, and those who mocked and scorned and tried Him today are of no account.' Asked by the *Daily Mirror* what any of that had to do with the Hitler statue, he replied: 'You can use your wits.'

Comparing Hitler with Jesus Christ was apostasy enough, but Robert's actions and comments were all the more repulsive for their timing. At their Nuremberg trials, top-ranking Nazis, including Göring and Robert's old pal von Ribbentrop, had just been made to watch film footage of the horrors of their Holocaust on their way to receiving death sentences for their war crimes.

Robert had recently also spent his money on legal defence for William Joyce during his treason trial in London. Unsuccessfully, as it turned out, with Lord Haw-Haw also condemned to death.

The *Daily Mirror* followed up with Robert at Hartpury House, which he was now sharing with fellow 18B detainee and Right Club founder Archibald Ramsay. Robert refused to say what he had done with the Hitler bust. Quizzed about his politics, he was similarly sinister and evasive. 'But I will tell you that we are working away quietly, awaiting our time,' he said. Sydney *Truth* visited shortly after, its headline leaving no doubt of the paper's opinion about him and Ramsay: 'The Best-Hated Men in All England: Two Fascist Stooges Mourn for Hitler'. When Britain's *Sunday Pictorial* went to Hartpury, it found that Robert was now despised by the once-loyal villagers. Yet he remained unrepentant. 'It was done as a gesture to show my political feelings,' he said of buying the bust. 'I still believe that Germany could have saved the world.' Robert's continuing love of Hitler was more extraordinary for the fact that if the war had gone the other way he would have probably been *executed* by the Nazis. In September 1945 the Gestapo's Black Book had been found and its contents made public. A pocket-sized directory, it was to have been carried by SS officers so they knew which British residents to arrest after the Nazi invasion of England. The roster was comprised almost entirely of British politicians, media owners, pacifists, leftists, communists and Jews, writers and artists. 'My dear, the people we should have been seen dead with,' Rebecca West quipped after learning she and Noël Coward had made the list. Yet Robert would likely have been hanged or shot alongside them. As a Hitlerite fascist, he stood out in the Black Book. A plausible explanation for his inclusion was his 1940 statement contradicting Nazi denials about the Tavistock peace plan. Either that or he had *really* rubbed the Führer up the wrong way on those visits to Germany.

Robert was making himself a hate figure while Phil was making himself an entrepreneurial inventor. His talent for engineering and fondness for a drink had come together in a cleverly designed chromium siphon that attached to the neck of a bottle so when tipped it poured one ounce of alcohol every one and a half seconds. This was just the thing for the post-war consumer boom, with Americans looking for new modern creature comforts to help them entertain at home. Phil set up the Modern Engineering & Development Company with his brother Rolland to manufacture and market his invention. The patent filed in January 1946 called it an 'intermittent siphon dosing device'. Generations of Americans would buy it as 'Mr. Bartender'.

As Phil set up his business, Mary dieted strenuously for her Hollywood comeback. It's not known which of her film friends she contacted to set up studio meetings. Miles was the most probable candidate. He had carved out such a successful career as a character actor – having recently appeared in the likes of *Murder, My Sweet* and *The Picture of Dorian Gray* – that he was averaging six studio pictures a year. Mary may also have called Joe Schenck.

Convicted in 1941, he had been sentenced to three years in prison but went free after four months in return for testifying against Willie Bioff and his accomplice. Joe saving his own skin was the first domino that ended up toppling the Chicago Outfit, with boss Frank Nitti blowing his brains out rather than face prison again. Hollywood recognised Joe as a hero who had taken the fall for everyone, and he was rewarded on release by walking back into power at 20th Century Fox. He even received a full pardon from President Harry S. Truman in 1945 – said to be in return for previous generous campaign donations to the man now in the White House. Knowing a thing or two about bad associations and redemption, Joe may have been willing to give his old girl-friend another shot at fame. In any event, it was a Fox film that Mary tested for.

Forever Amber had everyone in Hollywood talking. It was to be based on the 1944 novel of the same name by young Kathleen Winsor, whose depictions of female sexuality had scandalised the nation and seen her book top the *New York Times* bestseller list for seventy-five weeks. Production code boss Joe Breen said the story was 'hardly more than a saga of illicit sex and adultery, into which enters the elements of bastardy, perversion, impot-ency, pregnancy, abortion, murder and marriage without even the slightest suggestion of compensating moral values'. But Darryl F. Zanuck and Joe Schenck were determined to turn the 972-page novel into their *Gone with the Wind*. They even modelled the search for a leading lady on the process of casting Scarlett O'Hara. Budgeted at $3 million, the film told the sprawling tale of Amber, a seventeenth-century peasant beauty who woos her way into the English aristocracy. Mary had some natural affinity for the role and she likely tested for Amber – but then more than two hundred women did before it went to twenty-year-old Welsh newcomer Peggy Cummins. Director John Stahl nevertheless saw potential in Mary and asked her to try out for Bess, a highway-man's mistress, who's jealous of Amber and says things like, 'D'ye think I'll stand back and watch you throw yourself away on a milk-faced nanny goat like her?' Stahl also had her test for Beck, one of Amber's similarly jealous stage rivals, who'd snipe with, 'Look here, Mistress What-d'ye-all, you needn't strut like a cow in the gutter – the gentlemen will have a swing at anything new.'

'Both are good parts and either would provide her with a successful comeback,' reported Lon Jones for the *Sydney Morning Herald*:

> Mary told me that she is avoiding ingenue roles, preferring solid character parts to being a glamour girl, though she is only 27 and still beautiful. 'I think I'll do better and last longer as a character actress,' she said.

He also reported that Paramount was considering Mary for a role in its adaptation of the racy 1945 Dan Wickenden novel *The Wayfarers*. A contemporary Midwestern drama set between the wars, it is about a middle-aged father trying to reconnect with his grown children, including the son who turned fascist and married a nymphomaniac. It's not known whether Mary was in the frame for that wife role. She also told the reporter that she'd like to return to Australia for a trip if she received a suitable stage or screen offer. But going home wouldn't help her career. Australia's live theatre scene was moribund. The film industry was in an even worse state – between 1945 and 1950 only a handful of feature dramas were made. Pressed by Lon Jones, Mary 'refused to discuss her former husband, Captain Gordon-Canning, stating that he was a closed chapter, but said that she was not surprised by the news that he had purchased a Hitler bust'.

On 8 February Miles Mander died, aged just fifty-seven. The *Los Angeles Times* reported he had suffered a heart attack in his sleep, though a story would gain currency that he had dropped dead in the Brown Derby restaurant. Mary was shocked and saddened. He had been instrumental in her professional and personal life. After a memorial service at a funeral home, Miles was buried in British Columbia, Canada, having specified in his will that his final resting place be on British soil.

———

Mary didn't get a role in *Forever Amber*, with Bess and Beck going to younger beauties Fox was planning to turn into stars. Shooting began in mid-March. Even if Mary had landed a part, audiences would never have seen her. At the end of April – after thirty-eight days filming at a cost of nearly $1.9 million – director John Stahl was fired and Peggy Cummins was let go. Fox shut the film down and made preparations to reshoot it entirely with an almost completely new cast. And *The Wayfarers* never eventuated at Paramount.

Despite her bad luck, Mary still looked set to return to screens. In early May an escape attempt at Alcatraz turned into a two-day siege and battle that killed two guards and five prisoners. The newspapers couldn't get enough of it. Warner Bros. wanted to cash in by dusting off *Alcatraz Island*, adding a new opening and three scenes, and putting the film back into cinemas fast. Lon Jones reported: 'Mary is not sure that this particular comeback is beneficial, pointing out that she was only nineteen when it was made, and an inexperienced actress. But it will at least bring her before the public and other studios.' Mary's hopes or fears were for nothing: Warner Bros. didn't go ahead with their re-release.

Meanwhile, Mr. Bartender was shaping up nicely. Phil had trademarked a goofy cartoon mascot, and commissioned hip packaging and a catchy slogan: 'One jigger, 1 pour, no less, no more'. He launched his product in March 1946, stocking it at upmarket Gearys store in Beverly Hills for $2.95, and within months Mr. Bartender was being sold across the country. A *New Yorker* magazine ad featured a cartoon of entertaining made easy and a photo emphasising how perfectly shots could be poured.

The gadget would have delighted readers of *Cavalcade*, an Australian men's magazine, which in May 1946 ran an article on the fortunes of antipodean stars in America. 'All that is left of Mary Maguire's brief conquest of Hollywood,' it concluded, 'is a stack of out-of-date glamour shots and a two-page biography of her personal life, obviously manufactured by the studio publicity staff.' It was a brutal verdict but also an accurate one. Mary's time as a studio actress was over. Any further screen tests were unsuccessful and unreported.

Mary's career didn't need to end there. Poverty Row, as the low-budget studios were collectively known, would have snapped her up. Even Jocelyn Howarth, who by the early 1940s was working as a waitress, scored a few supporting roles in movies made by cheapie companies PRC and Monogram. But Mary would have thought this a big step down. She was a former star who had recently envisaged herself an enduring character actress. Nearly a decade ago she had turned down *Mystery House*, so why stoop now to appear in schlock with titles like *White Pongo* or *Devil Bat's Daughter*? Yet if Mary had extended her acting career with Poverty Row pictures – or even local theatre productions – she may have soon stumbled into the medium that saved and sustained many of her former peers: television. In 1946 there were only six thousand sets in the United States; five years later there would be twelve million.

41.

Mary became the housewife of her immigration form around the same time tuberculosis got an effective cure in the antibiotic Streptomycin. She wasn't famous anymore but once she could be treated with this miracle drug neither would she be sick. Mr and Mrs Legarra were also doing quite nicely thanks to Mr. Bartender. Though they had lived in a modest house near Santa Monica when they returned to California, by 1950 they had moved into a mansion with ocean views in the swanky enclave of Surfridge at Palisades Del Rey. Called a 'castle on the hillside', the estate overlooked Dockweiler Beach and was popular with the rich and famous. Phil's niece Betty recalled that her uncle was busy at the office with Mr. Bartender, while her aunt-in-law played lady of the house and directed domestic help and tradespeople. Mary still regularly hosted some of her old Hollywood friends. 'She liked to entertain and part of the people she entertained was his family so I'd see her quite often,' Betty said. 'She was beautiful and she was fashionable.'

But there were to be no children in their new American dream lifestyle. When Mary fell pregnant, she had an abortion. She said that she and Phil hadn't wanted the responsibility of parenthood, though her decision may have had much to do with her horrific experience of motherhood. Baby Michael's death haunted Mary – who, as a Catholic, also came to feel guilty about terminating her pregnancy.

———

Back in England, Mary's sisters continued their rise into high society, though their lives were far from free of drama and tragedy.

Following in Mary, Patricia and Carmel's footsteps, Lupe made a spectacular marriage in 1946. Family lore had it that Mick heard she was seeing a millionaire named Godfrey Davis. The old bruiser came crashing into their love nest and so scared Davis that he felt compelled to make an honest woman of Lupe. Thirty-four years her senior, the Welshman had been a WWI pilot hero before introducing the concept of car hire to Britain in the 1920s. He was now one of the country's richest men. The couple lived in a palatial residence called 'Melbourne' in London's fashionable Hampstead Lane. 'He had everything but a title,' Bina said. 'They had six servants and two gardeners – but you don't count them.' Lupe and Godfrey shared a passion for horseracing, and she became every bit as passionate for the sport as her dad. Following another Maguire tradition, she developed a fondness for alcohol.

Patricia and Peter also drank too much. She handled it better than he did. In August 1945 he had been caught so intoxicated behind the wheel of his car in Piccadilly that he was sentenced to two months in prison and disqualified from driving for two years – a special indignity for a motor-racing enthusiast. Patricia was then four months pregnant, giving her a small taste of what Mary had been through with a husband behind bars five years earlier. The couple's second son, Peter, was born in February 1946. Less than a year later, Patricia sued her husband for 'restoration of conjugal rights' – a type of legal reverse divorce in which a judge compels a spouse to return to the marriage. One time, seemingly after a fight with Patricia raised her father's ire, Peter turned up with a black eye. 'I forgot Mickey was a pugilist,' he told Lord Beaverbrook.

In August 1947 Peter's yacht ran aground in Stockholm and he suffered broken ribs in the water trying to stop it from being smashed against rocks. It's not known if alcohol played a part, though he had been drinking heavily for years. Returning to his hotel room and in pain, he summoned a doctor who administered an injection of morphine. Peter had a bad reaction and died of a heart attack at age thirty-five. A funeral was held at St Michael's Churchyard, Mickleham, with Patricia consoled by Mick as her husband was buried next to his mother. Lord Beaverbrook never spoke about Peter's death — though he would take a great interest in his grandsons.

'All hell broke loose,' recalled Peter Aitken, Patricia's son, in 2017, of the aftermath of his father's death. 'The world could have been her oyster but she was very stubborn and used to fight with him [Lord Beaverbrook], which, of course, he didn't appreciate. But he was always very supportive of her.' She took her sons to live in the exquisite seaside mansion that Beaverbrook owned on the Isle of Wight. The attractive 31-year-old widow wasn't alone for long. Patricia was visited by hard-drinking, high-living Lord John Wodehouse, the 24-year-old Earl of Kimberley and godson to Winston Churchill. Johnny had inherited his title in 1941 when his father was killed in the Blitz by a bomb that, in a strange coincidence, also injured Peter Aitken's hero brother, Max.

Young Lord Wodehouse's ancestral seat was Kimberley Hall, a 250-year-old mansion on a 5000-acre estate in Norfolk, and he owned more properties and estates in Cornwall. He had gone to Magdalene College, Cambridge, but his studies were cut short when, at nineteen, he got drunk in a nightclub and accidentally enlisted in the Grenadier Guards. Johnny ended up commanding a Sherman tank group in Europe and taking part in heavy fighting against Germany's fearsome Tigers, including the disastrous 'Operation Market Garden', depicted in the film *A Bridge Too Far*. Victory came at a personal price for Johnny. 'Helping to liberate Brussels in 1944 was the beginning of my downfall,' he wrote in his memoir, *The Whim of the Wheel*. Having captured an almost inexhaustible supply of Champagne, 'I spent much of the war tight and when it was over I couldn't stop.'

Returning home, Johnny married the daughter of the head of the King's household, with their 1945 wedding reception held at Windsor Castle and attended by the entire royal family.

Johnny had wanted out of his marriage from that very day. 'I couldn't stop it,' he would say of the wedding, 'because the King and Queen were there, and I was in my best uniform.' He thereafter gave himself a green light to philander – and now he wanted Patricia. 'She was quite attractive, and, well, as I never wasted much time, we ended up in the hay together,' he wrote. 'She fell in love with me, but though I was very fond of her, I couldn't return her feelings.' But Patricia's visiting sister was a different story. 'Then Carmel arrived on the scene,' he wrote. 'We met, were immediately attracted, I swept her away and we had a whirlwind romance.'

Patricia didn't lick her wounds for long, soon wooed by Richard Lycett Green, 23-year-old son of Lady Grimthorpe and a member of another very wealthy English family. Not one to waste time either, in July 1948 Patricia had her second secret wedding. 'We were married quietly because I don't like fuss,' she said.

In late 1948, Carmel divorced her seed heir, Derek – he was soon to marry *Forever Amber*'s original star Peggy Cummins – and Johnny ditched his wife. Taking a leaf from Patricia's book, Carmel and Johnny married in haste in February 1949 in St. Moritz, Switzerland. 'Still at It! "Marrying Maguires" Get Another Prize' screamed a *Truth* headline. The groom gave his bride a mink coat and diamonds, though his greatest gift was her title. Carmel, nicknamed 'the Duchess' as a child, was now an honest-to-goodness Countess. Almost as satisfying: during their honeymoon Carmel was twice mistaken for Rita Hayworth, who was then in St. Moritz learning to ski.

Back in their Berkeley Square flat in London, Bina and Mick were having a cup of tea when a telegram arrived. It read: 'Getting married today. Stop. Love Carmel, Johnnie [sic].' Mary St. Claire of *The Australian Women's Weekly* arrived soon after. Mick did the talking: he said how much he liked his new son-in-law – and how very down-to-earth the Maguires remained. 'We've been to the races together – he loves racing,' he said of Johnny. 'Mrs Maguire and I have been to Kimberley, his country seat in Norfolk, quite a few times. He's never once given the slightest hint he is an earl when we've been out with him.' Mick claimed he wasn't impressed to add a title to the family. 'Being parents-in-law to an earl doesn't make a bit of difference to us,' he reckoned. 'We live quietly here in Mayfair, and although they will have a cocktail party when they come back from Switzerland, it won't mean any high society life for us. We like living quietly. Carmel and Johnny will be living in Norfolk, but they'll often be popping in on us when they're in town.' His new son-in-law, a 'regular fella . . . the sort of bloke they'd like in Australia', had, he said, already taken to calling Bina 'Mumma'.

Carmel and Johnny moved into a cottage on his Norfolk estate, as Kimberley Hall was undergoing extensive repairs to fix damage done by the British Army, who had requisitioned it during the war to house German and Italian POWs.

Like Lupe and Patricia, Carmel drank heavily. 'There was always a lot of brandy being poured when Carmel was around,' Johnny recalled. Not that he was any sort of teetotaller – later admitting his decades of alcoholism in a speech to the House of Lords. It's not known whether booze played a part, but in April 1950 Johnny was behind the wheel of his car in Piccadilly when he hit and killed a seventy-year-old pedestrian. His memoir's title, *The Whim of the Wheel*, refers to his other addiction – gambling at the roulette table – and the book doesn't mention the death, for which he wasn't charged.

Only Joan, the most sensible and sober, the least tempestuous and troubled, was yet to become one of the 'Marrying Maguires'. But she was pretty, warm, clever and still popular as an actress. Though Joan was frequently away on tour, Bina and Mick hoped it would only be a matter of time until she settled down.

Bina and Mick spent a lot of time with their younger daughters and their impressive husbands. They visited Lupe and Godfrey each Sunday at their house in Hampstead Lane, where they talked about the races and the fine horses that the couple were breeding. When Bina and Mick called on Carmel and Johnny at Norfolk, they got updates on the prize pigs and golden labradors they were raising. They also heard how Carmel had set up Maguire family friend Angela Dowding, Lady Fox's daughter, with Johnny's good mate Gerald Lascelles, the King's grandson and cousin to princesses Elizabeth and Margaret. And it was especially lovely when Patricia came to visit from the Isle of Wight. Mick, never blessed with a son, was tickled to give his little grandsons Tim and Peter boxing lessons. The boys might be destined to be in big business and politics like their other grandfather Lord Beaverbrook, but Mick could teach them a thing or two about being fighting Maguires.

The clan continued to expand. By 1950, Patricia had two more children by her husband Richard and was pregnant with a third. Tragedy struck on 13 May when, in another awful echo of Mary's experiences, Patricia's son died at seven months.

The fight went out of Mick Maguire suddenly on 4 June 1950, two days before his fifty-sixth birthday. His death of unknown causes led to a smattering of tributes in the Australian press. Despite her immense grief, Patricia organised the funeral. As far as records and memories allow, Mary did not attend, likely due to the difficulty in getting from Los Angeles to London at short notice. But Bina soon visited California to commiserate with her and they had a holiday in Mexico, where Philip was doing business. 'She told me Mary was as pretty as ever, has given up any thought of making a comeback in films and is perfectly happy in her beautiful home at Playa [Palisades] del Rey,' reported an *Australian Women's Weekly* writer. Some consideration had apparently been given to Bina moving to California to live with Mary. 'Though I gave lectures at women's clubs and was given a warm reception everywhere I went in America, I felt London was really my home, so I came back,' Bina said. Carmel and Johnny wanted her to move into an apartment in their London townhouse. But she felt she needed her independence and took a brand-new Mayfair flat, where four servants looked after her.

Mr. Bartender was prospering, and Philip had expanded the range with a swivel spoon he invented. 'In the beginning it made money,' Betty recalled. 'It was popular and at one time people would have individual Mr. Bartenders for each bottle.'

In July 1952, Mary visited London, where she joined Carmel, Joan and Lupe at the wedding of the year. When Gerald Lascelles married Angela Dowding, it was in the presence of most of the royal family, save for the young queen-in-waiting, who was suffering from a cold back at Buckingham Palace.

The visit gave Mary a chance to catch up on everything that had been going on with her sisters.

Joan had finally taken her place as one of the 'Marrying Maguires'. In Nice in 1950 she had quietly married twice-divorced Tony Colmore, a very wealthy industrialist who had made his fortune from artificial sweeteners. The couple lived half the year at a mansion called 'The Mount', on the historic Penshurst estate in Kent, and spent the other half on the Continent, where he had business interests. Tony had asked her to give up acting – so ended the career of talented Joan Shannon.

In January 1951, Carmel, after numerous miscarriages, had given Johnny an heir, also named John. Despite their glamorous lifestyle – hobnobbing with Gerald Lascelles, going to the races and lots of dinners and dances, and chartering a plane for weekends at the casinos at Deauville – their marriage had disintegrated under the weight of their drinking and infidelities. Johnny was having a long-term affair; Carmel was sleeping with his best friend. The breaking point came when she whipped him across the face with a dog leash in front of startled friends visiting them at Norfolk. Their divorce in August 1952 was acrimonious, with Carmel collapsing in court before winning custody of their nineteen-month-old son. She moved into the ritzy Cumberland Mansions in London and would soon move on to her third husband, Jeremy Lowndes, a wealthy landowner. After they married, they took up residence in a sixteenth-century Norfolk mansion, 'The Nunnery'.

Lupe, still living in London on Hampstead Lane, was fast becoming one of Britain's most prominent racehorse owners. She was so obsessed that she had started the 'Fillies and Brood Mares Club' for society women who shared her passion. 'They meet about once a month for lunch, when the topics of conversation range from horses to horses and then back again to horses,' noted one wag. She was also completely blithe when it came to her immense wealth. 'Lupe doesn't care about money,' Bina said. 'Her husband lavishes presents on her. But when she is given

another diamond bracelet she says it only means more jewellery
to lock up.'

Mary doesn't appear to have seen Patricia, who was now living
in Switzerland with Richard, having left her sons Tim and Peter
in the care of Lord Beaverbrook and Bina, who developed a
strong regard for each other. The boys grew to love and respect
both grandparents and didn't reconnect with their mother until
their teens.

———

After Mary returned to California, Mr. Bartender started to
slip from Phil's grasp. In 1951, when granted his swivel spoon
patent, he had assigned half to James McPhee of Culver City. In
1954, McPhee patented his own addition to the ever-growing
Mr. Bartender range, whose home office was now in Culver
City, suggesting he had taken over the company. That the brand's
headquarters then moved to Kentucky indicates that Phil sold out,
as does McPhee launching a rival range that included products
Bar-Host and Bar-Gavel. However it happened, Philip had lost
Mr. Bartender.

But he had a bigger bottle problem: he was boozing more
and more. So was Mary. 'Drinking went from social to part of
life,' Betty recalled. 'They partied a lot. There was always alcohol
involved. It was easy for someone to become an alcoholic. There
were lots of restaurants and dinners. Their relationship and marriage had been a happy one, but as time went on the drinking
made them more irritable.'

That irritability might explain Mary again going to England
without Philip in 1953. She flew BOAC from New York to
London in late May, arriving a week before Queen Elizabeth II's
coronation, and didn't return home until the end of September. In

April 1955 Mary flew to London for a third time, again without Philip, though it's not known how long she stayed.

In 1957, Betty Legarra married Wilson Burtis, Phil's NAA buddy from the war. In one of their wedding photos, Mary, now aged thirty-eight, pretty and slender in a mauve dress, stands smiling at the side of the groom. Phil, wearing a blue suit, is paunchy, jowly and nearly bald, looking older than his forty-two years and like he wanted to be anywhere else.

That same year Bina returned to Australia for the first time in twenty years. She visited Brisbane, where friends found her still full of the old charm. Bina wasn't shy about discussing her daughters' wealth: Joan's husband had just built her a £190 000 house in South Africa, where she and Tony liked to winter; Lupe's husband had just invested £1 million building a new corporate headquarters near Buckingham Palace – after all, he was one of England's richest men. What Bina didn't say was that Patricia and Richard had divorced the previous year. Just as Patricia had all but abandoned her sons by Peter Aitken, she now left the children by her second husband in the care of their grandfather Commander David Cecil Lycett Green.

Going to Melbourne, Bina stayed at her sister Marguerite's hotel. Marea O'Brien, her then fourteen-year-old second cousin, in 2017 remembered meeting a charismatic livewire who was a lot of fun and who had the longest red-painted nails she'd ever seen. When Bina gave an interview to *Woman's Day*, the magazine described her as a 'tiny, fine-boned woman with creamy magnolia skin and snapping brown eyes'. Based on Bina's comments, the article described Mary as the 'wife of a wealthy aircraft-designing engineer who lives in a luxury mansion in Hollywood, California'. It made Phil sound like Howard Hughes rather than one of the thousands of engineers toiling in the aerospace industry. As for their residence, Mary and Philip had moved out of Surfridge by the next year, no longer able to maintain a movie-star lifestyle on his middle-class income. They took a more modest house in Westminster, Orange County, closer to his family and work.

Mary's celebrity had long since faded, and now she was no longer wealthy. Life had gone from extraordinary to ordinary. Her name only appeared in print when mentioned in articles about her mother or sisters, as they had once been afterthoughts in stories about her. Though she no longer moved in the Hollywood scene, Mary stayed in touch with one actress. 'She used to see a friend – a woman who she had a lot in common with, they'd both been in the movies,' Betty recalled. It may have been Jocelyn Howarth, by the 1950s also living as a Los Angeles housewife. Another possibility is Phyllis Barry, Jim Gerald's niece, though she killed herself with a phenobarbital overdose in 1954. In truth, the city had no shortage of faded starlets to fit the description.

Has-beens had been part of Hollywood since the start of the star system. But Mary now had a constant reminder that the parade that had passed her by was still going for many others. Her lounge room was visited daily by her former friends, lovers, co-stars and competitors. Ann Sheridan, Basil Rathbone, Peter Lorre, Paul Henreid, George Sanders, Bette Davis, Maureen O'Sullivan: they and many others were reaching huge audiences and finding new fans by working in television. Even Charles Farrell – who hadn't made a movie since 1942 – was a household name again. Still married to Virginia Valli, and now mayor of Palm Springs, he had in 1952 been cast as the lead in the sitcom *My Little Margie*. A surprise hit, it got him his own program, *The Charlie Farrell Show*, which debuted in 1956 and ran for four years.

Yet no one's small-screen television rebirth – and political career – was more extraordinary than that of Ronald Reagan. By 1951 he had been playing second banana to a chimp in the film *Bedtime for Bonzo*. After appearing in some of the earliest live television dramas and popular theatre programs, Ronald in 1954 became host of NBC's *General Electric Theater*. Over the next eight years he introduced 235 episodes, appeared in thirty-five of its dramas, became rich via part-ownership in the show and was made more famous than he ever had been as a movie star. As spokesman for General Electric, Ronald gave hundreds of speeches, reckoning he met a quarter of a million people in a process that turned him into the 'Great Communicator'. By the time he was fired by GE in 1962 for comments about 'big government', he was listening to his and Mary's old pal Jane Bryan and her multi-millionaire husband Justin Dart's suggestions that he should get into Republican politics.

Mary appeared on television when her old movies popped up on the schedule. She had to feel a little like Norma Desmond in *Sunset Boulevard*, drinking and chain-smoking and wishing she'd got another shot at fame as Gloria Swanson had in that very film. Seeing herself at the height of her beauty in *Mysterious Mr. Moto* or giving her best performance in *The Outsider* had to be bittersweet. The small screen also brought reminders of what could have been: *Jezebel*, *Angels with Dirty Faces* and *Alexander's Ragtime Band*. Some television listings for *Kid Galahad* even had her name instead of Jane Bryan's in the cast alongside Edward G. Robinson, Bette Davis, Wayne Morris and Humphrey Bogart. How different everything would have been if she and Mick had organised those working visas in Brisbane. They wouldn't have needed to go to Mexico, and maybe she wouldn't have got sick and would've been able to make that picture.

'I don't think she was ever as happy as when she was actually doing movies,' Betty said. 'It was like a lifeblood to her.' Phil, too, was disappointed in how his career had panned out, his work lacking the meaning of the P-51 Mustang or the money promised by Mr. Bartender. 'She drank too much and so did my uncle Phil,' said Betty. 'Why? The reason any alcoholic drinks – something has disappointed them in life. Not continuing in the movies disappointed her, not making enough money disappointed him. He was always able to earn a living but he never made big, big money, which I'm sure he always wanted. Of course, she would've approved of that, too. They weren't destitute, of course, but they wanted that big glittery life again.'

Around 1960, Mary took another break from Philip when Patricia flew her to England. By then Bina and Patricia were aware that, even for a Maguire, Mary was drinking too much; they hoped they could help her quit. Her nephew Peter Aitken, then a teen-ager, was shocked to finally meet his movie-star aunt, who didn't look like the young starlet in the photo frame Bina kept atop her television set in her London apartment. 'Alcohol had taken over with a vengeance,' he recalled in 2017. 'It was heartbreaking for my grandmother when she came over to the UK. You would have been frightened. Her looks had gone to pieces. Her great beauty had gone. Her face had turned into a road map by then. She was very skinny, which happens with alcoholism, I guess.'

Mary's sisters weren't the best people to deal with her addiction. All – except Joan – remained heavy drinkers and chain-smokers. 'When you deal with the Maguire sisters, it seems to have been a trait,' Peter said. 'They were fun but they were wild women. They'd had these extraordinary lives after coming from Australia. They were all fucking lunatics, you know, if you want to put it that way. My grandmother used to go nuts about it.' His saddest memory of Mary is her eyeing off the coins from his money box. 'I said, "Do you want all of those?" And she took them all and went and bought booze.'

Mary accompanied Bina, Patricia and young Peter for a two-week visit to stay with Joan and Tony in the South of France.

Carmel also popped in one night for dinner. Despite Mary's drinking, Peter thought her lovely. 'I really liked her,' he said. 'She was very soft and caring – she had a very warm heart. She was a very nice woman. When she was sober she was absolutely delightful.' When Mary hit the bottle, her resentment came out. 'There was a sort of clash with my mother. She was very competitive with my mother, and my mother was very competitive with her because she was a superstar and of course brought them all to Hollywood and England,' Peter said. 'If you want, Mary had made the family, which she always felt they didn't give her credit for. I heard that conversation take place: "The only reason you're here, that you married Beaverbrook's son and the rest of it, is because of me!" She felt that they all owed her something, which left bitterness in her.' Patricia, meanwhile, felt she wasn't getting credit for what she had done in the past two decades. 'My mother always resented Mary because she was Bina's favourite,' Peter explained. 'But my mother was really the support that my grandmother had. My mother and [Joan and Tony] supported Bina.' During those two weeks, Mary made an effort to slow her drinking. 'She straightened out a little bit,' Peter recalled. 'Joan had a good influence on her. Joan was very level-headed.'

Then Mary got a call from Long Beach: Philip had hit bottom. 'She went back to America because her husband had been put in a booze home,' Peter said. 'They got together again. They used to drink themselves into insanity, so I was told.'

———

Photos of the couple at Legarra gatherings from the early 1960s showed a façade of normality. Mary and Phil, along with Betty, Wilson and other family members, celebrated Christmases, Thanksgivings and birthdays. Mary still looked fashionable, taking care with her appearance and changing her clothes and hairstyle with the times. There she was smiling as she cut her forty-fifth birthday cake and happily hosting a Thanksgiving dinner later that year.

Yet in dozens of photos spanning more than a decade, Phil never smiled. Sometimes he was blank faced and seemingly bored; at other times he averted his gaze or even scowled at the lens. As the years went by, Mary sometimes couldn't help but stare at Phil in frustration and bewilderment. That these were all Polaroids meant his sourness was plain for anyone to see in a matter of minutes. 'Philip as a young man was handsome and active and a desirable husband,' Betty recalled as she turned the pages of these photo albums. 'But he didn't stay light-hearted as he got older.'

Philip wasn't drinking just to deal with the disappointments of his career. He was also dealing with grief, following the deaths of his mother in 1959 and father in 1961.

Back in England, Lupe's husband Godfrey, now seventy-one, was in poor health. On 20 August, their horse Laughing Cheese won the 2.45 p.m. race at Folkestone. Godfrey died the next day, leaving the better part of his £500000 (£11 million) fortune to his young widow.

Around this time, Bina, now seventy and also in failing health, came to stay with Carmel and Jeremy. Her twelve-year-old grandson, John, the future Lord Wodehouse and Earl of Kimberley, thought she was wonderful. 'She was a little lady with a lot of character,' he recalled fondly in 2017. 'She had a look, a sparkle in her eyes and a determination. She was always well dressed and you knew in the nicest way who was boss. She used a cigarette holder which she clicked with her teeth, and had the habit of leaving half-finished cigarettes around and starting another one.' Even though she was sick, Bina 'still had a tremendous character. Of course no one mentioned that she was not going to live a lot longer, so I never knew how ill she was and assumed she would get better in due course.'

In May 1963 Bina died, aged seventy-two, in Middlesex Hospital. 'Champion Match-Maker Dies: She Married Off Five Pretty Girls' read the *Daily Mirror* headline back in Sydney. Just as Bina would have wanted. 'She was ambitious and driving,' a friend remembered, 'but her daughters loved her very much, and so did her friends. One assumes that, indomitable as always, she is even now finding the right place among the right people.'

As far as memories and available records indicate, Mary didn't make it to Bina's funeral.

A few months later, Lupe became engaged to an American, James Camden, twenty-four years her senior. They appear to have moved to California, though Betty didn't recall her having contact with Mary. James died in April 1965, leaving Lupe widowed for the second time before her fortieth birthday. She was soon back in London and drinking away her sorrows.

Although mourning her movie career, Mary had to realise that even continued Hollywood success was no guarantee of a happy ending. Errol Flynn had only made it to fifty, dying in 1959, his body ruined by a life of excess. In August 1962 Marilyn Monroe died of a barbiturate overdose, aged thirty-six. The following January, heavy-drinking John Farrow, whose womanising had caused Maureen O'Sullivan to finally leave him, died of a heart attack at age fifty-eight, telephone in hand as he tried to make a conciliatory phone call to his furious daughter, Mia Farrow. In October 1963 Jocelyn Howarth died, aged fifty-one, with her first director Ken Hall cryptically alluding to 'sad circum-stances' that attended her passing. Never having quite kicked his morphine addiction, Peter Lorre died of a stroke in March 1964, aged fifty-nine. Ann Sheridan succumbed to the long-time smoker and drinker's double threat — oesophageal and liver cancer — in January 1967 at age fifty-one. Robert Gordon-Canning, who had married again and had a daughter, died that same month.

Mary's baby sister Lupe died on 23 February 1969. Despite the fabulous fortune she had inherited, she had drunk herself to death by age forty-two. Mary couldn't get to this funeral and nor could Carmel, who was abroad at the time. But John Wodehouse, by now a teenager, went with his aunty Joan, who had become the rock of what remained of the Maguire family. In the continued absence of his mother, Patricia, Peter Aitken had also become close to Joan. A few years earlier she had even helped his young friend Andrew Lloyd Webber by writing lyrics for the first musical he ever submitted to a theatrical producer.

———

Despite Lupe's death, Mary wouldn't again try to quit drinking. 'She didn't try to give up alcohol,' Betty recalled. 'Phil did at one time. But she didn't give up — and then he went back to it.' They were functioning alcoholics. He worked steadily, inventing a pressure-controlled bomb ejector for his bosses at aviation company Whittaker Corporation. She was happy to entertain and be entertained at family functions. When Mary's Australian cousin Tom Talbot visited from Australia in May 1966, she and Phil drove him around Hollywood so he could see the sights. 'We arranged to meet on my last night in Los Angeles before I flew to Mexico City,' he recalled in 2017. The pair picked up Tom in the early evening after Philip had finished work. 'As parts of downtown LA were no-go areas after dark in those days, they preferred to show me around by car than walk, although we did get out to see the stars' hand prints in the pavement in Hollywood,' he said. 'They showed me some of the studio sights and the homes of some of the film stars.' What really stunned Tom was Los Angeles's pollution.

'The whole city was blanketed by a dirty brown cloud of smog,' he said. Mary told him that the smog aggravated her respiratory problems – the legacy of TB and decades of heavy smoking – and that this was one of the reasons why she and Phil lived out in Long Beach. Tom spent two or three hours with the couple. Mary was warm and voluble; Phil didn't say much.

Long Beach, once a suburban idyll, had gone into steep decline in the late 1960s, with drugs, crime and poverty increasingly rife. In 1967 the decommissioned *Queen Mary*, which had thirty years earlier taken Mary to London, was berthed there in the hope it would become a tourist attraction. This relic from a bygone era did nothing to revitalise the area. Mary and Phil's fortunes seem to sink with those of Long Beach. 'When they were entertaining they had a nice life,' Betty recalled. 'But it gradually got worse. Excess drinking just permeated a great part of her and Philip's life. It destroyed the good things that they did have.' By 1968 they were living in a very modest apartment in a complex that looked like a two-storey roadside motel. Two years later, Mary and Phil – then working as a tool designer for a company called Shultz Steel – had taken a shabby three-bedroom house in Lakewood. 'As the drinking got worse,' Betty recalled, 'the houses got worse.'

In a series of photos from 1969 and 1970, Mary, wearing her hair in an Elizabeth Taylor-style mini beehive, appeared bored at a number of family functions. She looked like an ageing movie glamour girl confused at being teleported into such a dull suburban scene. Phil had lost more hair and gained more weight. One of the last photos of the couple, at a small family dinner in January 1970, showed them sitting on a curved white leather couch. Phil, in an apricot shirt, striped yellow-and-ochre tie and brown slacks, looked grumpy as ever – though, in a rare demonstration of affection, he had his arm around Mary, who, slender and tanned in a black dress, smiled at her husband.

Phil died of arteriosclerosis at Pioneer Hospital in Artesia, a couple of miles from their house, on 1 May 1971. He was fifty-six. Mary placed a small obituary for her 'beloved husband' in the *Long Beach Press-Telegram*. Phil was cremated. She attended a memorial service with friends and family in the Church of Our Fathers at Forest Lawn Memorial Park. Her husband was interred in a beautiful niche in the Columbarium of Prayer, just metres from the famed Last Supper Room, the centrepiece of the Great Mausoleum where so many of Hollywood's stars were at rest.

Mary's relationship with Phil had been tough. But despite all their troubles, it had been underpinned by love. 'She wasn't madly in love with Robert Gordon-Canning,' Betty said. 'But she was in love with my uncle. It just didn't manifest as much when they were drinking.' They had been together twenty-eight years – more than half her life.

Mary didn't have much, least of all a source of income, yet somehow – perhaps using life insurance or an inheritance – she flew to London in September 1971. Accompanied by an unidentified man, she had arranged to borrow Carmel's London flat. At Heathrow, they were met by her nephew: Carmel's son, John Wodehouse. For him, it wasn't particularly memorable, apart from car trouble on the way back from Heathrow, which dominated conversation. 'She was just glad to see me and have somewhere to stay in London,' he said. 'We were really just the taxi service that day.' It's not known how long Mary stayed in London, or the purpose of her visit, but John remembered his mother mentioning her sister's drinking problem.

Returning to California, Mary applied for social security. Peter Aitken recalled being told she was working as a maid, though Betty Legarra couldn't confirm this. No longer able to afford the Lakewood house, she moved into a studio in a one-level garden apartment block in Pasadena Avenue, Long Beach. For

$80 a month she had a murphy bed, a kitchenette, a bathroom and a front door beside a back gate that opened onto a menacing alley that became even more frightening after dark. The Bull & Mouth and Belle Vue hotels, her house in the Hollywood Hills and Sandilands estate, her swanky London apartments and the Playa Del Rey mansion: they were as far in the past as her movie career. Her studio had more in common with what Robert had endured in Brixton than any place she had lived.

Mary got rid of most of her belongings. She had no choice because they wouldn't fit into her little abode. But she kept the Vasco Lazzolo portrait Robert had commissioned all those decades ago; in it she still looked a regal beauty befitting of the manor. Mary also kept six film publicity photos in simple wooden frames. There she was at age seventeen in *The Flying Doctor* and looking fresh in one of the first shoots she'd done for Warner Bros. Another photo showed her holding close to her heart the man she had known as 'Dutch' and who was now California's Governor, Ronald Reagan.

Mary sometimes saw members of the Legarra family and a few of Phil's friends. But she disappeared from the photo albums and depended more and more on Betty. 'The more she drank the more she became introverted,' Betty said. 'When I first met her she was gregarious but now she wasn't really that interested in people anymore. I'd take her out driving. I took her out to dinner and shopping. She couldn't take care of herself that well by then. She'd gained weight. She wasn't doing well. She wasn't happy not being married. She enjoyed life with a man. She never had another relationship. She was losing strength and what not. It was age and too much alcohol. She just got worse. She wasn't happy with life.'

In addition to Betty, her painting and her photos, Mary had her television for company. As summer approached, she likely welcomed whatever distraction she could get from what was

happening to her. She would have been feeling increasingly naus-
eous and exhausted. Her appetite was all but gone and her weight
was dropping away. The right side of her abdomen ached and her
skin was itchy and yellowing, as though she was wearing the film
make-up she'd used long ago. If Mary was watching her TV on
the afternoon of 17 May 1974 she would have seen the sensational
live coverage of the Symbionese Liberation Army's shootout with
five hundred cops in South-Central, Los Angeles. The furious gun-
fight lasted two hours. It ended with the siege house burning and
five SLA members incinerated beyond recognition. Patty Hearst,
granddaughter of Mary's old friend W. R., had been kidnapped
and brainwashed by the group, and was thought to be one of the
dead. Meanwhile, Howard Hughes was facing legal action for not
paying $1 million he owed for leasing Las Vegas's Silver Slipper
Casino. And, in lighter news, Governor Reagan, who kept a jar
of jellybeans on his desk, was entering a frog called Jellybeans
VIII in the annual Jumping Frog Jubilee up in Calaveras near
San Francisco.

Mary died in her little abode just after 1 p.m. on Saturday
18 May 1974. It was one day shy of forty years since she had been
discovered by Charles Chauvel.

Betty Legarra called Peter Aitken, who broke the news to his
mother Patricia. She took it with seeming equanimity. He also
called Joan, who was very upset, and she contacted Carmel. Mary's
body was taken to the Los Angeles County Coroner's Office. She
was still in the company of the right people: her autopsy was to
be performed by 'coroner to the stars' Thomas Noguchi, who had
performed his duties on the likes of Marilyn Monroe, Robert F.
Kennedy and Sharon Tate, and who would soon inspire TV hit
Quincy, M.E. But Mary's autopsy had to wait a few days because
Noguchi was busy examining the remains of the five Symbionese
Liberation Army bodies; Patty Hearst wasn't among the dead.

When he examined Mary, he found she had died of 'acute liver insufficiency' brought on by her 'chronic and acute alcoholism'.

Betty placed a small notice about Mary's passing in the obituary pages of Long Beach's *Independent Press-Telegram*.

LEGARRA, Helene T. (Mary) Rosary Sunday, 5:30 p.m. Dilday Family Chapel, 1250 Pacific Ave. Funeral Mass Monday, 10 a.m. Holy Innocents Church.

Mary's sisters couldn't make either service, and no one from her Hollywood days came either. 'It was a small church for her service,' said Betty. 'Just immediate friends and family.' Betty took her ashes to Forest Lawn so they could be interred next to those of Phil and his parents. With the Great Mausoleum the resting place for so many stars – from Carole Lombard and Jean Harlow to Clark Gable and W. C. Fields – she would now be surrounded by the right people for eternity.

While she had been born Hélène, become famous as Peggy, sometimes signed her name as Ellen and been known as Mrs Robert Gordon-Canning and Mrs Helene Legarra, the name on the rectangular bronze niche plaque reads: Mary Maguire.

AFTERWORD

Patricia Maguire came to Australia in 1975, visiting relatives in Melbourne, with their reunion photographed and chronicled by *The Australian Women's Weekly*. She told of her experiences in Hollywood and London. Mary's death the previous year was mentioned in passing – and said to have been from tuberculosis.

Patricia lived until 1995. 'My mother came through all right, though she used to drink like a fish,' Peter Aitken said. 'She gave up drinking in the end, and went until she was seventy-nine.'

Joan and Tony remained in France for most of their lives, moving back to England to enter nursing homes in the 1990s. Though more temperate in her youth, Joan also succumbed to the Maguire fondness for alcohol. 'She started into the booze really in her late sixties,' said Peter Aitken. 'It was unbelievable to watch.' Joan died of Alzheimer's in 1999, aged seventy-eight.

In the early 1980s, Carmel's third husband, Jeremy Lowndes, succumbed to depression and attempted suicide by shooting himself in the head. He survived, though was never the same. The couple moved to Sotogrande, Spain, taking a villa and drinking heavily. On 21 July 1992 they were visited by Carmel's son John Wodehouse. A boozy dinner party followed. After the guests left, John and Carmel went upstairs to their bedrooms to sleep. Sometime later, he awoke to find his stepfather in his room. 'I think I have killed your mother,' Jeremy said. In a fit of drunken rage, Jeremy had punched Carmel and then bludgeoned her to death with a blunt instrument. After confessing, he tried to commit suicide by jumping off a first-floor balcony, succeeding only in breaking both legs. Tried for murder, Jeremy claimed no memory of the night and tried to insinuate someone else there that night – perhaps John – might have killed Carmel. Jeremy was found guilty and sentenced to nine years in prison.

The central Melbourne hotels that the Maguires ran were all demolished. The biggest architectural loss related to the family, however, was that of Brisbane's Belle Vue Hotel, shamefully knocked down in the dead of night by Sir Joh Bjelke-Petersen's government in 1979. The site is now occupied by an ugly office block – a small bronze plaque commemorates the magnificent historic building that once stood there.

After decades of near inactivity, the Australian film industry came back to life in the 1970s. Bruce Beresford's *Don's Party*, Peter Weir's *Picnic at Hanging Rock*, Gillian Armstrong's *My Brilliant Career* and George Miller's *Mad Max* were but a few of the movies that spearheaded this renaissance. In 1977, the Australian actor Peter Finch – whose early film career included Ken Hall's *Dad and Dave Come to Town* and Charles Chauvel's *The Rats of Tobruk* – posthumously won Australia's first Best Actor Oscar for his role as Howard Beale in *Network*.

In the next ten years Judy Davis and Mel Gibson made it good in Hollywood – and didn't fade out quickly in the manner of so many of our early stars. In the decades that followed,

Australians in American and British films have become increasingly commonplace. Nicole Kidman, Geoffrey Rush, Cate Blanchett, Hugh Jackman, Chris Hemsworth, Margot Robbie, Ben Mendelsohn, Isla Fisher, Eric Bana, Naomi Watts, Rose Byrne, Joel Edgerton, Rachel Griffiths, Sam Worthington, Toni Collette, Hugo Weaving, Abbie Cornish, Rebel Wilson, Jason Clarke, Mia Wasikowska, Emily Browning, Rachael Taylor and Jacki Weaver: they and others have more successfully navigated the territory that Mary Maguire tried to blaze. Sadly, the death of Heath Ledger, Australia's other posthumous Oscar-winner, was a reminder that young stars can still pay a steep price for chasing their Hollywood dreams.

Mary Maguire never achieved critical or commercial success anywhere near that enjoyed by her successors, and she never found much of a place in books about Australian film history. If she was mentioned, it was usually in passing in older volumes devoted to the early days of the industry. But some of her work can still be seen. *Diggers in Blighty* is available on DVD from the National Film and Sound Archive, and *Heritage* was re-released a few years ago, though the screen rehearsal footage included in the extra features is not of Mary but is one of Charles Chauvel's newsreel promo stunts using a stand-in seen only from the back.

The Flying Doctor was for decades thought lost, and its rediscovery ranks as something of a miracle. In Sydney, workers demolishing a building found a safe and, thinking it might contain something of value, cut into it with an oxyacetylene torch. Remarkably, the film canisters inside were undamaged – though the workers thought them worthless and loaded them onto a truck with other rubbish bound for the tip. An eagle-eyed motorist saw the cans and, having heard of the National Film and Sound Archive's quest to find Australia's lost films, chased down the truck and rescued the canisters. Five of six reels of *The Flying*

Doctor were thus saved – and, in a remarkable coincidence, a canister containing the missing reel was found in Britain a year later. Sadly, the film has yet to be restored or released in any format.

Of Mary's American films, only *Confession* and *Mysterious Mr. Moto* have merited DVD release, though *That Man's Here Again*, *Sergeant Murphy* and *Alcatraz Island* make the rounds on the Turner Classic Movies Network. *The Outsider* and *Black Eyes* have recently been made available on disc in the UK, and an unauthorised release of *This Was Paris* occasionally pops up on eBay. The British Film Institute holds a viewable print of *Keep Smiling*, along with the only known footage from *An Englishman's Home*, the film's first reel, which runs for eighteen minutes.

Australia's Sweetheart isn't an attempt to claim that Mary Maguire's work in these films qualifies her for rediscovery as a great forgotten actor. This is why critical commentary – for better or worse – has mostly been left to contemporary reviewers, who saw her films differently to how we are able to perceive them. *Heritage*, for example, is incredibly creaky by today's standards, and Mary's performance often barely adequate, though many critics at the time thought her a refreshing and colourful change from previous Australian screen actresses.

Mary does show gradual improvement across her films, particularly in scenes where she was able to play with a lighter touch and what one reviewer called 'Puckish humour'. She was more natural in *The Flying Doctor* and better still in *That Man's Here Again*, *Confession* and *Alcatraz Island*. She did backslide – her performances in *Sergeant Murphy* and *Mysterious Mr. Moto* are more often flat than charming – but her British work shows continued dramatic development when given roles with complexity and substance, as she was in *The Outsider* and *Black Eyes*. She was also charming in *Keep Smiling*. As anyone who has seen Errol Flynn's debut in Charles Chauvel's *In the Wake of the Bounty* can attest, he began his career as wooden as that ship's mast. But sticking with Warners made him a polished performer, and a huge and enduring star. If Mary had been able to make better decisions – not easily done in an era of studio control – and enjoyed better luck and health, then this might not be the first biography of the woman once called Australia's Sweetheart.

SOURCES

Mary Maguire left behind no known diaries or letters. *Australia's Sweetheart* is a work of creative non-fiction based on five years of archival research, interviews with relatives and the use of secondary sources. While Mary's thoughts and feelings about events in her life were often recorded in contemporary interviews, on other occasions no such record exists; in some of these instances, I have inferred her mental and emotional state based on her previous reactions and what I hope are reasonable assumptions. For example, it's recorded that she burst into tears upon leaving Brisbane and cried herself to sleep after arriving in Hollywood; from this I believe it permissible to extrapolate her mixed emotions on departing Sydney as described in the prologue. When it comes to more complex questions on which she gave only short answers, such as her relationship with Joe Schenck or her view of Robert Gordon-Canning's hate-politics, I have marshalled the evidence and provided possible interpretations, but otherwise left it to the reader to make up their own mind.

Newspapers and magazines were accessed through: the marvellous National Library of Australia digital resource Trove (https://trove.nla.gov.au); New Zealand's Papers Past (https://

paperspast.natlib.govt.nz); United States resources Newspapers. com, Newspaperarchive.com, and the film fan/trade magazine archive Lantern (lantern.mediahist.org); United Kingdom's The British Newspaper Archive (www.britishnewspaperarchive.co.uk) and the Express archive (www.ukpressonline.co.uk), which also contains digitised versions of fascist newspapers *Action* and *The Blackshirt*. Further newspaper microfilms were accessed at the State Library of New South Wales, the State Library of Victoria, and the Los Angeles and London public libraries. Immigration, addresses and other family records were accessed through collections held by Ancestry (www.ancestry.com) and Genealogy Bank (www. genealogybank.com). Information on Robert Gordon-Canning's internment, interrogations and appeals came from surviving declassified MI5 files KV2 877/878, held at the National Archives of the UK. Further information was found in John Beckett's MI5 file KV2/1511. Home movie footage of *The Flying Doctor* and production memoranda related to that film were found at Australia's National Film and Sound Archive. Comparable documents about Mary Maguire's work in Hollywood were found in the University of Southern California's Warner Bros. archive, the 20th Century Fox archive, and the Margaret Herrick Library, all in Los Angeles. *Keep Smiling* and the eighteen-minute fragment of *An Englishman's Home* were viewed at the British Film Institute, London.

SELECT BIBLIOGRAPHY

Abrahams, Olga, *88 Nicholson Street: The Academy of Mary Immaculate 1857–2007*, Melbourne, the Academy of Mary Immaculate, 2007

Aitken Kidd, Janet, *The Beaverbrook Girl*, London, Collins, 1987

Aldrich Jr, Nelson A., *American Hero: The True Story of Tommy Hitchcock – Sports Star, War Hero and Champion of the War-Winning P-51 Mustang*, Guildford, Connecticut, Lyons Press, 2016

Baker, Sarah, *Lucky Stars: Janet Gaynor & Charles Farrell*, Albany, NY, BearManor Media, 2009

Beckett, Francis, *Fascist in the Family: The Tragedy of John Beckett M.P.*, London, Routledge, 2016

Behlmer, Rudy, *Inside Warner Bros. (1935–51)*, London, Weidenfeld & Nicolson, 1986

Bellamy, Richard Reynell, *We Marched with Mosley: The Authorised History of the British Union of Fascists*, London, Black House Publishing, 2013

Bingen, Steve, *Warner Bros. Hollywood's Ultimate Backlot*, Lanham, Maryland, Taylor Trade Publishing, 2014

Bynum, Helen, *Spitting Blood: The History of Tuberculosis*, Oxford, Oxford University Press, 2012

Carlson, John Roy, *Cairo to Damascus*, New York, Alfred A. Knopf, 1951

Carlsson, Susanne Chauvel, *Charles & Elsa Chauvel: Movie Pioneers*, Brisbane, University of Queensland Press, 1989

Chauvel, Elsa, *My Life with Charles Chauvel*, Sydney, Shakespeare Head Press, 1973

Chisholm, Anne, and Davie, Michael, *Beaverbrook: A Life*, London, Hutchinson, 1992

Clayton, Tim, and Craig, Phil, *Finest Hour*, London, Hodder & Stoughton, 1999

Collins, Diane, *Hollywood Down Under: Australians at the Movies: 1896 to the Present Day*, Sydney, Angus & Robertson, 1987

Cross, William, *Lady Carnarvon's Nursing Homes: Nursing the Privileged in Wartime and Peace*, Newport, UK, William P. Cross, 2011

Custen, George F., *Twentieth Century's Fox: Darryl F. Zanuck and the Culture of Hollywood*, New York, Basic Books, 1997

Davies, Marion, *The Times We Had: Life with William Randolph Hearst*, New York, Ballantine Books, 1977

Dorril, Stephen, *Blackshirt: Sir Oswald Mosley and British Fascism*, London, Viking, 2006

Eliot, Marc, *Reagan: The Hollywood Years*, New York, Random House, 2008

Fitzpatrick, Peter, *The Two Frank Thrings*, Melbourne, Monash University Publishing, 2012

Folsom, Robert, *The Money Trail: How Elmer Irey and his T-Men Brought Down America's Criminal Elite*, Washington, DC, Potomac Books, 2010

French, Philip, *The Movie Moguls: An Informal History of the Hollywood Tycoons*, London, Weidenfeld & Nicolson, 1969

Frith, David, *Bodyline Autopsy, the Full Story of the Most Sensational Test Cricket Series: Australia v England 1932–33*, Sydney, ABC Books, 2002

Fury, David A., *Maureen O'Sullivan: 'No Average Jane'*, Minneapolis, Artist's Press, 2006

Gillies, Michael T., *The Regent: Brisbane's Motion Picture Cathedral*, Brisbane, CopyRight Publishing, 2014

Gordon-Canning, Robert, *Flashlights From Afar*, London, Elkin Matthews, 1920

Gordon-Canning, Robert, *The Holy Land: Arab or Jew?*, London, 1938

Gordon-Canning, Robert, *The Inward Strength of a National Socialist*, London, 1938

Gordon-Canning, Robert, *A Pagan Shrine*, London, E. Macdonald, 1922

Griffiths, Richard, *Fellow Travellers of the Right: British Enthusiasts for Nazi Germany 1933–1939*, London, Faber & Faber, 2015

Griffiths, Richard, *Patriotism Perverted: Captain Ramsay, The Right Club and British Anti-Semitism 1939–40*, London, Constable, 1998

Griffiths, Richard, *What Did You Do During the War? The Last Throes of the British Pro-Nazi Right, 1940–1945*, New York, Routledge, 2017

Guinness, Jonathan and Catherine, *The House of Mitford*, London, Hutchinson, 1984

Gussow, Mel, *Darryl F. Zanuck: Don't Say Yes Until I Finish Talking*, London, W.H. Allen, 1971

Hemming, Henry, *Agent M: The Lives and Spies of MI5's Maxwell Knight*, New York, PublicAffairs, 2017

Jackson, Robert, *Dunkirk: The British Evacuation, 1940*, London, Rigel Publications, 1976

Kazan, Elia, *A Life*, London, Andre Deutsch, 1988

Kear, Lynn, and Rossman, John, *Kay Francis: A Passionate Life and Career*, Jefferson, North Carolina, McFarland & Company, 2006

Korda, Michael, *Alone: Britain, Churchill, and Dunkirk: Defeat Into Victory*, New York, Liveright Publishing, 2017

Leaming, Barbara, *Marilyn Monroe*, London, Weidenfeld & Nicolson, 1999

Lowe, Malcolm V., *North American P-51 Mustang*, The Crowood Press, UK, 2009

Luke, Michael, *Hansel Pless: Prisoner of History*, London, Mary Ashdown, 2001

Mander, Miles, *To My Son – In Confidence*, London, Faber & Faber, 1934

Mant, Gilbert, *A Cuckoo in the Bodyline Nest*, Sydney, Kangaroo Press, 1992

Mosley, Leonard, *Zanuck*, London, Granada, 1984

Mosley, Sir Oswald, *My Life*, London, Nelson, 1968

O'Brien, Duncan, *The Grand Manner of Matson*, Victoria, BC, Pier 10 Media, 2014

O'Brien, Duncan, *The White Ships, 1927–1978, A Tribute to Matson's Luxury Liners*, Victoria, BC, Pier 10 Media, 2008

O'Brien, Stephen, *Kay Francis: I Can't Wait to be Forgotten – Her Life on Film and Stage*, Duncan, Oklahoma, BearManor Media, 2013

Ramsay, Archibald Maule, *The Nameless War*, London, Britons Publishing Company, 1952

Reade, Eric, *The Australian Screen: A Pictorial History of Australian Filmmaking*, Melbourne, Lansdowne Press, 1975

Rice, Christina, *Ann Dvorak: Hollywood's Forgotten Rebel*, Lexington, University of Kentucky, 2013

Sandwich Local History Society, *Sandwich Recollected: An Oral History, 1914–1950*, Sandwich, 2000

Simpson, A. W. Brian, *In the Highest Degree Odious: Detention Without Trial in Wartime Britain*, Oxford, Oxford University Press, 1992

Smith, Gary, *Forever Amber: From Novel to Film*, Duncan, Oklahoma, BearManor Media, 2014

Stansky, Paul, *The First Day of the Blitz: September 7, 1940*, Carlton North, Scribe Publications, 2007

Summers, Anthony, *Goddess: The Secret Lives of Marilyn Monroe*, London, Victor Gollancz, 1985

Tate, Maurice, *My Cricketing Reminiscences*, London, Stanley Paul, 1934

Tate, Tim, *Hitler's British Traitors: The Secret History of Spies, Saboteurs and Fifth Columnists*, London, Icon Books, 2018

Taylor, A. J. P., *Beaverbrook: A Biography*, New York, Simon & Schuster, 1972

Ungerson, Clare, *Four Thousand Lives: The Rescue of German Jewish Men to Britain, 1939*, Stroud, UK, The History Press, 2014

Wagner, Ray, *Mustang Designer: Edgar Schmued and the P-51*, New York, Orion, 1990

Wiley, Mason and Bona, Damien, *Inside Oscar: The Unofficial History of the Academy Awards*, New York, Ballantine, 1993

Willetts, Paul, *Rendezvous at the Russian Tea Rooms*, London, Little Brown, 2015

Wodehouse, John (The Earl of Kimberley), *The Whim of the Wheel*, Cardiff, Merton Priory Press, 2001

Youngkin, Stephen, *The Lost One: A Life of Peter Lorre*, Lexington, University of Kentucky Press, 2005

ACKNOWLEDGEMENTS

The generosity and patience of dozens of people made this project possible. Norman Archibald, Mary's second cousin, called me in early 2014 and left my jaw on the floor with what he could tell me of Mary and the Marrying Maguires. Thanks also to his daughter Caitlin Archibald for facilitating that initial contact.

Betty Legarra Burtis twice welcomed me into her Long Beach home to share her recollections of life with Mary after 1945. Thanks also to Betty's carer and friend Kathy Bumer.

Peter Aitken spent several hours recalling his encounters with his aunt Mary and mother Patricia in the early 1960s. I'm indebted also to John Wodehouse, Sir Edward Lycett Green and Timothy Aitken for their recollections of the Maguires. Louise Gordon-Canning kindly spoke to me about her father. Mary Redvers, Robert Gordon-Canning's second cousin, kindly hosted me at her house in Gloucestershire. Thanks also to her sister, Sally Codrington, another of Robert's nieces. On Mary's Australian side of the family, thanks to Mary's second cousins Tom Talbot, Marea O'Brien, Bronwyn Ingleton and Margaret Hine for sharing their recollections.

Thanks also to: Simon Drake, of NFSA, for his research assistance and encouragement; Dianne Byrne, formerly of the State

Library of Queensland and a fellow Maguire family enthusiast, who generously shared her research; Duncan O'Brien, for his wonderful books on the Matson liners and for reading early drafts; Mic Looby, for suggesting the title and early reads; Tim Keen and Candice Fox, for their hospitality and driving services in Los Angeles; Brett Service for his assistance accessing USC's Warner Bros. files; Ned Comstock at USC for help finding non-digitised newspaper clips and further Warner Bros. and Fox materials; Matthew Yongue, for help accessing 20th Century Fox's archive; Danny Murphy, former editor of *Empire* magazine, and James Jenning, present *Empire* editor, for their enthusiasm for the project; Maureen McAuley, archivist at Academy of Mary Immaculate, and Kieran Donnelly, archivist at Loreto College, for material on Mary's education; Sister Ellen Marie Quinn, of the Carmelite Monastery Melbourne, for information about Mary's aunt Marie; Tony De Bolfo of Christian Brothers College, Melbourne, for putting a call-out to Old Paradians for information about the Maguire family; Barry Nicholls for his Bodyline insights; Naomi Hall, for research advice; Sophie Johnson of the Wiener Library for the Study of the Holocaust and Genocide for information on the Right Club; Hector Perez at CBS News and Eric Graf at the Library of Congress, for permissions/digitisation of the 'Forecasting 1938' radio broadcast; Michael Yaikatis, for supplying the Hearst seventy-fourth birthday party footage; Rich Lorenz at Trinity County Historical Society for material on the Weaverville premiere; Christina Rice, for her encouragement and Ann Dvorak research; Paul Willetts, for supplying additional material on Robert Gordon-Canning not found in Willetts' excellent book *Rendezvous at the Russian Tea Rooms*; Ronald Reagan biographer Marc Eliot, for confirming Mary's relationship with Dutch; Michael Pinckney at the Ronald Reagan Presidential Library; Jeanne McCombs, Presidio archivist; John Fredrickson of

Boeing, for information about and photos of Philip Legarra; Grant Newman, for his Mustang P-51 expertise; John Davis, former butler to Carmel Maguire; Elizabeth C. Borja, of the National Air and Space Museum, Washington, DC, for providing Vernon Dorrell's scrapbook with information about the *Mariposa* voyage; Stephen Youngkin, author of *The Lost One: A Life of Peter Lorre*, for his insight into Peter Lorre and the *Mr. Moto* series; Mike Baard, for his friendship and for opening archive doors in Los Angeles; Steve Tollervey and Kathleen Dickson of the BFI; Anna McFarlane, who initially encouraged me to add an Australian angle to my historical novel; Simon Fraser, who said something along the lines of, 'Hey, you should write Mary's story instead of your novel.'

For their friendship, support and encouragement: Charlie Tapper; Luke Goodsell; Colan Leach: Rachel Carbonell; Paul and Leonie O'Farrell; Bruce Beresford; Jo-anne McGowan; Matt Johnson; Dan Creighton and Charlotte Pache; Rebecca Wallwork and Sam Barclay; Simon Houghton; Kylie Short; Dora Weekley; Kirrilly Brentnall; Elissa McKeand; Bruce Permezel; Jeff Siberry; Trent Chapman; Damien Parer Jr; Ric Chauvel Carlsson; Cassie Hamer; Melissa Wilson; Kaz Boalch; Oscar and Shahida Hillerström; Sally Jackson and Miguel Gonzalez of the NFSA.

Enduring thanks: Noel, David and Tina Adams, for lifelong support; Melanie Ostell, for mentorship and navigation of the publishing world; Daphne, Mark, Brett, Kate, Monique and the rest of the Nichols clan, with whom I was reunited through this project; David, Susan, Sam and Max Lone; Michael, Sarah, Charlie, Oscar and Leo Thompson; Denzil Joyce; Sophie Hamley, Karen Ward, Klara Zak and the entire Hachette team for returning Mary Maguire to the spotlight.

Love always: Clare and Ava, who make everything worthwhile.

INDEX